CHURCHILL'S SHOTGUN BOOK

CHURCHILL'S
Shotgun Book

by ROBERT CHURCHILL

A guide to the successful use
of the smooth-bored game gun

FOREWORD BY MACDONALD HASTINGS

ALFRED A. KNOPF: NEW YORK

1955

L. C. catalog card number: 55-9278
© Robert Churchill, 1955

S. B. C.

Originally published in Great Britain by Michael Joseph Limited under the title of GAME SHOOTING.

To

all the sportsmen—good shots, born shots, and especially the bad shots—who have taught me everything I know

Foreword

An everlasting monument to his unrivaled genius is already established in every quarter of the globe, by his celebrity as the greatest artist in firearms that ever the world produced, as the founder and father of the modern gun-trade, and as a most scientific inventor in other departments, not only for the benefit of his friends and the sporting world, but for the good of his King and Country.

THAT's the epitaph which Colonel Peter Hawker composed in 1835 in honor of his friend, the great gun-maker Joseph Manton. I'm not sure that it wouldn't do equally well, in our own time, to describe the achievement of Robert Churchill.

In some ways, Churchill's contribution to his trade has been even a larger one than Manton's. Certainly his fame is the greater. In every police department in the world the name of Churchill is already a legend as the pioneer, and the unquestioned authority, on the identification of bullets in criminal cases. He has been called as expert witness in almost every important murder trial involving a shooting in this century, and his evidence— based on his own original methods in the scientific examination of firearms and bullets—has usually been decisive.

His reputation as the world's expert on firearms in police courts is unchallenged. But whether or not he is also "the father of the modern gun-trade," as Manton was, is a matter of opinion and of controversy, too. In the years 1910 to 1920, when Churchill was introducing and perfecting his newly designed game-guns with short barrels, the argument for and against was so embittered that people on the same shooting field could scarcely discuss the subject with equanimity.

Today I think it's true to claim that Churchill's 25-inch-barreled guns have won the day. The other gun-makers are increasingly imitating him, and, much more important, the younger generation of sportsmen (who can afford them) are tending to prefer Churchill, and Churchill-type, guns.

He is the only one of the top half-dozen great London gun-makers whose reputation is of his own making and uninherited from a previous generation. When he took over, E. J. Churchill Limited had a small and specialized business in making pigeon guns. Today his firm is one of the biggest and most prosperous of those who still make their weapons entirely by hand. And it's sad to think that, with the passing of the old craftsmen, Churchill, the latest of the great gun-makers, may well be the last of them.

But Churchill the gun-maker, Churchill the firearms expert, is only a part of the man. All of us who have had the privilege of being personally coached by him know that he is also the greatest shooting instructor of our day.

For a long time I have been trying to persuade him to put down his own particular system of teaching straight shooting for the benefit not only of sportsmen all over the world who are denied the opportunity of "going to school" with Bob Churchill himself, but also for the benefit of generations of shooting men to come.

The only authoritative book I know on how to shoot, apart from a library of books on what to shoot at, is a manual written by Charles Lancaster in the past century. In the fashion of the time, Lancaster teaches the old system of shooting at moving targets by telling the sportsman to make varying "forward allowances" at birds traveling at different speeds and angles. It's an appallingly complicated way of teaching shotgun work, and, in practice, the man who tries to make arbitrary calculations of "forward allowance" usually pokes his weapon and shoots yards behind.

FOREWORD

The essence of Churchill's coaching is that he tells his pupils to swing straight on the bird; to trust the unerring ability of the eye to make the necessary forward allowances, and to leave it to the gun to do the rest.

It works. Churchill, who on his day can still hold his own with the best shots in Europe, has helped to "make" a new generation of shooting men by his methods.

Learning from a book is obviously a more difficult way of learning than by taking lessons at a shooting school. But it can be done: I taught myself how to use a fly rod that way. And not everybody has the opportunity of going to school.

Some of the notes in this book were published in a brief guide to shooting which Churchill brought out many years ago, and which is now out of print. In my capacity as a sort of Dr. Watson to the master, I have persuaded him to enlarge them and to incorporate them here. In my view, it gives this volume a definitive flavor.

Here is the round-up of a lifetime's experience and knowledge by a man who, in his own specialty, is as much a legend in his time and in his way as that other Churchill whose name he shares.

MACDONALD HASTINGS

Contents

[xi]

hand—grip only at the instant of firing—balance the gun between the two hands—common faults explained.

Point your left hand at the bird—put your shoulder to the stock—common faults explained.

Keep your eye on the bird—avoid head movement without equal body movement—the head should only move with the body—individual styles—young sight *v.* old sight —how to test the fit of your gun—cures for gun headache —where to look.

Speed of bird *v.* velocity of shot charge—how the eye can be deceived—the natural overthrow allied to perfect gun-mounting and body swing which automatically makes the correct allowance although you apparently shoot at the bird—ballistics in theory and practice—judging distances —judging heights.

Shooting discomforts and cures—bruised second finger— bruised cheek—bruised mouth—bruised arm—bruised shoulder—bruised chest—how to open, load, and close gun at express speed yet with perfect safety—shooting rules— the danger zone—the poacher—some notes on etiquette.

If they care to learn, women can shoot as well as men—a correct beginning half the battle—the approach to full-size gun must be carefully carried out—the small bore gun— the new 2-inch gun—gun drill—shooting clothes.

PART TWO

Gun Know-how

The all-round increase in hidden strength to meet modern conditions—the new Zenith Under-and-Over gun—single

shooting, the varieties of stance and bodywork for the eight different stands and sixteen different kinds of birds —the layout of a shooting ground.

PART FOUR

Field Notes

The environment and conditions of hunting in America are only outwardly different from those ruling in Europe —the English system as a model for American hunters— shotgun or rifle?—hunting fatalities—the universal code of shotgun work.

The interpretation of the Code varies in different company—shooting etiquette—shooting accidents—ricocheting pellets—syndicate shoots—eight very important rules for your safety and enjoyment—your legitimate field of fire —how to dispatch wounded game—shooting averages— keepers' tips.

The right clothes for the shooting party are still anybody's fancy—the choice of your wardrobe will have a direct and noticeable influence on performance—the best jacket for shooting with a specification for your tailor— footgear—camouflage clothing—cartridge bags and belts.

Habits and environment—walking up over dogs—driven birds—the grouse butt—on the alert—where to look—always pick your bird—when to shoot—unsafe butts—unsteady shots.

What not to do—analyzing the expert shot—stance and footwork—effortless gun-mounting—where to look—how to mark your birds—some important "don'ts"—walking up: everybody must help in marking birds—how to mark and gather birds.

The important difference between shooting grouse and pheasants and partridges and pheasants—it is not a snap shot—indoor drill for overhead shots—high pheasants in theory and practice—the confusion of "conscious" allowance—the born shot analyzed—some important "don'ts" and a few very simple rules.

Even the most experienced shot is tempted to take chances —some shooting "don'ts"—some shooting hints—ferreting rabbits—rabbits bolting across a ride—hares—how to make quick snap shots.

Dawn excursions and night attacks—the choice of gun, ammunition, and clothes—the best wild-fowlers are always first-class naturalists—shooting from boat or hide—the value of camouflage—leave those tall birds till last.

The odd and interesting additions to the main bag—the woodcock flight—the knack of snipe shooting—wood pigeon decoys, jays, magpies, crows, rooks, gray squirrels, and other vermin.

Conclusion

Old and dangerous guns—teaching the young idea how to shoot—when to start a boy—shooting is indeed a great field sport—summing up for the last time.

[xv]

Illustrations

Straight Shooting

NOBODY expects to play golf well without proper coaching and regular practice. Yet, although "swing" is as important in game-gun shooting as it is in golf, and although there are other notable similarities in the two sports, such as, for example, the prime necessity of keeping your eye on the object you are aiming to hit, most men who get an occasional day with a gun are disappointed with themselves because they fail to put up a good performance. The secret of straight shooting, like playing scratch golf, is constant practice, a steady temperament, and a knowledge of the game.

Shooting knowledge can be acquired by anyone who takes the trouble to learn that there is more to shooting than being able to distinguish which end of the gun to keep clear of. Temperament, unhappily, is more difficult to control. But in shooting, as in other sports, coaching and sheer gunmanship can do a great deal to combat it.

The essential, and encouraging, difference between shooting and most other sports is that, under the guidance of an expert coach, a complete duffer can be made into a fair shot after a few hours' practice.

In the first place, unlike most sports, age is a very small factor in game shooting. As muscles become set, limbs stiffen, it becomes more than ever important to use a gun which has been tailored to fit the user. But, with good coaching and a gun that fits him, a man of seventy is capable of "wiping the eye" of a stripling; and, in fact, often does. The mistake that so many men make, who take up shooting late in life, is in thinking that any old gun will do and that they learned all about it when they handled a rifle in the army. In fact, a knowledge of rifle shooting is a questionable introduction to handling a shotgun. A shotgun is a weapon of movement. A rifle is a weapon of immobility. And it is rare, in my experience, for a man to excel with both. Normally, it is advisable to concentrate on one weapon at a time.

Secondly, unlike most sports, keen eyesight in shotgun shooting is comparatively unimportant. A man who cannot hit a golf ball to save his life, can shoot game with fair precision, provided only that he can see well enough to distinguish a flying pheasant from a partridge at about thirty yards.

In practice, shotgun shooting takes place at such short ranges that faults of vision which debar a man from accurate rifle practice won't make any material difference to his performance in the coverts, on the marsh, or in the stubbles. A good deal has been talked and written about the master eye. In my view, the simplest outstanding fact has been overlooked.

In the normal man the degree of emphasis on the master eye is slight. What is not so well known is that fatigue of the master eye rapidly transfers the mastery (temporarily of course) from one eye to the other.

If you strain and weaken the command of your right eye by putting your head down to the stock of a badly fitting gun or by a bad habit of gun-mounting you tire the eye. After a few shots, the right eye is fatigued and the left then takes mastery.

This phenomenon is recognized by rifle shots who close, or half-close, the left eye in order to prevent the disturbance of vision consequent on fatigue of the right, or aiming, eye. Yet it has not, so far as I am aware, ever been noted as an important factor in shotgun shooting.

[4]

In other sports this eye problem does not cause trouble. Left-eyed tennis players and golfers probably exist; but only in shooting do we hear of it as a difficult physical problem.

If you learn to shoot without worrying about your eyes, you will be in the same position as the ordinary man who uses his eyes all day without any perceptible strain or discomfort. By adopting a natural head position 75 per cent of the master-eye difficulty is solved.

If you are very slightly left-eyed, shooting from the right shoulder will not worry you and will, in fact, train the right eye to function as master.

If you are, on the other hand, completely left-eyed, or have lost the sight of the right eye, there is a type of stock which will compensate for this trouble and allow you to shoot comfortably with the head turned slightly more to the right than is usual.

So, whether you wear glasses or not, providing you can see well enough to identify, for example, the number of a streetcar in time to raise your hand to stop it, vision is going to present no difficulty to you in the shooting field.

If you are not too old for the gentle exercise of shooting in coverts, you are young enough to use a shotgun as well, if not better, than a young man who is in good enough physical condition to play a hand game of football.

But you can't be a good shot unless you're prepared to practice as thoroughly as a good golfer practices for his game, and unless you realize that just knowing how to put a gun to your shoulder and pull the trigger isn't enough to be an average, never mind a first-class, shot.

While the shooting school can never reproduce the actual conditions of the shooting field proper, it's safe to say that a man who can hit clay pigeons consistently is unlikely to make a complete "blot" of an important day in the coverts. And, if his gun fits and the coach knows his job, he will be hitting clay pigeons—if not consistently, at any rate often enough to give a wonderful lift to his morale—before he has fired a hundred rounds. The fact is, if you present a well-fitting shotgun properly to the shoulder, and keep your eye on the quarry, you cannot possibly miss.

The reason that all of us do miss—much too often—is entirely the consequence of bad style. We drop our heads or fail to bring the gun well in to the shoulder. We shoot off balance through bad footwork. We fail to hold the barrels of the gun straight in the cup of the left hand. We "poke" instead of swinging. We hang on to the trigger. Every miss is a fault in style. So much so that it is comparatively easy for an expert to tell whether a man has killed his bird or not simply by watching his gun handling and without looking at the target at all.

Obviously, faults can never be entirely eliminated. If that were possible, there would be no fun in shooting. But nobody can hope to improve performance without recognizing that, providing the gun fits and is throwing an even pattern of shot, a miss is always the consequence of bad style. The moral is that, if you wish to improve your shooting, the first necessity is to recognize your own weaknesses. Anybody can miss. Everybody should know, every time, why he misses. When you can say, with precision, that you shot high or low, too far in front or too far behind—which is not a very difficult thing to do—you are more than halfway to being a good shot.

When first-class shots are asked how they do it, they often have considerable difficulty in explaining their technique: what conscious allowances they make for the speed of the bird; how they judge the moment to fire; and how they deal with targets at various angles. The answer is that they don't have to think about it because they have largely solved this problem of style.

The footwork, bodywork, and gun-mounting of a first-class shot is as pretty to watch as a first-class baseball batter. But although stylish shooting is difficult to achieve, there need be no mystery as to how it is done.

[6]

There are two techniques of learning shooting at game. The older method (and, I think, the archaic method) is based on the principle of "forward allowances." The shooter is supposed to calculate the speed and angle of the target, and then swing the gun ahead of it, or above or below, so that the charge and the target meet. Many gun coaches still teach on this principle.

You will find in this book that my method is to tell you: "Keep your eye on the ball," swing your body with the target, and shoot straight at it, varying the speed of the swing with the speed of the bird. Admittedly, it is easier to write about it than to achieve it. But in my experience it is far simpler to shoot in the way of my school which tells you "to stroke the birds out of the sky" than the one that suggests a different lead to every bird that comes. The truth is that a mental calculation of allowance will let you down again and again. The man who shoots straight at his bird, and automatically overthrows as he fires, is leaving his eyes to work out allowances for him. The eye is never wrong. If you miss, you can blame your failure on faulty body movement, bad gun holding, erratic trigger pulling, or a similar error.

The purpose of this book is to put down, in practical terms, the reason why we miss and to teach a technique of straight shooting.

Simply reading this book won't make you a better shot. You won't improve your average performance, whether you are an experienced shooting man or a novice, unless you build muscle memory.

Your mind may accept the new knowledge, but only practice with the lesson in mind will ram it forever into your subconsciousness. Take my instructions, especially in the first section of the book, as drill; accept them, practice them, and, above all, master them, not only in abstract theory but in actual practice. Concentrate on the rules and practice the technique; then, like swimming, you will never forget it.

When a child masters the difficult feat of walking he forgets how to walk—he knows how—but he is unaware of his knowledge, as it is forgotten by his conscious mind. He does it, in fact, without thinking. If anyone starts thinking about walking, such as when crossing a narrow plank over a stream, he immediately does it unnaturally and without confidence and is apt to falter. Until the motions of swimming become a habit to a man, the learner is awkward, clumsy, and lacks confidence. But as soon as the motions become a habit to him, when he is expert, he does it without thinking. In other words he has forgotten how to swim.

All this is to assure you that if you will practice the drill I recommend to you, you will gain muscle memory and you will be able to mount your gun properly without conscious thought or effort. Accept my teaching as you accept any formal drill. Practice what I tell you as a purely physical technique—without argument—and you will find that your shooting has emerged from the mist of hazard to a very steady average basis upon which you can build your individual style.

There is no fixed standard of style in shooting as there is no fixed standard in any other sport. When all is said and done the personal equation is always paramount. A long-armed, narrow-chested tall man will inevitably have a different style as compared with a short, broad-chested, short-armed man; but, when you come to analyze comparative performance, there is very little, except the purely physical difference, to influence the mechanics of the process. The methods I advocate suit all physical variations, are easily learned, and once learned never forgotten.

A secondary but no less important characteristic will always intervene—temperament. This is a more disconcerting quality, for you will meet the quick, impatient type and the slow-velocity, enduring, patient slogger. The first is the hardest problem for himself as well as for the gun coach because he is always in antagonism to himself. Mind outreaches his physical performance, and he is likely to swing to the other extreme, becoming casual, half-hearted, and disappointed. Here discipline counts; practice and success will cure that man. His biggest enemy is his own despondency, his quick reaction to failure. But if a mercurial spirit like this once sees that he is getting better, there is no more adept pupil and the mastery once gained lasts.

Your low-velocity, patient slogger presents another condition; yet in a sense his shortcomings are his virtues. Slow to put into practice what he learns, yet once there it remains forever. Nothing will shake it. He will always be a sound, clean shot.

In brief, there is no fixed style in shooting; every man must develop his own style, but the basis of shooting is always and invariably dependent on first learning the routine which I outline in this book. First, learn to play the game in the classic style. If you do that, there's plenty of room for you to develop your own special technique.

Not until you make a critical survey of the wealth of books on shooting and sporting subjects which have appeared, do you realize how few of them contain any practical instruction on how to handle a shotgun.

The English language, so rich in its output of technical and sporting literature, is strangely lacking in an authoritative treatment of the science of shooting and the sort of detailed analysis of the sport that has been accorded to style and performance in other sports and other games.

This, in essence, is due to the radical difference which exists between games which can be witnessed by a large audience and the comparative seclusion in which shooting is practiced.

The average sportsman who shoots is seldom able to criticize, or rather analyze, the performance of his brother guns in the field. He is too busy, and his attention must necessarily be concentrated on his own sector of the beat or drive. His own style, in nine cases out of ten, is a standard of unconscious proficiency, joint product of a well-fitting gun, a good eye, and past experience. Questioned by an eager novice he can find few golden rules to explain "how to shoot" and in most cases admits that it is more a matter of knack than any conscious formula or system of technique.

But as I am a gun-maker who, as well as being a practical shot, is accustomed to studying the actual performance of men at the shooting school, I naturally approach the problem from a different standpoint. I am teaching you from my experience not only as a shot but as a critic and analyst of individual styles. What I am telling you in this book is not limited to casual glances at field performances during the shooting season but is based upon a routine of experience throughout the year. You can approximate me to the coach, amateur or professional, whose value and authority are admitted in every other branch of sport from lawn tennis to boxing.

At the beginning of this book, I am anxious to persuade you that the art of shooting is one that is just as capable of being taught or learned from fundamental points of style or technique as golf and tennis. In such games the attention paid to such matters as grip, position, and stance is rightly recognized as the highway to proficiency. It forms the basis of training which, with practice, develops into satisfactory achievement and a good style. My method is to deal with the use of the game gun and the attainment of shooting skill on these modernized lines. Expert rifle and pistol shots have long since insisted on correct physical technique as the basis of all teaching in their particular branches of shooting. Careful study of shotgun shooting over many years has taught me that certain fundamental rules, which can be defined, are at the bottom of all good shotgun work, and the disregard of these rules accounts for nearly all the bad shooting attributed to bad luck or other impersonal causes.

Good shooting is an indefinite term at best, for we all have varying standards by which we gauge our own and other people's performances. But in shooting there is no system of gauging proficiency like handicaps at golf. We just form our own impressions of the people we see at the game.

We all know bad shots, poor shots, ordinary shots, fair shots, good shots, brilliant shots, and those happy beings known as born shots. But these are all purely comparative terms. Personally I would make a difference between "good" and "brilliant" shots. A "brilliant" shot is a man whose standard of accuracy is as high as that of the "good" shot; but, where the latter is cautious and does not fire at difficult birds, the "brilliant" man takes chances and, as a result, shows a lower percentage of kills to cartridges expended. On the other hand, he probably kills more game in the day than the "good" shot, who is content only to take birds at easy angles. And, of course, the man who takes sporting chances gets a good deal more fun out of it.

The "born" shot is the rare man who enjoys the consistent accuracy of the "good" shot in combination with the less calculated style of the "brilliant" shot. The success of the "born" shot is, however, due to the fact that consciously (or far more probably entirely unconsciously) he automatically obeys the underlying rules of the art and achieves perfect co-ordination of muscular movement and aim.

Having read as far as this, the average-to-bad shot may well ask: "Am I too old or too set in my bad habits to develop into a good shot as late as this?"

Certainly he can. In fact, the man who is used to handling a gun, even inaccurately, will improve far more speedily than an absolute novice. The absolute beginner is perhaps the most difficult of all people to teach because he makes hard work of each shot. In a word, he uses far too much physical energy in his movements and expends too much mental calculation on his aim. He looks at the gun rather than the bird, tries to improve his first aim. He puts enough vigor into his swing and "follow-through" to lift a steam engine and finally he stops to pull the trigger, shooting behind his target.

Faults of style are easier to correct in men who have done at least sufficient shooting to have got over the preliminary troubles of awkward muscular action with the gun, who no longer flinch from fear of the noise or recoil, and who have overcome the feeling of strangeness inseparable from an introduction to any new sport. Experience proves that bad shooting habits can be eliminated at almost any age and that the experienced shot learns, on the whole, very swiftly.

The next question which might be asked is "Can a man teach himself to shoot?" He can, and a careful study of this book will help him enormously. But, of course, he can never see his own faults as clearly as a bystander, and inevitably an expert coach can teach a man more in half a dozen lessons than he is likely to learn by himself in three times the time.

If a man cannot find opportunity for a little work with a skilled coach, he can do a good deal for himself by persuading a friend to go over with him the technique laid down in this book and then go out with him in the field. The friend, if he is an alert critic, will be able to indicate what appears to be the shooter's faults in the light of what he has just read. One of the best ways in which a shooting man can double-check himself and compare his actual performance in the field with the instruction laid down in this book is to persuade a friend to photograph him in action with a cine-camera. Using a home movie you can make a point-by-point examination of the individual gun action. I have already used the cine-camera a great deal myself and found it invaluable for demonstrating to the sportsman his idiosyncrasies. For example, a gun may fit perfectly but a momentary hesitation, or an error in mounting, will negate the result of the best-fitting weapon which ever left a gunsmith. Yet, if you know where your own fault lies, you are three-quarters of the way to curing it; the cine-film shows precisely where the error lies, and, once it is known, a correction is easy.

I want to emphasize that the teachings in this book are not directed either to the novice or the expert in particular. They are for all shooting men. A lot that I have written in the earlier chapters will seem familiar to experienced shots, but any man who ever misses a bird—and who doesn't?—will find that his own failures can be corrected by referring back to the drill. On the other hand, I like to think that the novice with little or no experience in handling a gun will find that he can start here right at the beginning.

I have already referred to a man with a well-fitting gun. Ideally no man can expect to shoot at his best unless his gun has been tailored to fit his own physical conformity as carefully as his suit. But this drill will be equally valuable even to someone who can't afford to have a gun specially made to his own measurements. The man who can't afford it will almost certainly be a younger man. All I need say to him is that gun-fit is not so important to a man when his muscles are limber and he is able, to a very large degree, to fit himself to his gun. Gun-fit becomes increasingly important as a man grows older and his muscles get set. But whatever old gun you use—providing you take care to see that it's proofed for modern shells—you will shoot the better for taking my advice.

Finally, blame nobody but yourself if you bruise your fingers on the trigger guards, get a sore jaw, or suffer from what is called "gun headache." Gun-makers will be delighted to sell you various accessories to relieve the trouble. But, if you held your gun properly, you wouldn't need them. The proper cure is to find out what you are doing wrong. If your style improves, you will not need rubber padding and the birds you shoot at will mysteriously discard "their tin drawers."

INCORRECT METHOD

The right hand is too far over the top of the stock. The knuckle of the middle finger is hard against the gun. Faulty gun-mounting will result.

The gun cannot be mounted without raising the elbow, thus causing head movement. Finger and arm are likely to be bruised on recoil.

THE CORRECT METHOD

The right hand is well under the stock, thus straightening the trigger finger and clearing the knuckle. The shooter is balanced to meet recoil.

The gun is mounted without head movement. Note that the trigger finger is extended protectively along the guard until the actual moment of firing.

If the muzzle of the gun is held too high in the air . . .

. . . the barrels usually drop below the mark on gun-mounting.

If the muzzle of the gun is held pointing to the ground . . .

. . . the butt reaches the shoulder before the muzzle is on the target.

The adoption of this position in readiness for gun-mounting is one of the basic rules of sound, safe shooting. The stock is pressed tight under the right arm. The muzzle in the left hand is pointing towards the target. Note carefully that the gun is not held across the body. The left hand holds the barrels on a line with the right shoulder and at a right angle to the torso of the shooter. To hold a gun across the body in the ready position is dangerous.

If the left hand is too far for-ward . . .

. . . the barrels will mount ear-lier than the stock.

If the left hand is not forward enough . . .

. . . the stock will mount earlier than the barrels.

THE INCORRECT METHOD: *The fingers of the left hand encroach over the rib, causing the gun to cant or throw too high on the object. The right finger is bent in an unsafe position over the trigger guard.*

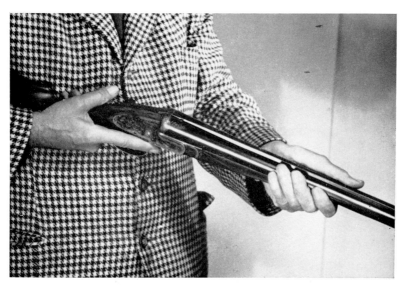

THE CORRECT METHOD: *The left thumb, lying along the left barrel, encourages a pointing movement; it checks "up-jump"; effectively stops the finger-tips covering the rib; and allows the ball of the thumb to stand out prominently, thus blocking the gun sight from the sight of the left eye and insuring right eye domination.*

Everyone knows that, with every kill, the gun-muzzles must have been pointed correctly at the target as it moved through the air.

But many people fail to realize that, as the barrels lie in the left hand, the left hand must also have been pointed in the right place.

The left hand must not be considered simply as a lifting lever. You will shoot just wherever you put it. Therefore, the left hand must point the barrels at the target during the whole movement of gun-mounting and trigger-pulling. If you misuse your left hand simply to lift the gun and then, in a separate movement, try to poke it at the target, you will miss. If the left hand is moving continuously on to the mark as the gun is mounting, the barrels will be on the mark too.

It is unsafe *to shoulder a game-gun with the trigger guard resting on the shoulder and without taking proper care to see that the barrels are held pointing skywards.*

It is unsafe *to nurse a gun across the forearm in the style of the man on the left. Between drives a gun should be carried open at the breech and unloaded.*

When you are walking-up game, it is a most dangerous position to carry a gun across your body instead of pointing the muzzles straight in front. If you hold a gun in this fashion . . .

. . . what happens is that every time you put the right foot forward the muzzles of your gun will swing and point directly at the next man in the line. The left hand should push the muzzles to the front.

From this natural and relaxed stance the shooter is in position to take any flying shot that offers.

The left heel is lifted and the gunbarrels move smoothly to meet a middle-height incoming pheasant.

The left heel is well up and the weight of the body on a stiff right leg to take a tall pheasant.

The shooter is well back, with his weight on the right leg, to take a high pheasant overhead.

A pivot on the right foot and the weight on the left leg to take a partridge on the left in front.

A pivot well round on the right toe to take a partridge behind. A typical second barrel shot.

With a pivot of the right leg, the shot is taken on a firm left leg at a high pheasant on the left.

With a pivot of the left toe and the weight on the right leg to deal with a back partridge, right.

(Starting from the ready position, the exercises on these pages should be followed, gun in hand, in dry practice with snap caps.)

Turn, with a pivot of the right toe, forward partridge, left.

Make an almost complete turn to take a back partridge, left.

Make a reverse turn to take a forward partridge on the right.

Swing round as far as you can to take a back partridge on the right.

*The weight is on the right foot to take a high pheasant on the right.
Note that the whole body shapes like an additional stock behind the
gun. Further, that the body is balanced so that recoil is taken by the
whole frame. In tall pheasant shooting, you should present the actual
physical appearance of stretching to stroke your bird out of the sky.*

A back view of the moment of firing at a high pheasant on the left. The inset reveals the problem of guessing the height of tall pheasants. The three posts are erected ten yards distant from each. The first or lowest board is 1 yard in length, the second or middle one 2 yards in length, the third 3 yards. To the eye they all look alike (see pages 63–64).

The three upper photographs show variations of the American beaver-tail grip, which is probably the most satisfactory fore-end so far devised (see page 99). The lower photograph illustrates the metal leather-covered handguard which can be slipped on to any double-barreled gun. The handguard assists gun-mounting and protects the fingers when the barrels get uncomfortably hot through constant shooting, or uncomfortably cold in hard weather. The ordinary handguard is inclined to slip unless fitted to the barrels with a special clip.

1. The grip of many modern guns, although graceful, is too straight for practical mounting. 2. The grip of Churchill Short-Barreled Guns is designed to preserve a graceful design but to keep the eye parallel to the line of sight. 3. The "roach-bellied" shape is copied from the old muzzle-loaders. It has a pleasant contour and a comfortable grip. 4. This is the notched stock of a trap-shooting gun specially adapted to the needs of competition shooting. 5. A traditional stock which is handsome but impractical for modern driven-game shooting.

6. An example of a full left-eyed gunstock which is often the most suitable stock for a man with abnormal sight. 7. This is the pistol grip which, in its various degrees, is very suitable for single trigger guns. 8. The half pistol grip is suitable for the trap gun or for walking-up game. 9. The full pistol grip is another form which is favored for specialized shooting but which is normally unsuitable for ordinary driven-game shooting. 10. An example of a gun with a deepened fore-end. It is sometimes a palliative for bad gun-mounting.

(Gun-stock variations are discussed in greater detail under the figures in the chapter "The Measurements of a Gun.")

The chief objection to the Under-and-Over Gun in the past, in which the strikers gave a glancing blow, has been overcome in the Zenith model in which the whole of the action face is free for the internal hammers to give a central blow. The model is "easy-opening" and the bolts lock into the upper barrel instead of the underneath one. The Zenith overcomes the objections to the usual Under-and-Over.

PART ONE

DRILL

CHAPTER I

The Elements of Gun-Handling

Unlike the muzzle-loaders of our forefathers, loading and letting off a modern shotgun is a simple matter. So simple that, although the mechanism of game-guns today is as safe as human ingenuity can devise and the mere process of charging and discharging calls for no explanation, the temptation to use a gun carelessly is greater than ever before.

In the nineteenth century, in the days of Colonel Peter Hawker, the father of modern game-gun shooting, the muzzle-loading flintlock and percussion gun of the period involved so many hazards to the user that the wonder is that there weren't more accidents.

If you read Colonel Hawker's diaries, you will find that it was a fairly common occurrence for shooting men to blow off their hands loading black powder into the muzzle of a barrel in which the spark from a previous charge was still burning. Powder flasks blew up in the shooter's hands and pockets. Barrels burst when somebody forgetfully put in a double charge.

Sometimes, when a man had fired with one barrel and stopped to reload, the second one went off in his face. In moments of excitement the shooters forgot to draw out their ramrods and fired ramrod and all at the departing quarry. The back flash from a flint gun occasionally blinded the user. Badly made copper caps in percussion guns exploded like shrapnel. Not surprisingly, the

[17]

most important lesson a novice had to learn before the coming of the breech-loader, in the latter years of the past century, was to avoid flinching when he pulled the trigger.

With modern game-guns and modern smokeless cartridges the only dangerous factors the shooter needs to consider seriously are himself and the other gun.

The first and most important convention of the shooting field prescribes that in no circumstances shall a gun, loaded or unloaded, point towards anyone. The second rule is that, in theory at any rate, a gun is always loaded.

Every gun with what is called a safety catch carries the legend "SAFE" when the catch is engaged. It is a dangerous word; but the gun traders, and the shooting men who patronize them, are a conservative breed and custom rules that the word "safe" remains: "check" would be better. The safety catch simply checks the trigger. The sears and tumblers of the actions are *never* locked.

I recommend you, as a drill, to use your safety catch. But I beg you to regard it as an extra precaution rather than a basic one.

The best of guns can become unsafe through neglect or climatic causes. Slight swelling of the wood, for example, may prevent the sear from fully entering its bent and the gun can jar off when closing. A very old "springy" stock may cause the sears to be partly lifted during closing. I remember one of our famous gun-makers could take one of his own lock plates and, with a sharp flick on his bench, jar off the lock.

In my time, as an expert witness called in many civil and criminal cases, I have had to examine I-don't-know-how-many faulty guns. In one case heavy damages were awarded in a civil action to a sportsman who lost his leg as a consequence of an accident in which a gun, which another guest was carrying quite properly under his arm, went off unexpectedly. The safety catch was engaged; but the lock failed. A stranger case, fortunately without serious consequences, was one in which the owner loaded, put his gun at "safe," and was astounded, a few minutes later, when it went off. He emptied his gun and put it under the back seat of his car. A few minutes later he heard a click. Once again the action had operated of its own accord.

When the gun was brought to me, I found the right lock had been fired. Closing it very carefully, I laid it down while I made my notes. To my own great surprise, it went off again after several minutes. Before stripping the gun I had a record taken of the time lapse over several days. This varied from two to eleven minutes and, on examination, I discovered that a combination of chances had been at work; the safety work, sear spring, and sear nose and tumbler bent had all contributed to the main fault which was that the gun was, as we say, "wood bound." The consequence was that the sear nose could only hang on the bare edge of the tumbler bent whilst pressure from the mainspring caused the sear to slowly creep until the tumbler (internal hammer) was released. I think that was the most extraordinary case of gun trouble I have ever experienced; but it shows what *can* happen.

Whenever I am handling a gun myself, demonstrating as I am daily to other people, I make it a rule as soon as I pick up a gun to break it and show the empty chambers to the person who is with me. As I do so, I say: "Empty."

You may believe that I am over careful, but a very large part of my professional career has been occupied studying the evidence, and giving my opinion, on the causes of gun accidents of one kind or another. The commonest cause is that somebody didn't know that his weapon was loaded.

You will never be criticized, just the opposite, for being punctilious in your gun-handling. When you are carrying an empty gun, as every game-gun should be unless you are in readiness to shoot, make a practice of carrying it under your arm WITH THE BREECH OPEN. Let everybody see, including yourself, that an accident cannot possibly happen. Incidentally, the most comfortable way of all of carrying a gun is in this manner, broken across the crook of the arm.

There are two basic positions in which sporting guns are customarily carried when shooting is not afoot:

(1) In the crook of the elbow, in the manner I have described to you, with the muzzles pointing downwards.
(2) On the shoulder, with the muzzles pointing skywards, not horizontally inclined.

The former is the favorite method of carrying a gun and though, theoretically, it is slightly less safe than the shoulder position, it is as good in practice.

When walking up game, the gun is held, tilted slightly upwards and forwards, in both hands in easy position. Even the most experienced sportsman, walking in line or in company, should constantly check himself to make sure that, in his concentration, the barrels of his gun have not swung across his chest, which is the more natural position, but the position in which anybody on the flank will receive the full charge if the gun goes off by accident.

Drill yourself to hold your shotgun on the march in the field not at the port arms position of army drill, but pointing straight out in front of you.

Shooting in covert, or from any sort of stand, the technique may be a little different. Sitting on a stick seat, the most comfortable way to carry the gun is to hold it in one hand with the butt on the knee and the barrels pointing straight in the air. When you are expecting birds, rise to your feet and present the gun forward and tilted upwards in the ready position. Apart from considerations of safety, the gun is thus correctly poised to come on to a bird with the minimum of delay, and, in the case of birds at an angle, the turn of the body carries the arms with it and so achieves the correct alignment without motion of the arms themselves.

You may be seated with muzzles erect, you may be walking with a gun under your arm, you may be holding your weapon in any of the comfortable and safe positions, but when it comes to actual shooting you must learn before you mount the gun to your shoulder to assume the correct "ready" position.

Some of my readers will be left-handed shots. It is important to point out here that in the following sections the drill applies to right-handed shots only. Left-handed men will appreciate that they must reverse my instructions, from right to left, to meet their own personal requirements.

CHAPTER II

The First or "Ready" Position

IN READINESS for gun-mounting, the stock must be tucked in well under the arm. You are inviting a miss if you hold the gun slackly with the butt at elbow level. Place the stock with the small of the butt just forward of the right armpit, and squeeze it between biceps and ribs.

The man waiting to shoot with his gun under his right arm and his left hand free should naturally reach this position before he raises the muzzle in readiness to shoot. In any other position, there is an inclination to rush the gun to the shoulder with the result that it never comes to the same place twice running. To do that is to invite a miss. Consistency in style is the vital concomitant of consistent shooting. The method I advocate, practiced until it becomes automatic, will compel you to do the right thing.

Tuck the stock well under your arm because (1) I want you to *push* your left hand forward as you mount, not merely raise it. (2) I want you to push your left hand forward because I am going to show you that the left hand is the aiming hand. (3) By pushing your left hand into the aim, you take a proportion of the recoil of the charge through your left arm and thence to your body rather than take it all on the shoulder. (4) In squeezing the gun under your armpit, you are taking some of the weight off your hands and encouraging the muscles in your arms to relax.

(5) This method will train you to put your shoulder to the stock instead of making the common error of putting the stock to your shoulder. (6) It's the quickest form of gun-mounting, because the butt simply slips from the underarm to the shoulder without losing contact with your body (that is important) and the gun comes easily and smoothly to eye level. (7) The gun comes up to your face instead of the head going down to meet the stock, and faulty head movement is one of the commonest causes of poor shooting. (8) The system checks hasty gun-mounting and encourages correct timing. (9) It prevents the incidence of bruised cheek and jawbone from the recoil. (10) It encourages the right hand to adopt the correct position on the side of the stock and so prevent a bruised middle finger. (11) It not only keeps you squarely onto your target (as your body is checked from turning too much sideways) but it also encourages you to adopt a natural stance.

Finally, and this is most important of all, it encourages you to start your body swing whilst the gun is coming up.

With that I hope I have given you sufficient good reasons for asking you to begin by adopting a "ready" position for shooting which may at first seem odd and unfamiliar to you.

Practice the ready movement and, at the same time, don't be ashamed, however long you have used a gun, to check yourself on the rest positions, too. Are you sure that you are instinctively carrying a gun safely and correctly? Do you always break and unload it when you cross wire or a ditch or a hedgerow? Are you sure that when you are walking in line you never swing the muzzle towards the man walking beside you?

It is always dangerous to walk up game with the gun cradled in your left arm or to proceed with the barrels pointing any-where but in the region of your own feet. Walking potato ridges, for example, the natural body sway is enough to make a gun held horizontally between the two hands point down the line every time you put your right foot forward.

When you shoulder your gun, if you adopt that position, do you always carry it with the trigger guard uppermost? You should. Normally, I myself never shoulder a gun except when following single file. There is a reason for it when walking in single file. In single file, there is a risk that mud flying off the heel of the man in front will plug the barrels of the man walking behind if he is carrying his own gun muzzles pointing downwards in the crook of his arm. I've seen it happen; and it was lucky I was there to notice it. If the mud-plugged gun had been fired in that condition, the barrel would certainly have burst.

As you practice the ready and the rest positions, accustom yourself to another safety habit.

Never let your finger touch the trigger until the actual moment of firing. In the ready position the trigger finger should lay straight along the right lock plate. And it should stay there until the barrels are aligned on the target and the butt comes into your shoulder.

Under actual shooting conditions you will often find that you come to the "ready" in anticipation of a shot which doesn't materialize; that you are "on your toes" and in those circumstances it is unnecessary and often unwise to go back to a full rest position. But you have a loaded gun in your hands.

This is the time to adopt the semi-rest waiting position. Keeping the stock well up between your upper arm and hip, lay the gun sideways in the palm of your right hand, keeping the trigger finger straight out as an extra cover to the guard, using the second, third, and fourth fingers to hold the small of the butt with the thumb crossing to meet them. The barrels are held sideways in the left hand with the left thumb on the side of the left barrel. (*See Further Comments on Walking Up Game.*)

Some experienced shots cock their gun by slipping the safety catch forward as soon as they assume the ready or semi-ready position. I can't recommend the practice. It's so easy to acquire the habit of pushing forward the safety catch as part of the drill of actual gun-mounting. But it must be a habit. Nothing is more exasperating than to align on a bird, pull at the trigger, and then find that nothing happens.

You mustn't slip off your safety catch too soon and neither must you leave it too late; too soon is any time when the quarry is not in sight, too late is any time after the gun is raised to eye level. If you actually shoot with your thumb pushed forward on the safety catch, you will pull it back again with the recoil of the discharge.

Practice slipping the safety catch on and off with the side of the first joint of the thumb, not the ball of the thumb. If you use the ball of your thumb—and most people do—there is a risk that if you happen to pull the trigger at the same time, you will get a jolt from the lever. But, more important, if you use the ball of your thumb instead of the first joint, you are altering your grip, which is never to be recommended. The whole of your right hand should always remain in its correct position on the stock.

CHAPTER III

Feet

YOU will often notice that experienced shots, standing in a plowed field, waiting for a drive to begin, are at some pains to select a position where there is no obstacle to impede their stance and footwork. They tread down a ridge, or select a wide furrow, to secure a position for their feet which is both firm and free from obstructions such as would prevent their pivoting.

Like a good ballplayer, the wise shooting man gets himself set before he begins. And, like the golfer who makes a practice swing at the ball before he hits it, expert shots, long before the shooting starts, seize the opportunity to limber their muscles, practice their gun-mounting, footwork, and swing, and get themselves into a proper condition to give their best.

I mention this because I can imagine an impatient reader thinking that by this time we ought to be getting on with the actual shooting. I can only assure you that, if you master the proper way to use your hands and feet and practice it until the drill becomes automatic, you will find that the problems of hitting what you are aiming at become relatively easy.

In shooting, as in most other sports, stance, footwork, and poise of the body are all married together to blend into one smooth action. Above all, the balance and poise of the body must be firm and comfortable, with the weight supported evenly on *both legs.* The only exception occurs when using wildfowl guns or unusually heavy charges, in which case the greater proportion of the weight may be thrown on the left leg.

The toes of the feet should be about nine inches apart and the heels about three inches apart, although this distance will of course vary slightly with the general build of the individual. But, generally speaking, it is better to take too narrow a stance than too wide a one.

I have introduced a series of figures here because that is the simplest way of demonstrating the commonest faults in stance as compared with the correct position.

Fig. 1   Wrong

Figure 1 shows the common fault of standing with heels too close together. The result is that the bulk of the recoil is taken by the shoulder without assistance from the legs. This is not only unnecessarily wearing for the shooter, but also prevents him firing a successful second barrel until he has recovered his poise. In addition, it is a frequent cause of bruised cheek or a bruised second finger. Shots who may suffer from these troubles should always suspect their stance and be at pains to correct it.

Figure 2. Another fault. Right foot immediately behind left. This twists the body in such a manner that the gunstock is not firm to the shoulder. As a result, the recoil of the discharge of the first barrel causes the butt to shift from the shoulder to the arm muscle. Thus the second barrel cannot be fired with true alignment. This fault is perhaps the most frequent cause of second-barrel misses. The butt must bed squarely into the shoulder.

Fig. 2   Wrong

This is also an "infirm" stance which will cause the shooter to drop the right shoulder and shoot underneath the bird crossing on the right, but with the reverse effect on his left where the left shoulder will be uplifted and shoot well over the top of the bird crossing on the left.

Fig. 3   Wrong

Figure 3. Another common fault. The stance is too wide. The shooter is unable to transfer body weight from one foot to the other without a sway of the body, with the consequence that he will drop a shoulder on side shots and shoot underneath them. On uneven ground the recoil can even knock him over or drive him back a pace or two; which of course means a risk to the neighboring guns.

Figure 4. The correct position. The balance and poise of the body is even, weight can be transferred left or right without body disturbance; it allows the shooter to put his right shoulder

Fig. 4   Right

to the stock and to absorb recoil bodily instead of all on the shoulder. Any turn is easily and quickly accomplished and the heels are about three or four inches apart.

Having placed your feet in the correct stance, assume the ready position. Now take your own gun and practice moving your trunk to the right and to the left. The turn of your body to the right should compel you to transfer body weight on to the right leg. The turn of the body to the left should transfer the weight onto the left leg. Practice this body swing at angles of 45 degrees right and left where only a transference of weight is required.

Having mastered this movement, increase the body swing to a full 90 degrees right and left and it will be found that the opposite foot, instead of being firm and flat on the ground, will quite naturally begin raising its heel around the 45 degree mark and will turn outwards to allow you to get to 90 degrees and beyond.

Do not mount your gun yet. Remember that part of this body and foot movement must take place before gun-mounting. A short, heavily built man may notice that heel-raising begins before reaching 45 degrees, whereas a tall, thin man may almost reach 90 degrees before it happens. Regardless of this, you will find that it is a natural swing which will allow you to pivot on

[29]

your toes and to cover much more than one-half of the circle without alteration of stance. With a forward inclination of the body, practice a low shot at a rabbit on the right or left. Then, with a backward inclination of the body, practice shooting at an imaginary pheasant crossing in front of you. Finally, although I have a personal distaste for the "eye-level" bird which, in the interests of safety, must be shot at with caution in front or behind and never down the line, it makes very good dry practice to try the swing for the whole 180 degrees all around you.

A middle-aged man especially may find it difficult to swing more than three-quarters of the complete circle. In that event, it is proper in certain circumstances to move one foot more to the rear of the other one. For example, when birds are immediately behind, you may be able, on firm ground, to move one foot more to the rear with the toe turned as much as is conveniently possible in the direction of the bird; and then raise the other heel and pivot.

To get round to the right, shift the right foot a few inches to the rear of the left and the reverse for the opposite side. Do not take a step with the foot, since to lift it off the ground disturbs the balance, rather "scrape" it round to the back of the other one.

SWINGING TO RIGHT BEHIND   SWINGING TO LEFT BEHIND

(*1*) *Scrape right foot behind left.*   (*1*) *Scrape left foot behind right.*
(*2*) *Pivot on left toe.*   (*2*) *Pivot on right toe.*

In partridge driving, fast birds often get out of range before a gun can get round, and this movement should be practiced in your room against your usual method to enable you to decide whether you can adopt it for such shots. It is difficult at first, but after practice you will become more confident and will be able to do this movement very smartly whilst retaining your balance. With a little indoor drill the motions become automatic.

When walking up game, as apart from waiting at a stand for game to be driven over the guns, the essential footwork is unchanged but, on sighting a target, the walking gun must accustom himself to a routine movement which will place his feet in the correct position.

As the gun is mounting, the shooter should simply scrape back the right foot to bring himself into the position shown in *Figure 4*.

Again, with gun in hand, held in the ready position with the barrels pointed straight ahead, walk up and down a room, or a lawn, and practice the movement of stopping in your tracks, scraping back the right foot so that you assume the correct position as the gun mounts to your shoulder.

If you shoot as you put your left foot forward, you will shoot under the mark. If you shoot with both feet together, you will take recoil without assistance from your legs and you will be off balance and miss with the second barrel.

Don't fool yourself that you can remember your foot drill—like all the other drill in this book—without dry practice.

This business of indoor drill is important. Just as a boxer uses a punching-bag for practice and exercise, so a shooter can improve his style and get into better muscular trim for field work by indoor gun-handling.

The preliminary manual of rifle exercise of the army is not solely to teach the recruit how to open and load his rifle. It is very largely designed to accustom him to the muscular exercise involved. If you give a man unaccustomed to guns a weapon to handle, his movements are relatively slow and uncouth. He has to exert far more energy than the trained man.

Normally, we put our guns away at the end of January, and when August or September arrives, even if we have been accustomed to shooting all our lives, we are to a certain extent slack and out of this particular form of training. That is why very many of the very best shots, men with established reputations as leading performers, go down to the clay-pigeon schools and fire on one, two, or three successive days in order to get into training. The practice braces them and accustoms them to recoil, and it must be remembered that the physical effort of lifting a 6½-pound gun or more and firing a hundred or so rounds is considerable. It puts them into physical training as well as "getting their eye in." Not everyone can spare the time for these visits, but indoor drill, although it lacks the element of actual practice and the reality of recoil, is by no means a waste of time. It is sound physical training.

Those who live in the country, or pay frequent visits there, can find many more opportunities for carrying a gun and firing a sufficient number of rounds than a townsman. They attain what I might term contact with their weapon. If you want to shine as a shooting man, you must make an effort to keep in reasonable practice all the year round.

You are bound to be disappointed with yourself if you only take up a gun on the occasion when somebody sends you a shooting invitation or somebody lends you a gun for a day's sport in the country. There is no game on earth in which you can achieve a mastery without constantly playing it and giving your attention to it. But, oddly enough, shooting is one of the sports in which I notice that singularly few men are prepared to take the same trouble as they take over their golf.

❦ CHAPTER IV ❧

Hands

Now that you have found your feet, or I hope you have, take your gun and go over this section carefully with the weapon in your hand. Grip is a very important matter and it is necessary that the detail should be understood.

Right Hand. Most people think that they grip a gun naturally and correctly. All too often they do not. The tendency is to carry the right hand far too much round the top of the stock. This checks it coming up and forces the knuckle of the second finger hard against the rear of the trigger guard (another cause of bruised finger).

Make this test: lift your gun to your shoulder with your thumb purposely too far round the top of the stock. You will find that you cannot lift the gun without raising the elbow as well. That in itself causes muscular constraint and awkwardness.

And, again, starting with your usual grip, readjust so that the finger-tips of the right hand are rather more round the stock than usual. You will find that the gun fits comfortably into the hollow of the hand and that it can be lifted without any elbow work far more quickly and comfortably than usual. You will also be able to bring the gun up to the cheek instead of having to put your cheek down to meet the gun.

A frequent cause of bad grip is the tendency for shooters with a short thumb to keep it in contact with the top lever. This is not necessary, as the fraction of time lost in shifting the grip of the hand is immaterial, whereas a bad grip means bad shooting.

The strength, or pressure, with which the stock is held should not be exaggerated. The gun should be brought up with a fairly light grip which should be tightened *only* at the instant of trigger pressure. If you grip too tightly while mounting the gun to the shoulder, you may relax on the instant of firing. Bruised cheek or finger is sometimes an indication of too light a right-hand grip at the instant of firing, though more usually it is due to the error in stance indicated in the previous section.

Sometimes a man may use a gun which he has inherited or bought second hand. It *may* fit, but, more likely, it does not. Stock length, bend, and castoff represent only approximations to fit unless we also take into account the circumference of the narrow portion of the stock where the right hand grips it. Men's hands vary considerably. One man may have a long-fingered, trim, and flexible hand; another a broad-palmed, capable hand, that of a surgeon rather than an artist; while a third may have a short-fingered, podgy hand. Even if all these three are relatively the same in the circumference which they can grip, the width of the hand varies. When fitting a gun I pay considerable attention to this factor. One man may need the comb of his stock cutting back half or three quarters of an inch more toward the heel than another, simply in order to make a comfortable bedding for his hand. There is no particular novelty about this attention to manual anatomy, for, in the old days, when dueling was in vogue, a gentleman would be measured for his pistols, the selection of an appropriately shaped stock having been part and parcel of the gunsmith's craft. They had to fit perfectly in the individual hand. Similarly, in these days, we must ensure that our game-guns are stocked to fit not only the bodily dimensions of shooters, but also fit their hands.

In my opinion the grip of every normal gun should be tapered from the direction of the breech; that is to say, it should be thicker in front of the hand than at the rear and thus offer a cone to prevent the hand slipping forward on recoil.

Very often one sees a grip tapered the reverse way. Such guns tend to slip through the fingers on recoil, with bruised second finger for result.

Left-Hand Grip. The right and left hands should each do an equal share of the work of mounting the gun to the shoulder. The correct point of reach is found by balancing the gun between the two hands until the point of equal distribution of weight is found.

If the left hand is too far back, the stock will mount earlier than the barrels, which will "sag"; also the recoil will be more heavily felt on the shoulder.

If the left hand is too far forward, the barrels will come up before the stock. This is almost as bad.

The gun should be balanced to encourage horizontal mounting, so that, by the time the butt touches the shoulder, the barrels should be pretty well parallel to the line set by the eyes.

A badly balanced gun has no right place for the front grip, but one properly balanced will allow firm grasp to be taken near the front of the fore-end.

The left thumb should not be curled round the barrel but, rather, be held lengthwise and made to project, or, at least, be noticeable. This serves a double purpose, for it cuts out disturbance of aim due to left-eye vision and prevents the fingers covering too much of the barrel and encroaching on the sighting rib; it also prevents the barrels jumping out of hand on recoil, another cause of bruised cheek.

While lifting the gun the barrels should only be held lightly; but they should be gripped at the instant of firing.

You may adopt a correct stance and you may also take a perfect grip of the gun, yet you can still miss certain birds if your body or legs are wrongly braced. The rifle shot holds or expels his breath as he shoots: but the man with the shotgun does, or should do, something more.

Perhaps I can explain it most effectively by pointing out a few of the differences that I notice between the expert shot and the novice.

You can always recognize the expert as he takes his stand to shoot, because his feet are never too wide or in an unnatural position; his toes are pointed at their usual walking angle, the forward foot is not much in advance of the other, and the shooter's balance enables him to transfer his body weight from one leg to the other without disturbing his bodily control. In conjunction with legs and body, he can take recoil properly.

The novice, you will notice, may never stand twice alike. He puts one foot behind the other, with the effect that it turns his body sideways. His toes are turned unnaturally, which means an insecure foothold, and, if his stance is too wide, it causes a drop of the shoulders in the side shot.

The expert shoots with a stiff knee, either left or right; or, to be more precise, if he is taking a going-away shot on the left, the left leg is very firm or stiff and the right is the reverse. All the weight is on the left leg, and the right leg, with heel slightly raised, is helping to push the weight forward. Of course, everything is reversed for the overhead shot and for the crossing shot on the right.

The novice often bends both knees, or simply stands free, without really using his legs as part of the machinery to ensure rock steadiness, regardless of wind. He hasn't learned how to take up recoil without disturbance and so allow a quick recovery for the second shot.

The expert braces up his body by means of both arms and legs. The stiffening of the knee tightens the leg muscles and thus serves to stiffen the hip joint, consequently stiffening the whole side. The action of gun-mounting, with elbows and both arms kept down as much as possible, helps to stiffen the back muscles and, altogether, the body is very rigid.

The novice, with his bent knee, is also loose at the hip. If his elbows are outwards, he can wobble about so much during his gun-mounting that the odds are very much against his ever making a consistent performance as a shot.

The expert clenches his teeth, slightly inclines his head, and slightly shrugs his shoulders to stiffen his neck muscles. The novice may keep his mouth open, hold his head loose, or be out-breathing at the instant of firing, all of which aggravate looseness in general, causing irregular gun-mounting.

In its proper place, I am emphasizing in this drill the necessity of keeping the eye on the bird, pushing out the left hand, relaxing the right-hand grip, and putting the shoulder to the gun. For that reason, the shot must plant himself firmly, not only to withstand recoil, but also to allow perfect gun-mounting.

All the good shots I have ever known have been men who, perhaps without thought, have naturally braced themselves at the instant of firing. Some of them, whom I have seen emerge from the ranks of the mediocre and middling-to-fair-class shots, have altered with practice from a nervous and jumpy style to one of firm rigidity which, without a shot being fired and simply by gun-mounting alone, shows the onlooker that here is a man who has perfect control of his gun, who is keen, and who, if given the right tools, will shoot well.

Again, and you must not overdo it, this whole muscular bracing progress occurs during gun-mounting. Confidence, plus keenness, causes the majority to do it more or less properly, and the perfect action is a smooth gradual mounting culminating in rigidity at the instant of recoil. Nothing here, of course, refers to the grip of the hands. We brace up the body yet relax our grip, as explained in the next chapter.

Gun-Mounting

THIS is perhaps the most critical process of shooting, for it co-ordinates all the mechanical functions of stance, footwork, and grip with the conscious function of aim.

When you point your finger at an object, you aim at it and there is unconscious adjustment of the line of vision with the axial line of the pointing finger. Point at an object, glance along your extended finger, and note how, without conscious sighting, you have taken a true aim.

The left, or forward, hand must not be considered simply as a lifting lever for the gun. You must, so to speak, mentally aim, or point, at the object with the left hand which holds the gun. You point just as straight with your left forefinger as you do with your right. Drive the left hand forward with a rather vigorous pointing movement, pointing at the bird the whole time.

The left hand does the real aiming. But the right must keep pace with the left, doing its share of directing the muzzle on the object the whole time that the gun is coming up.

Here is where gun-fitting and, to a lesser extent, the clothes worn need consideration. The gun must not be too long in the stock or the clothes bulkier or tighter than those normally worn while shooting. On the other hand, though the stock should not get in the way of the coat, neither may it be too short. In practice, the butt should scrape your clothing as it travels up your arm to bed in your shoulder. The slightest clearance between butt plate and shoulder is all that is necessary or desirable; and the *thrust* of the left arm automatically provides it.

At the completion of the mounting movement or, rather, this first portion of it, the gun is up to the eye level and the butt of the stock in touch with, but not home on, the shoulder. The left arm (hand) is pointing at the object in subconscious co-ordination with the sight, or line, of vision from the eye.

Now put your shoulder forward to the stock and at the same time contract the trigger finger so that, as the gun is firm against the shoulder, the trigger is pulled exactly at the limit of the movement. Swing is combined with this movement.

It is in appearance almost a "snap" and the jar of the shoulder against the stock aids the trigger finger in precise timing of its pull. Analyzing this simple yet complex movement we find that the left arm pushes forward while the right finally neutralizes the push and adds the bit extra that brings the gun back. Thus the left arm absorbs a large proportion of the recoil which would otherwise be received on the shoulder.

The pressure of the stock against the shoulder by the right hand involves the necessity of gripping with the right hand and so avoids the occasional trouble of too slack a grip. You should actually be *pulling* the gun between your two hands as you fire. With practice, the opposing movement of the two arms becomes so automatic that the trigger finger can remain in a semi-rigid position and trigger pressure to fire can be made (indeed should be made) part and parcel of the butting of the gun to the shoulder. Trigger pulling is thus timed to occur at the instant that the butt of the gun is met by the thrust of the shoulder coming forward to meet it.

If you perform this mounting movement correctly—thrusting the shoulder forward to meet the butt, butting the gun into the shoulder with the hands, and applying trigger pressure at the moment the two meet—you won't feel the kick of recoil from the gun.

The analogy is the old one of grasping the nettle. If you handle your gun indecisively, it will "sting" you. Handle it firmly and determinedly and you'll know you're handling it right because you won't feel recoil.

The precise position where your shoulder should meet the butt of the gun in the instantaneous action of completing mounting and applying trigger pressure can be established by folding your arms. When you fold your arms, you will notice that your shoulders come forward, in just the way that your right shoulder should come forward to meet the butt, and that you create a muscular bed between your collar bone and the ball in the shoulder socket. That natural bed in your shoulder is the point where the butt should meet it as you fire.

The proper movement in gun-mounting is, in fact, the precise reverse of what many novices, and nearly all women, tend to do when they lift a gun warily to their shoulder for the first time. They draw the shoulder away from the butt. They're unable to take recoil and can easily be bowled off their feet, or lose a tooth, on discharge.

As an experiment—but choose a safe place to make it—try firing a gun, held firmly in the hands, without lifting it to your shoulder. It will remind you what an ugly kick a 12-bore has when it is held improperly. But, held properly, the arms and shoulder absorb the full shock and do so without the shooter being aware of it.

What the novice does is to hang on to his gun with grim determination at all times when he isn't actually firing it. But when he fires, he loosens his grip, draws away his shoulder, and catches the recoil on his jaw.

The expert carries his gun, except at the instant of firing, with a relaxed grip. But as he fires, his muscles tense in perfect time with the action of gun discharge.

From the foregoing you will see that the eyes have been left nothing to do but look at the bird. The hands and arms automatically obey the eyes, and if the gun is mounted correctly, discharge occurs automatically and in perfect time as the butt comes to the shoulder.

Provided the gun fits and that the quarry is within range you will shoot exactly where you are looking and should kill every time.

Obviously every bird killed is proof that the muzzle must have been pointed in the right place. Next, that, as the barrels lie in the left hand, the left hand also was pointing in the right place. Combining the two propositions one shoots wherever the left hand points. If weakness or injury prevents, or makes, this ordinary procedure at all difficult, there are remedies which are dealt with in another chapter.

When this formula is properly carried out, misses occur from one cause (and one cause only): not looking at the proper place. Curiously enough, when you have mastered the knack of correct gun-mounting, misses which you could not analyze or diagnose before, but attributed vaguely to some fanciful cause, are easily resolved. You know instinctively what you have done wrong and are able to correct the error. The only explanation I can offer is that the shooter knows where he is putting his charge because the slightly upward movement of recoil lifts the muzzle of the gun into view and the eye takes cognizance.

A common complaint of shooters is that they "do no good with their second barrel." This is often caused by a disturbance of the grip or shoulder-bedding of the gun brought about by the recoil of the first discharge. The method of gun-mounting I am teaching you eliminates this. If the left arm is correctly pushed forward, it not only serves to keep the butt from catching against the clothes (so that an extra heavy coat in hard weather does not so seriously disturb or upset the fit of your gun) but, acting as a girder under compression against the backward pull of the right hand, it takes the main stress of recoil and absorbs it without transmitted shock to the body. A bad mounter, on the other hand, takes the full recoil shock on his shoulder instead of on his left arm and in consequence is swung slightly round, so that for his second shot he has perforce to correct his aim again.

Needless to say, bad footwork is another reason for second barrel misses. The shooter fires when, as a consequence of bad style, he is off balance.

But, although shooters themselves have a common tendency to complain that they miss with the second barrel, I fancy that the complaint is more often that they are looking for an alibi for poor shooting all round.

A man who can consistently kill with his first barrel can usually put up a good show with his second. Under the test conditions of the shooting school, what we usually find is that a pupil who is "trying too hard" misses with his first barrel because he pokes at the bird and makes a clean kill with his second (once we've taught him not to be afraid to use his second barrel quickly) because he hasn't got time to stop and think, makes a natural swing onto the target, and fires at "first aim."

It's a paradox of game-gun shooting that, if you see the barrels as you fire, or indeed hear your gun go off, you have missed. There is no mystery about that. If you see the barrels, it means that you can't be looking at the bird. If you hear the gun go off, it means that you are not giving the target, which is all that matters, your undivided attention.

To cure that trouble we use various coaching devices. We tell the shooter to try and miss the bird; just behind, or just in front. It doesn't matter where. By making him concentrate on hitting a particular part of the target, we make sure that he looks at the target and not at his gun.

If you are missing in the field, it is always an effective corrective to make up your mind to place the charge not at the target in general but at a specific part of it. Promise yourself to shoot that next pheasant in the eye, or in the left leg, or in the beak. Look at that, and nothing else, as you fire.

A man with his eye on the bird can often kill clean, if his foot-work and gun-handling are correct, by pulling the trigger before the butt of the gun is into his shoulder. Some snipe-shots shoot that way for choice; although I wouldn't recommend it, except as an experiment, to anybody but a very experienced gun-handler.

Most of the foregoing remarks deal with the "going-away" bird, perhaps the simplest shot of all; but the subsequent instructions, detailing the adaptation of the technique to more difficult shots, are all dependent on this first mastery of the knack of correct gun-mounting.

A novice is inclined to snatch the gun to his shoulder. This is wrong. The whole sequence of movement for ordinary shots should be easy and steady, becoming in time so purely mechanical that once learned it is never forgotten.

Contrast this technique with the practice, so often seen, of raising the gun at an angle rather than parallel to the line of vision, then bringing the muzzle down on the bird. In this practice it is obvious that not only is the line of vision temporarily intercepted by the barrels, but that the gun is spinning windmill fashion and has to be got out of its spin before firing takes place. With proper technique, the muzzles are finding the bird during the whole process of mounting, and even a slightly premature, or belated, trigger pressure does not necessarily involve the miss that is unavoidable in the case of the man "tipcatting" his gun or otherwise not keeping his muzzles in the general direction of the bird.

In the field it is not possible to ensure a succession of simple "straight away" shots for practice purposes, but a good deal can be done with simple manual exercise in one's room at home. Practice simple gun-mounting with a pair of "snap caps" [1] in the barrels, and you will, in a day or so, get the necessary muscular control or "knack" which is half the battle.

Timing the discharge is rather more difficult at the start and can really only be learned by practice, preferably at clay birds. In essence there should be a ratio between the speed of the bird and the speed of mounting the gun to the shoulder. The swifter birds need a quicker movement.

After a little practice this soon ceases to be a matter of conscious calculation. It becomes an automatic or reflex effect accomplished instinctively and without thought.

Those who are dogged by persistent failure are sure to ask the question: "Does my gun fit me?" It is not one that can be answered in general terms, but, if you do not shoot well and your gun-fitter has not seen you shoot, it is highly probable that some alteration is needed. Never have the stock of a gun bent or cast-off to compensate for faults in gun-mounting. These should be corrected not by deforming the gun but by improving your style. Unless a man has been properly trained or has unconsciously and naturally evolved a good consistent technique of his own, his very errors are inconstant and it is useless to try to attempt a fit until a standard or basis has been established.

A perfect fit with a gun is dependent on the establishment of a preliminary normal method, or standard, of shooting, with subsequent small alterations and adaptations to suit the maturing style. No gun-maker or fitter, however expert, can hope to make a gun a perfect fit by forecasting what a pupil will become when he has mastered the groundwork of gun-handling.

I realize, too, that many good sportsmen who read this book will be using guns that haven't been specially built, or fitted, for

[1] Snap caps are dummy cartridges used for dry practice. They are necessary because, unlike a rifle, the action of a shotgun is jarred, and can be severely damaged, by releasing the pins on empty chambers.

them. The majority, perhaps, will perforce have to use a weapon which they have inherited from somebody else or purchased in circumstances when skilled alterations for fit were out of the question.

Ideally, I must insist that no man can shoot at his peak performance without a gun that suits him. But I admit it is possible to fit a gun to yourself, especially if your muscles are supple and you study how to get the best out of the marriage between you and your gun. As a professional, I'm shooting for test purposes with guns of all shapes and sizes. I am able to use them effectively because I make allowances of grip and presentation to correct the misfit factor.

Much more important than gun-fitting are the basic requirements of good shooting: proper stance, grip, and a stylish technique of gun-mounting. A man who looks after that will always outshoot the bungler with the best-tailored pair of game-guns that can be produced.

Further, any shooter with a gun that he himself finds is comfortable to use will be at no significant disadvantage, whatever his weapon, walking up in a rough shoot or pot-hunting along the hedgerows or in the marshes. Where a man's gun-fit will find him out is in a really hot corner at driven partridges or in the coverts, when pheasants come taller than the trees. But a man who can afford that sort of shooting can afford to have his guns made to measure. He will never get the best out of himself until he does.

CHAPTER VI

Position of the Head

IT IS said that head movement is the cause of one half of the misses in shooting. This saying is true of the "going-away" bird, when, with your eyes on the quarry, you move your head by burying it down on to your gunstock.

Begin this lesson by making a simple experiment. Point your finger at some distant object. You will find that, on first aim, you come straight onto it every time. Now, lower your head as you raise your finger and you'll notice that you are all over the place, never on the mark.

The cause of head movement is, commonly, that the shooter is using a gun which is too heavy for him. He puts down his head to meet the stock instead of allowing the stock to come up to meet his head. In that event, the cure is to practice gun-mounting until this bad habit has been eliminated. Another fault, which may be yours, is to put the head down and subsequently re-sight the bird; few shots made in that fashion make a successful kill.

THE HEAD SHOULD ONLY MOVE WITH THE BODY. Never shoot "out of the corner of your eye." And, if you find that you are shooting underneath going-away birds, don't mistrust your gun until you have made absolutely sure that head movement isn't the reason why you are missing. How often it happens that a sportsman reports that he is missing underneath the target and, as a consequence, the gun-maker sets up the stock with the object of making the gun shoot higher. Yet, in practice, it has absolutely the reverse effect if head movement is the real cause, because, when the head goes down, it arrests the stock from coming up. In such cases, the higher you build up the comb of the stock, the lower the shooter will be on the mark.

Head position varies very much with the individual. The short-necked man doesn't move his head about nearly as much as the long-necked individual. The tall man has a natural tendency to use his neck like a swan. The desideratum to aim at, when you are shooting, is to be stiff-necked rather than otherwise. If you can keep your head from moving about and retain this during gun-mounting, you should come up on the mark every time.

Oddly enough, the position of the shooter's head is closely associated with eyesight. A boy will usually lower his head to meet the stock, but a middle-aged man will hold his head erect and raise the gun to his face.

These two classifications cover the difference between "young sight" and "old sight." Nothing is commoner than a marked falling off in shooting due to an unsuspected change in eyesight in middle age. A man may have been shooting all his life with a straight-stocked gun. A change of vision occurs and he finds that he is right off his shooting. The cure is not glasses, but a bending down of the gunstock about a quarter of an inch at the heel or bump. This will compensate for an alteration of alignment due to the new head position.

While on the subject, it is as well to mention that a relaxation of the muscles, from age or sedentary habits, also alters gun-fit, and, generally speaking, a shorter stock will be found more comfortable with increasing age. Similarly, a novice, who has yet to learn how to extend his arms fully and naturally in the normal shooting position, should begin with a gun which is rather short for him. When properly practiced, he can be fitted for exact length, a simple matter of different depths of heel plate.

To test your own gun: first, follow out the section on correct gun-mounting and note if, at the moment you press the trigger, the rib and muzzle of the gun are correctly leveled "on" the object.

The best position for the head is fairly erect and turned very slightly to the right.

If you have to put down your head too much to the stock, you are not properly fitted. Above all, your head must be naturally, normally, and comfortably poised. It is hopeless to try to adapt the poise of the head and the neck to a badly fitted gun, for it induces rapid fatigue and a consequent falling off in shooting performance. A proper grip of the right hand will allow the stock to come up to the face. The head is inclined slightly, to avoid the cheekbone or jawbone pressing hard on the stock, and the cheek should touch midway between the two.

Head position is an arbitrary matter which varies with the individual. It should be first and, above all things, "natural"; very erect and definitely firm. Gun headache is due, in nine cases out of ten, to neglect of one thing only: the neck muscles are not braced and the head is held "loose." The shock of recoil jerks the head and the effect is that of a minor "knockout" blow. The old remedy of holding a rubber band between the teeth is a good one, for the act of clenching the teeth steadies the head and stiffens the neck muscles, so that the automatic throwback of the head is lessened. Most shooters automatically retract their neck muscles and bring their head down to their shoulders when firing. A minority—and particularly the swan-necked minority—do not do this and complain of headache in consequence. Alter the attitude and alter the gun to fit is the real remedy for headache. It is a curable trouble.

Sometimes, indeed very often, one finds people who believe

that, by adopting one particular load, or one particular brand of powder, they escape from headache. But you will find upon inquiry that they do not agree about the powder. One will claim that he is headache-free when he uses, say, 42 grains of Schultze; another says that that is the worst possible load for him, and that, for his part, he cannot use other than 33 grain E.C. without a headache. Recoil, the note of vibration of the explosion, are all called into account for the trouble; but, actually, it comes from one and the same cause: taking the recoil shock with a loosely-held head. Set the head down into the shoulders, though without raising the shoulders, stiffen the neck muscles, and gun headache will vanish.

The position of the head and, above all, the rigid maintenance of that position are vital matters in shooting. In golf, it is recognized that head movement, while a shot is being taken, will seriously affect its direction; a lift of the head may cause you to miss your ball, a slight inclination may lead you to hit below it. Golfers know that if they look at the ball as a whole, they are prone to "top" it, whereas, if they concentrate on the back, on a point on the ball, greater precision is achieved.

The underlying principles apply in a similar sense to head movements during gun-mounting. A great many of those unaccountable misses of seemingly easy "away birds" are due to too much head movement during gun-mounting. One's vision is centered on the bird, and, as the gun is raised, there is a risk of a final unconscious squeeze of the face down to meet the stock. In consequence, there is a loss of the instinctive accuracy of *first aim*.

Remember that, if you lift your head, you tend to shoot over the top of your bird. If you lower your head, you tend to shoot low.

To summarize, you must remember that, once the eye has found the object, the head should be carried rigidly and not moved independently of the body. This requires practice and, at first, concentration; but, once learned, it becomes instinctive and will often show both improvement in speed and in accuracy.

Keep your eye on the bird; but don't make the very common error of looking at birds which aren't there. There is no more certain way of tiring your eyes and assuring that, when the target comes into range, you will miss. If you are shooting in open country where you may see a mile or so ahead of you and you are continuously focusing and re-focusing your eyes, searching for birds that possibly won't be put up for another ten or twenty minutes, the odds are that, when a covey passes over you, it will be absolutely unseen and gone before you can throw a shot.

If you are continually looking up and down the line in partridge driving, you can count on it that when the birds come they will seem to be traveling twice as fast as they really are and disappear over the next hedge before you can bring your gun to them.

You will never be any good as a snap shot at rabbits in a narrow ride if you persist in trying to anticipate where you're likely to see them.

REMEMBER THAT IF YOU FOCUS ONE OBJECT, IT TAKES TIME TO RE-FOCUS ON ANOTHER OBJECT.

There is nothing which is so fatal to good shooting as lack of confidence. If you allow your eye to roam or get into a panic because birds came over you or because a rabbit ran across your path which you were unprepared for, all the faults of style which I have talked about will show themselves. You will be caught making the hasty snatch, the elaborate swing, and the steam-roller effort. You will miss again and again and again. Your faults will multiply the more you try to get back into form.

The secret is to master yourself. All you have to do is to concentrate; keep your eye on the bird, count it dead before you pull the trigger, trust your first aim, and remember you only have to kill one bird at a time. I know it is very much easier to write about it than to do it in practice. But, in practice, you can master yourself to an enormous degree by realizing what is going wrong.

Of all the faults which are the consequence of over-anxiety, the commonest is checking the swing of the gun. It is what you do when you see the first bird of the day or the last, or the one you have promised the kitchen for dinner. You make too sure of it, and, nine times out of ten, you miss behind. Good shooting is never hasty, never over-cautious.

I have often helped temperamental shooters by telling them that every cock pheasant flying towards you gives you time to say slowly to yourself "What a beautiful fellow you are" before you shoot at him.

The reason why some men are born shots, and others perpetually erratic, is almost entirely a state of mind. The great shots are usually phlegmatic shots. Most of us have occasional serene days when we could hit anything. Most of us, too, know the other days when we are shooting with increasing exasperation all over the shop.

I have a friend who, on his day, is a first-class shot, but he is such a chronic victim of nerves that he hardly ever shoots well if he is out with people who are strangers to him. The trouble is that he is much too conscious of his company. If you find that you are off form, almost the first thing to convince yourself of is that it doesn't matter (as, of course, it doesn't). Pretend that you are quite alone. Next, make up your mind not to be in a hurry. Finally, concentrate on shooting not at a given bird but at a part of the bird. Shoot off his tail or prick his beak. This has the effect of forcing the shooter to concentrate on the target instead of fluffing about trying to look after the other guns' business. If you remember some of these tips, and if you are a reasonable shot, you ought to get back into form before the day's shooting is over.

[51]

In addition, never try to pull off a showy shot at the beginning of the day. A fine partridge shot once told me that he always shot the first bird of the day behind him. The idea was to get his eye in. After the first kill he went on to shoot birds on the flanks. Only when he was mounting his gun sweetly did he shoot his birds well out in front and calculate on killing a brace. And he was a man who could put two birds down out of a covey before most of us could get our guns to our shoulders.

If you are missing driven pheasant, it is quite a good policy to wait until the birds are almost over your head so that you have to bend backwards to reach them. You will often kill them directly overhead because, in that position, you have no time to hang on the trigger and no choice but to keep your eye on the bird.

I have discussed all these matters again, in greater detail, in subsequent chapters; but I have no hesitation in repeating myself because repetition is the secret of instruction. I like to think that, when you are out shooting, you will remember an occasional phrase from this book; and that an occasional phrase from this book may be enough to bring you back into form during one of those black moods when you feel you couldn't hit a haystack.

The best illustration of the right attitude of mind on a shooting day is the story of a friend of mine who was invited shooting after a lapse of many seasons when he hadn't handled a gun at all. It happened that the company he was in was composed almost entirely of first-class shots. He went through the entire morning without hitting a bird. Subsequently, when the party was moving from one stand to another, his car was in front in a narrow lane where only one car could pass at a time. Half-way up the lane my friend came to a haystack. He stopped the car, got out, slowly produced his gun, loaded it, and, while all the cars at the back were hooting to encourage him to get on, he raised his gun to his shoulder and fired two barrels into the hay-stack. Then he solemnly turned round and made a rude gesture to all the men behind him. He was quite right. He had cultivated that happy frame of mind which banishes all fear of missing. In that mood, anybody will very quickly become a very good shot.

CHAPTER VII

The Theory of Allowance

THE MAN who has mastered the technique of dealing with the straight-away shot will find that it applies equally well to crossing and overhead shots as soon as the need for extra allowance in these cases has been appreciated.

The action of keeping the left hand pointing at the moving bird automatically compels a correct swing of the whole body. And the gun comes to the shoulder without a check for aiming, or trigger pressure, but all in one harmonious movement.

Contrast this with the style of a man who shoulders his gun and chases the bird with the muzzle, making either a calculated or an empirical "allowance" forward of his target. His endeavor to compensate for speed may be justified in theory, but bad trigger pulling results in practice.

The allowance principle, when permitted to enter into shooting as an abstraction, is quite unsuited to the average sportsman and, if imperfectly understood, is a prolific source of irritation and error. Take a simple demonstration of its difficulty.

A charge of shot takes one twentieth of a second to travel twenty yards; one tenth, thirty yards; one seventh, forty yards. A bird traveling at forty miles an hour covers one, two, or three yards respectively in the same time intervals (one twentieth, one tenth, and one seventh of a second), and we know that the gun must be pointed these distances ahead to score or kill. But measure out the ranges in straight line, in an open field or paddock, and erect three poles twenty, thirty, and forty yards apart. Now attach a piece of whitewashed board one yard in length as a crosspiece to the pole at twenty yards, a two-yard one to the thirty-yard pole, and a three-yard one to the forty-yard pole. Then return to the firing point and look at them.

They will present a very neat example of how easily the eye can be deceived, for in perspective they all look about the same size and they all look far shorter than they really are. The inference to be drawn is that a constant angular allowance suffices —to be modified and made more precise as experience increases.

A short study of the example will convince you how hopeless it is to attempt to calculate precise allowances for varying ranges in the heat of shooting.

Once you appreciate that allowance is needed, let eye and swing collaborate to produce the correct measure.

The whole secret is to regularize your movements and mount the gun properly to the shoulder so that the hand and eye coordinate. Your barrel must always be aligned precisely where your eye is looking. The eye learns its job quickly enough. Apparently you are shooting straight at the bird, but, unconsciously, you will be making all necessary allowances.

PRACTICE THE POINTING OF THE LEFT HAND AND BODY AT THE BIRD FROM THE READY POSITION UNTIL YOU ARE DOING IT INSTINCTIVELY WITHOUT BEING CONSCIOUS OF DOING IT.

The difference between shooting at birds overhead and crossing, as compared with going-away, is that, besides being in more rapid flight, their line of travel is more or less at right angles with the line of fire. Therefore, theoretically, the gun must be directed further ahead than with the going-away bird.

What I propose to teach you is that the more rapid gun movement, caused by the body swing, automatically carries the aim more forward. If you mount your gun at a speed that is equal to the speed of the bird—or, in other words, if you keep your left hand pointing at the bird during the whole of the gun-mounting—then, if it is a slow incomer, the unconscious over-throw is very slight, but all that is needed for correct forward allowance. On the other hand, if it is a very fast crossing shot, your own speed is increased, the overthrow is proportionately greater, and is, again, the correct forward allowance.

TRAIN THE EYE AND HAND TO TAKE CHARGE OF THESE MATTERS AND LEARN THEIR JOB WITHOUT BRAIN INTERFERENCE.

Once again, remember the remark on hands and feet.

If your technique is sound, you will find that the right angle target, whether overhead or wide out, presents no difficulties. Once again, dismiss all ideas of calculated allowances. Look at the bird, pivot easily and smoothly, and complete the movement as for a straight-away shot, but without in any way checking your swing.

If it seems difficult to begin with, then adopt a slow, smooth body swing before mounting the gun. Above all, do not mount the gun and then swing. This procedure is hopeless.

You will note that, in the foregoing sections, I have never told you to look along your barrels or to keep the sight in view. *Don't.*

In practice, the shooter should not be conscious of his gun-muzzle, the rib, or sight. His eye, or rather his attention, should be fully occupied with the bird, and, if he holds his gun prop-erly, he will hit whatever he is looking at.

When the gun has been fired, recoil jars the barrels up and the shooter may then see them, but, with proper action and a well-fitting gun, he should not be conscious of them until he has fired.

The scientific basis of this is the fact that the eye cannot pay attention to objects at different ranges at one and the same time.

In rifle shooting it is necessary to focus the target, and yet at the same time see the front sight. The back sight intrudes up to the foresight first of all and then deals with foresight and bull, usually by means of an intermediate focus. Shotgun practice is different. There is no time for focus to pass from one object to another. Gun-fitting gets breech and sight into line with the eye. For the rest, the close range and the widespread circle of pellets will compensate for any small inaccuracy of alignment or centering.

At the moment of striking, a billiard player looks at the object ball, not at the cue tip or his own ball. The golfer, after he has adjusted his stance and rehearsed his swing, has to keep his eye on the ball and not on his club. In tennis, baseball, and, in fact, all such sports, the eye must be kept on the object. So the shooting man must keep his eye on the bird and ignore his gun.

If your eye is focused on your gun, you will mount behind an incoming bird and will have great difficulty in catching up with him.

If I haven't already persuaded you, let me explain to you in greater detail the difference between aim in theory and aim in practice.

Figures are all right on paper. They can be immensely valuable in theoretical calculations. But I want to prove to you how ridiculous it is, in practice, to suppose that everybody can calculate the intricacies of muzzle and shot velocity in relation to a variably moving target in the actual field.

A ballistician, knowing the recorded decrease in shot velocity for a cartridge from initial muzzle velocity to ranges of twenty, thirty, and forty yards, can calculate the *time* occupied by the shot charge in covering different ranges, and he can also calculate the distance covered by a wind moving at the rate of twenty, thirty, or forty miles an hour in equivalent time. Normally, these would be computed for a bird crossing at an absolute right angle to the line of fire but can, of course, be calculated for any angle.

Let us take a simple example. Consider a shot from a standard 12-bore cartridge at ranges of twenty, thirty, and forty yards used against a crossing bird flying at thirty miles an hour. Twenty miles an hour is about the rising velocity of a pheasant bustled out of a hedge by a spaniel. Forty miles an hour is the average speed of a driven pheasant in full flight.

Now let me confuse the mathematicians by recording that the lateral movement of the gun-muzzles by one inch makes a difference of thirty inches at thirty yards. From that it can be calculated that the gun-muzzle movement necessary for forward allowance is:

$1\frac{1}{2}$ inches at 20 yards
$1\frac{5}{8}$ inches at 30 yards
$1\frac{3}{4}$ inches at 40 yards

From this we may calculate that, in general terms, the slow bird needs only half the allowance of the fast one and the birds of the short twenty-yard range only require 40 per cent of the allowance theoretically necessary to the forty-yard bird. Even these figures only relate to the birds crossing at right angles. For a bird quartering at 45 degrees all figures have to be halved. The bird seen straight in front, unless it is climbing steeply, needs even less allowance, and, if a bird twists as you lift your gun, no calculation is any good at all to you.

But, for the record, all theoretical forward allowances may be calculated from the following tables:

A shot charge in flight, traveling at a thousand feet a second, takes approximately:

0.06 of a second to reach 20 yards
0.09 of a second to reach 30 yards
0.12 of a second to reach 40 yards

A bird traveling at thirty miles an hour travels:

44 feet per second
11 feet in 0.25 second
8 feet in 0.18 second
6 feet in 0.13 second
4 feet in 0.09 second
2½ feet in 0.05 second

Therefore a calculated forward allowance for a bird crossing at thirty miles an hour is approximately:

2½ feet at 20 yards
4 feet at 30 yards
6 feet at 40 yards

These figures, of course, are calculated from the gun-muzzle. The shooter should add the length of time he takes to pull the trigger, in addition to the time taken by the lock mechanism and primer to explode the charge. If all the birds flew across at this level speed of thirty miles an hour, if we had a range finder, and provided we did not hesitate in pulling the trigger after having made our mathematical calculation, then all might be well. But I hope I have said enough to establish that it is beyond the capacity of even the most expert shot to work out forward allowances on a mathematical basis.

Forget all about them. Leave them where they belong, in the pages of this book. Your job is to keep your eye on the bird; forget all you ever knew and heard about the thousands of different allowances and the thousands of varieties of shots and let your eye and the natural overthrow of the gun take care of everything else.

My considered opinion is that these tables of allowances, which I give here simply to prove to you how confusing they are, are not only misleading, because very few people can interpret them properly, but they are one of the basic causes of bad, and sometimes dangerous, shooting. It is high time that the whole allowance system was deposited in the wastepaper basket. It is not practical, and it establishes an entirely false foundation of thought at the back of the shooter's mind.

It can never be practical, for, among a thousand men, it would be impossible to find half a dozen who were alike in their judgment of distance, their sight and reaction to speed, or their timing. The time taken to press the trigger is another factor which varies enormously with the individual and, indeed, varies from shot to shot according to empirical factors such as how soon the target was sighted.

All systems founded on allowances are inherently unstable and unscientific. Indeed, it is only in the sport of shooting that the matter even arises. I have never heard the question raised in any other form of sport where the hitting of a moving object, such as a ball, is involved.

Ballistics, so far as rifles are concerned, is a fairly exact science; but shotgun ballistics are far more a matter of compromise based on a theoretical "mean of average." Even in matters which do not concern ballistics, matters of sight displacement in minutes of angle, we should find some tables stating that the lateral movement of gun-muzzles should be 2.5 inches to give a forward lead of forty inches for twenty yards and three inches to give a forward lead of seven feet six inches at forty yards. Now this lateral movement obviously varies with the length of the gun, and it also fails to take into account that this lateral movement is carried out in a different way by different people. The pivotal point of time may be with the stock home or it may be a far looser movement with the left hand as the pivot, and it is very often accompanied by head movement as well. It is indeed difficult to resolve this 2½-inch movement into anything really practical unless a great many other factors are taken into account.

Now consider the question of timing, the precise adjustment of forward allowance, in terms of the ordinary shooting man.

Take the man who, with the best will in the world, is trying to improve his shooting or to correct his faults and is studying the thousands of figures involved in any moderately full table of allowances with his potential variations in range, angles, speed of birds, loads of varying velocity, and all the other technicalities. Assuming that he gauges the distance right (of which more later), one man will jump the required distance but stop to press his trigger; the next will fire before he has really completed the movement; while a third, and dangerous, type takes a long time to get to the desired point of lead and, by the time he reaches it, has swung round and is pointing down the line of guns before he is aware what has happened.

Now let us come to the question of judging distances. It is an enormously variable factor and is undoubtedly affected by a purely physical consideration in the individual. A shortsighted man, or one whose eyes are relatively wide apart, is, as a rule, slow at focusing distant objects (and, oddly enough, a one-eyed man can, as a rule, hardly judge distances at all). To people with this disability, a bird thirty yards away but near the ground looks far nearer than the one thirty yards almost overhead, although the distances are equal.

This is a very common fault, and it is concerned with background. A low bird is seen against some form of a subconsciously imaged "measuring stick." In a way its size is related to the hedge, a tree, or some object; it is seen in proportion, and the range is based on that. Against the sky, of course, there is no standard of proportion.

In addition to the physical limitations of the individual, we have to take into consideration normal "optical illusions." We traditionally see things in our own perspective, although the Japanese, for instance, have an entirely different value of perspective, as can be seen in their prints. In one of his experiments, Payne-Gallway fitted a measuring device to his gun-barrel, and a dead pheasant, at forty yards horizontally, appeared to measure more than twice the length of the overhead bird hoisted to forty yards in the air. It was clearly a matter of optical illusion; for the same bird at the same range is clearly the same size.

A man may be a fair judge of distance but not good at judging heights. The reason is, perhaps, that most men have some mental standard of distance: a miniature range, or some familiar unit of longitudinal measurement. Height, though, is less familiar, and the average man is usually sadly out in his guess at the height of a tree or a T.V. mast. Very few men realize that the average oak or elm tree, which looks quite tall, is seldom taller than some thirty-six to forty *feet;* that is, twelve yards or so. And may I remind you that the effective range of a shotgun is somewhere between forty and sixty yards. So much for those out-of-range pheasants that shooting men talk about. You will constantly notice stories in the papers of falls from third-story windows in which the report says that "the victim crashed sixty feet to the street below." The fact of the matter is that the average third-floor window-sill is twenty-four to thirty feet above ground level.

With a 20 per cent factor of error in horizontal range judgment, and a 50 to 60 per cent factor of exaggeration for height, we are unlikely to judge very accurately the matter of widths at a distance. Here again, an optical illusion operates. An interesting experiment, which will afford you an opportunity of testing your friends' judgment as well as your own, is to paint a board forty inches long and four inches wide with white paint and erect it crosswise on an upright thirty-five yards away. Then set up a similar board forty-eight inches long but *eight* inches wide. Paint the second board black on a lower post, some twenty or so yards to the side of the white one, but forty-five yards away from the observation point. You will very seldom find anybody who can make a correct guess as to the distances, and, in most cases, people insist on pacing them out as they literally can't believe their own eyes.

[62]

Practical experiments of this nature, and some practice in checking and estimating ranges and the size of objects at a distance, will soon give you sufficient experience to decide whether calculations are the least help at all in the field, or whether a more practical method isn't to subscribe to the system of shooting that I personally advocate.

In my method there is no question of trying to compute muzzle movement, allowance, or any other complicated matter. All I ask you to do is to look at the bird, and, by correct mounting and body work, shoot naturally without constraint or effort *apparently* straight at the bird; but, subconsciously, overthrowing a little and so giving the necessary lead, or compensation, for time flight; and, in that way, arriving at what, in any other terms, is a complicated mathematical problem.

When I say "look at the bird," I mean it. You must glue your eyes to it, focus it, and see nothing else. At first it is not easy to forget the gun, but, once proper concentration on the bird is achieved, you are two thirds of the way to becoming an expert shot. It is more difficult to do it at long ranges than short ones, for, thinking it over, you will realize that we all look things "straight in the eye" at short distances.

In the law courts, I have noticed how the jury shift their gaze from counsel to witness as questions are put and answered. All twelve heads move like automatons. Yet the crowd in the stands at a race meeting are all stiff-necked. I know the field of view renders movement unnecessary; but, to get down to the refinements of shooting, if you want to hit a pheasant in the neck, you must look at his neck and not at the bird as a whole. There is a lot to be said for a steady eye as well as a steady hand.

Finally, I must tell you, once again, never to be afraid of missing. I am reminded of Wild Bill Hickok, the great gunman of the frontier days of the West, who had a remarkable reputation as a marksman. Yet, in his biography, it is stated unequivocally that Wild Bill was never a good shot. He couldn't cut ace pips out of playing cards. The secret of his success was that he could shoot whilst he was being shot at. If you can cultivate that attitude of mind, if you can resist the temptation to get excited and can use your gun at game when you are in no danger yourself of being shot at with the same coolness that Wild Bill could handle a gun in a fight in a saloon, you'll be well on the way to become the calm and collected shot that I want to make you.

CHAPTER VIII

Practice in the Field

ASSUMING that you have carefully studied what I have so far said and endeavored to build up your *muscle memory* by practicing at home, you will be anxious to test out your technique in the field. Unless you are a natural stylist, or you have been particularly economical in your use of ammunition, the chances are that you will be bothered by a number of trifling discomforts which are common to everybody who uses a gun, except those experts whom all of us envy and so few can emulate.

If your shooting style is perfect, you shouldn't be bothered with minor bruises caused by the recoil of the gun. Gun-makers can provide various material sedatives to mitigate various conditions, but you would do much better to know the cause and, by style, try to correct it. Here are the commonest troubles with their cause and the proper way to overcome them:

Bruised second finger. This is caused through loose grip, relaxing grip on firing, badly shaped stock, or the bad habit of using the pressure of the second finger against the back of the guard to squeeze the trigger pull-off. If the stock is gripped too lightly, it will occasionally slip through the hands after firing and so knock the finger.

You may wear a finger guard or unscrew the guard and roll onto it a rubber umbrella ring (doubled) that will hold it in the spur of the guard and take off most of the blow. But if you will only study what I have told you about right-hand grip, you will notice that the pulling back of the right hand and the pulling off of the trigger with a semi-rigid finger, helped by the jar of the gun when it beds home in the shoulder, will completely clear the finger. If you follow this style of shooting, you will never bruise a finger again.

Bruised cheek. If the face is, for example, half an inch off the stock, the recoil is likely to jar the head into forcible contact. If the head is too erect and too square, the jawbone comes on to the top of the stock and the jar of recoil will bruise the flesh. Further, if the head is too much "down," the cheekbone comes onto the top of the stock.

Avoid sandwiching your flesh between either jawbone and stock or cheekbone and stock; and note that the head should be pivoted slightly to the right to avoid jawbone or cheekbone coming into contact, and that the gunstock should firmly touch the cheek midway between the two.

Bruised mouth is more often than not caused by the fingers of the right hand coming back with the recoil. What this means is that you have taken an incorrect stance, or that the stock is too short by at least half an inch.

Bruised arm is due to incorrect stance or too long a stock.

Bruised shoulder is due to incorrect stance or too wide a butt. A recoil pad should cure this ill. Get one that is rounded at the corners, smooth and well varnished, and always soft and pneumatic (not hard, as the wood itself is).

Bruised chest is due to incorrect stance or too short a stock or, alternatively, insufficient castoff at toe or too much toe on the stock of the gun. Sometimes an unsuspected suspender buckle is the cause.

Shooters should pay particular heed to the position of the buckles of their suspenders. Myself, I recommend all who can to dispense with this article while engaged in shooting. A little attention to the fit of the trousers round the hips and the avoidance of a long waist cut, such as necessitates a high lift of the buttons, will usually render any support, other than perhaps a belt, unnecessary. The shoulders are more supple without the confining effect of suspenders and the body less liable to perspiration. But, if suspenders must be worn, the buckle should on no account be situated where the butt beds into the shoulder. If the elastic has stretched so as to necessitate this position, the remedy is to remove some inches of the webbing and have the fitting resewn. I have discussed this matter in rather greater detail in the latter part of the book, but I want to emphasize here that shooting clothes can be very important. Rifle shots are so particular about it that many of them won't go to the ranges unless they are wearing the same clothes which they always wear when they are shooting at the targets. I know one prize-winner who, even in the hottest weather, always wears the same old mackintosh to make sure that the feel of the gun in his shoulder never varies, whatever conditions of weather he may have to shoot under.

This may seem late in the day to talk about the proper method of opening and loading a gun; but, generally speaking, I don't bother my pupils with matters of that kind until they have mastered the more elementary elements of gun-handling. When you know that you can hit what you are shooting at, when your confidence has been built up, that is the time to think about the finer points of gunmanship.

Of course, anybody can open a gun; but few people effect the operation in the smooth and effortless manner in which it should be conducted. More often than not, one sees a man who ought to know better hurriedly fumbling, dragging on the barrels, and attempting to break the gun before the lever has been completely opened.

To open the top lever, knurl the first finger against the right lock plate. With thumb on lever, squeeze both the lock plate and the lever together. The leverage will be sufficient to open the stiffest lever you are likely to come across.

To open the breech, hold the stock under the arm with barrels turned slightly sideways to give body leverage to assist easy opening. Draw down the barrels with the left hand whilst the stock is gripped between the right side and right forearm. Don't try to do it with your right hand, as this should be just leaving the lever to reach bag or pocket or belt for fresh cartridge or cartridges. Handled in this way, a self-ejecting gun will throw the cartridges away to the right and not immediately over your right shoulder.

Whether you have your cartridges in a pigskin bag or in your pocket, begin by giving the pocket or the bag *a good shake* before shooting. The heavy weight of the lead shot in the head of the cartridge, compared with its much lighter base, will cause it to turn "head uppermost." It is consequently long odds that, when you put your hand in your pocket or cartridge bag, you will find that the heads are waiting in the position in which it is easiest to handle them.

If you have only expended one cartridge, picking a second one out of your bag and popping it into the chamber of your gun is a quick process. Where time and effort is so often wasted is in fumbling with a second cartridge when both chambers of the gun have been expended. It may be that you are in no hurry to reload but, in game shooting, it is always wise to assume that the best chance of the day will come at the moment when you are the least prepared for it. Get into the habit of reloading your gun in the field as quickly as possible.

Following is the method which you should practice until, like everything else in shooting, you can carry it out without thinking:

When you break your gun to eject the fired cases, your right hand should be on its way to your pocket or bag at the same time. Two cartridges are taken and, if you have shaken your bag or pocket as I recommend, you will find that they come to your fingers easily. Take two cartridges and, as you collect them in your hand, make a movement of your fingers to provide that the lower one is more prominent than the top one by about three quarters of an inch; in other words, pick them up out of your pocket or your bag between your fingers in an over-and-under position. Insert the nose of the under cartridge into the right barrel but don't let go of it. Using it as an axis, twist your wrist so that the other cartridge turns over the left barrel. Let both go and the gun will be loaded at express speed without barked knuckles.

I don't expect you to master this trick just by reading what I have said about it. Practice it carefully, following the instructions. Once you have mastered it, you will get a reputation for quick loading which will be the envy of your fellow shooting men.

Closing a gun is an important matter because the factor of safety is involved. Never close your gun by lifting the barrels to the stock because the process involves raising the muzzle of the gun to what can so easily be a dangerous angle, if, by accident, you release the charge. The proper method of closing the gun is to lift the stock to the barrels. This is the way it is done: having dropped the cartridges into the chambers, grasp the stock of the gun with the right hand, making sure that the fingers are well clear of the trigger. Pressure of the right hand against the grip of the stock, with a slight forward inclination of the body, will close the gun. Alternatively you can close the gun by holding the barrels pointing towards the ground and raise the stock to meet them with a lift of your forearm.

Having learned the drill and adopted all the safety precautions that I have emphasized so strongly, you will still be an unwelcome guest at a shoot unless you also master the etiquette of the shooting party. The etiquette isn't merely a matter of ceremony;

it is based upon sound principles of safety and good sportsman-
ship, too.

When you are shooting birds in an organized party there are
certain rules which must be carefully adhered to.

The first is that, in the normal course of events, a line of men
will be driving the ground in front of you putting birds forward
so that they will fly over the guns. At a certain point in every
drive it is extremely dangerous to shoot at an angle below forty-
five degrees in front of you. When the beaters are close in, it is
the duty of every shooting man to be very careful indeed about
any shot he takes in front. Normally, especially if a low-flying
pheasant, flushed out of covert, or a rabbit, makes a last-minute
rush as the beaters come up with the guns you, should take the
shot, if you take it at all, behind you.

At any time, when you are in an organized drive, examine the
ground and the landscape carefully before you start shooting.
For example, if you are standing in a plowed field which is heavily littered with stones, it can be extremely dangerous to shoot
at any ground game which isn't well behind anybody else in the
vicinity. Pellets can ricochet in the most dangerous and devastat-
ing manner. If you are shooting in hard weather, remember that
the ground itself can ricochet pellets like a steel plate. And never
fire your gun unless you are perfectly certain where the charge
will finish. To shoot into foliage at ground level, however far
away you think the beaters may be, is inviting an accident.

One of the most rigorous rules of organized shooting is that
you mustn't steal another man's bird. It is your bird only when
it is coming to you more than to anyone else, or is otherwise in
your own proper angle of fire. Shoot only at an angle of 45 degrees right or left; do not shoot immediately in front of, or just
behind, adjoining gun.

Most of the great shots pride themselves on their courtesy.
That doesn't mean that, among friends, it isn't permitted to have
a bang at a bird which your neighboring gun may have missed

DRIVEN GAME SHOOTING: DANGER ZONES AND LEGITIMATE FIELDS
OF FIRE

In this diagram it is assumed that guns are standing thirty yards apart and well back from a high hedge during a partridge drive. Except when standing close to cover, when an inevitable "gap" will occur in front, all birds are covered while still well in range (forty yards). The legitimate fields of fire (the white areas) for each gun are 90 degrees in front and 90 degrees behind. The shaded portions are the Danger Zone.

It is permissible to shoot at a high-flying partridge covey in a Danger Zone or to pick the nearest of a bouquet of pheasants to the gun. But it is a matter of etiquette to be certain that you are not poaching a fair bird from your neighbor. Ground game should never be shot in the Danger Zone. *Above all, the shooter must train himself* never to follow through *into the shaded areas. Whilst turning to shoot behind, the gun should be down from the shoulder and the barrels pointing skywards during the 90 degrees traverse of the Danger Zone.*

with both barrels altogether. It is a part of the etiquette that, if that happens, you are fully entitled to have a go to "wipe his eye." And, if he is a good sportsman, he will be the first to congratulate you on doing it.

Remember that, in the sport of shooting, you are there not

only to enjoy yourself; you also have a responsibility to your host to help him harvest an important food crop. You also have a humane duty to see to it that you kill your birds clean, and if, by chance, you wound them, to take every precaution that the game is ultimately picked up by the beaters or the dogs.

As you shoot, it is your responsibility to mark your fur or feather as it falls, making a note of how many head of game fall in front of you, on your left, or on your right. Some men are exceptionally good at this, others cannot remember whether "it was five or seven" that they got down. Never hang up the field to hunt for a mythical bird. Alternatively, if you are certain that you have got a bird down, tell the keeper, or the head beater, where you think it is. It won't hold up the shooting and the keeper will be grateful to you for telling him where to look when he is going round on the pickup afterwards.

Even in the best organized shoots, with the most proper guests, it often happens that two men fire at the same bird. Always let the other man claim it; it goes into the bag just the same. And, anyhow, the lookers-on see most of the game.

The most important rule when you are walking up game—as opposed to occupying a stand and waiting for it to be driven towards you—is always to keep in line. Remember to walk in line "as steady as a farm laborer." Remember that birds usually prefer to run than fly. Partridges, if gently pushed forward, will run until they are tired to get into cover and will then squat. But, if you walk fast, they will run fast and, in all probability, rise out of range. If men could remember the number of times they have chased partridges all day without much success and on walking home tired had found birds sit for them, they would realize the importance of slow walking.

To sum up, it is far better to miss a chance of a bird than to take the slightest risk or to earn the reputation that you are a poacher of another man's sport. Never shoot horizontally into hedgerows or cover; some very remarkable accidents have happened through the shooter not seeing where his shot was going to end.

Don't fool about with your safety catch, working it to and fro until you don't know whether it is on or off. Accustom yourself to push it up with the first joint of the thumb as the gun reaches the ready position.

Whether you shoot well or badly during a day in the field, make sure that at the end of it you can congratulate yourself that never for a single second were you caught off guard in your safety precautions or did you do anything which might have caused a fellow gun to think to himself that you are a jealous shot or that you don't know the rules of the game.

Over-keenness, which is such a virtue in most sports, is one of the things in shooting which mysteriously results in your host refraining from inviting you to share his sport again.

CHAPTER IX

Shooting for Women

I HAVE deliberately refrained, up till now, from making any reference to women as shots, although quite a lot of women shoot really well, and with enthusiasm. The trouble is that very few women are properly taught how to shoot. This is the more regrettable as a correct beginning is half the battle.

If they care to learn, women can shoot just as well as men; but, in most cases, their approach to the sport is from a different angle to a man's. Boys, as a rule, like guns and noise, but girls, as a rule, have a distinctive dislike of firearms and fireworks; and, whereas a boy comes to a gun with a natural desire to be able to use one, girls usually have a doubt at the back of their minds.

I think many more women would shoot but for the unfortunate factor that, in many cases, they have tried the experience of a few shots from a borrowed gun and found it a painful affair; as a result of this, they abandon all desire to use a gun again. This is exactly as if, in an endeavor to learn swimming, they tried to dive off the highest springboard for a start. On a modern properly-equipped shooting ground, special provision is normally made for women. They begin with practice in proper gun-mounting and snapping with an empty gun at various marks. For this purpose a very light .410-bore try-gun is the best weapon. This is a measuring gun which is adjustable until the individual need is fitted. As the gun is a very small bore, it can be fired without any perceptible recoil and is indispensable for the first steps in shooting.

These early exercises have to be taken steadily at first, for they are bringing into play muscles not usually exercised and can be a little tiring. As soon as muscular familiarity is realized (this means perhaps a lessening of rigidity, for one always exerts too much energy in an unfamiliar effort), a beginning is made with recoil discharges at stationary birds set up in front of big steel targets. This is where the instructor teaches the importance of proper grip and stance, and co-ordination of hand and eye, during the rests in practice.

Women are inclined to flinch from an anticipation of the noise; but this is very easily cured, and they usually regain complete self-confidence in half a dozen rounds.

Within six lessons, at the most, a novice has probably graduated to the next size gun, again an adjustable try-gun, but of a larger bore.

This approach to the full-size sporting gun has to be very carefully carried out, as no risk can be run of bruising the shoulder. Women have a much more easily marked skin than most men, and though recoil may not in any sense be felt as uncomfortable, slight bruising may occur from any error in gun-mounting or firing before the gun was properly set to the shoulder.

The tendency of most women is to square their shoulders much more than men. This also throws out the breast which is exactly the attitude we want to avoid for shooting. We do not want a woman to stiffen her back, square her shoulders, and bring the gun up. She must not stand square, but very slightly sideways, and she must practice putting her shoulder to the gun rather than the gun to the shoulder. The reason for this is that, in the rigid position, there is no natural shoulder abutment for the gunstock. She will probably fire the gun with the stock against the arm muscles, which is wrong and painful.

Take anything—a walking-stick will do—and keeping the shoulders and the arms-folded-on-breast, simply move the arms from the elbows to allow gun-mounting. You will note the following:

(1) The breast is perfectly clear of the toe of the gunstock and safe from the risk of injury.

(2) A proper "bed," or abutment, for the stock is made within the right shoulder.

(3) This is not a rigid braced affair of bone and muscle but cushioned and elastic and free to move back with recoil and absorb it.

In fact, the body is, so to speak, poised to catch the recoil, whereas if the woman stood square and rigid, backing away from the gun rather than leaning towards it, she would experience the recoil. But as she would not "give to it," it would punch harder than was comfortable. If the stock of the gun rests on the bone of the shoulder joint, a thin layer of skin is pinched between unyielding bone and hard wood by the recoil and extensive and painful bruising may result. If, however, the correct position and method of gun-mounting is properly drilled home, any woman can fire normal-sized game-guns with absolute confidence. The main thing to remember is that nothing must be rigid; the shooter relaxes rather than stiffens and she must not grip her gun tightly but hold it as lightly as a riding switch. There is no bracing to withstand recoil, but an easy yielding to it. All muscles have to be relaxed, not tensed. The only bracing, or contracting, movement is that tightening of the right-hand grip which occurs as you press your trigger.

The new 12-bore two-inch chambered gun is excellent for women. It is a modified version of the standard 12-bore shotgun with two-inch cartridges. But in every case women should begin with a small bore gun and work up gradually. The 20-bore try-gun—a very nice gun to handle—can never equal the performance of the larger bores and its slender barrels are not adapted to some rather long and graceful hands; they tend to slip through the left and the recoil of the 20-bore is often more perceptible than it is with the more massive 12-bore.

For shooting clothes for women nothing is better than rough tweed with pivot sleeves loose cut at the elbow, as most practicable golf jackets are now cut. As women tend to wear thinner materials than men, it is also always a good idea to have a quarter-inch-thick pad of fine rubber sponge sewn into the shoulder of a light-weight shooting coat, inside the lining. This will take the sting out of any careless shot fired in a moment of excitement.

It is not easy to lay down any hard and fast rules for women, as their physical capacity to handle the weight of a gun is variable to the individual; but, in general, anyone who can drive a moderately powered car without fatigue will not find the slightest difficulty in a day's shooting, providing that they begin the right way and learn the essentials first.

So far as footwork and grip and all other matters are concerned, the rules are the same as for men, but it cannot be too strictly stressed that this matter of a correct shoulder resilience is vitally important in the interests of a woman shooter. The proper fit of a gun is even more important to a woman than to a man. Silhouettes may change with the march of fashion but the exact setting of a stock to fit perfectly, yet allow for changes in figure and fashion, is rather a skilled art. It may take a little longer to get a woman fitted to perfection; but it is really vital to her success in the field.

PART TWO

GUN KNOW-HOW

CHAPTER I

Game Guns of Today

THERE has been very little progressive development in sporting guns since the modern conventional double-barreled sidelock ejector became more or less standardized in the last decade of the nineteenth century. There has been a certain amount of detail improvement such as steel barrels replacing Damascus, but to all intent many makers are still regularly turning out a gun with little, if any, variation from their model of a half century ago.

Most modifications of design have been in the nature of a simplification of lock and ejector mechanisms. New steels have been selected and particular attention has been paid not so much to reduction of weight, as to its better distribution in barrels and action. Coincidentally, there has been an all-round increase in hidden strength to meet conditions liable to be imposed by modern powders. These matters are important, but they do not strike the eye; their effect on external appearance is practically nil.

Broadly speaking, the modern gun may be pronounced 20 per cent better balanced, 30 per cent stronger, and 40 per cent less likely to fail in functioning details than the guns of our fathers.

The under-and-over gun is a variation which is really a "throw-back" to the oldest type of double-barreled construction. These guns have always been popular with continental sportsmen; but it is certain that they present no great feature of convenience or utility such as may enable them to supplant the side-by-side gun. On the other hand, the older types of under-and-over guns suffer from very definite mechanical handicaps.

For those sportsmen who have a liking for under-and-over guns, I developed my Zenith model. This model overcomes the chief objection to under-and-over, which is that the top lever has to have a spindle and the strikers give a glancing blow. In the Zenith, fitted with a side lever, the whole of the action face is free for the internal hammers to give a central blow. The model is easyopening, and the bolts lock into the upper barrel instead of the underneath one. For those who favor this type of gun, the Zenith overcomes the objections to the usual under-and-over.

The single-trigger action represents a detail improvement of considerable utility. Detachable locks are, at best, a refinement. Neither variation represents definite radical progress comparable with the developments of the past.

Within recent years a certain improvement has been made in barrel boring. Constant experiment has enabled us to evolve methods which give an improved pattern at forty yards. What was unusual in the old days has become common since. For instance, it was exceptional, fifty years ago, to find a gun which would consistently give 70 per cent patterns at forty yards. Today we are able to get this standard of 70 per cent of pellets in the thirty-inch circle at forty yards with absolute certainty. Very often we exceed this average by an additional 5 or 10 per cent. Corresponding improvement has been effected in the lesser degrees of choke now necessary.

This interesting progress in boring is associated with the modern development of the short-barreled gun. In the matter of shotgun design, the development of the twenty-five-inch barreled gun is associated with my name. I regard it as the most significant contribution that I have been able to make, personally, to the improvement of the sporting gun in my time.

Many years ago, when I first introduced my short-barreled

guns, they aroused a great deal of controversy, and I shall always be grateful to the sportsmen who were the first to take them out into the field and prove, in a practical way, that my theory was right.

When the controversy about short-barreled guns was at its height, it was said that the velocity of the charge would be seriously affected by reducing the barrels from thirty or twenty-eight inches to twenty-five inches. Other older sportsmen, who had been accustomed to using guns with barrels of thirty inches or more, protested that my short-barreled guns didn't "look right."

Today, forty years after, the short-barreled gun is so widely used in the shooting field that it is the man with barrels thirty inches long under his arm who carries a weapon that looks out of date. But as a well-made shotgun is an arm which will last a generation or more, a great many people are still using the twenty-eight and thirty-inch barreled guns which were in fashion when I introduced my own shorter and lighter model. For that reason it may be as well if I state, once again, the reasons that led me to introduce the short-barreled gun and the advantages in shooting which this type of shotgun design affords.

Modern conditions call for maximum strength and shooting qualities, minimum weight compatible with low recoil, perfect balance, and something beyond the poise and ease of manipulation characteristic of the best examples of ordinary guns. The old thirty-inch barrel is a relic of past ages and is purely a survival from the black-powder period. It has long been common knowledge that smokeless powder will permit a very radical reduction of barrel length, but conservative tendencies amounting to prejudice suggested that this reduction could only be made at the expense of pattern and penetration.

In point of fact, almost all velocity is generated in shotguns with smokeless powders within a few inches of the chamber and is not materially increased as the charge approaches the muzzle.

[83]

The shooting or pattern is regulated at the muzzle end of the barrel, independent of length. It does not matter whether the muzzle is thirty or twenty-five inches from the breech; velocity of the charge is not affected and the pattern has to be regulated by the usual methods of control.

A century ago, a barrel of less than thirty-six inches long would have been derided. With the establishment of the early breech-loaders, firing the same charge of powder and the same kind of powder as the old muzzle-loaders, barrels shortened to thirty inches. At the close of the century, the demand for light guns for driven game reduced the length to twenty-eight inches. Today, the modern twenty-five-inch is as good as the longer barrels; it shoots as strongly and gives as good a pattern. In addition, the short-barreled twenty-five-inch gun shows an improvement in weight, in balance, and in ease of handling. The reduction of effort needed in gun-mounting allows steadier yet quicker shooting.

It is self-evident that you can bring the muzzle of a gun which is only twenty-five inches long quicker onto the target than you can barrels of twenty-eight or thirty inches long. And, in fact, what we have learned from experience is that the shorter barrel tends to have an upward flip on delivering the charge just as thirty-inch barrels have a definite downward flip as they are fired. As the commonest error in shooting is to miss behind, it follows that the short-barreled gun is more likely to make you lift up your charge to meet the target and the long-barreled gun more likely to cause you to miss behind.

There is a very slight difference in the velocity of the charge from a short-barreled gun and a longer one. But shotgun velocities are never taken as muzzle velocities. Over twenty yards, the commonly occurring difference between twenty-five and thirty-inch barrels is usually well under forty feet per second. Muzzle velocity cannot be measured, it can only be inferred, but while this inference is exact in the case of rifle bullets, the changing form of a shot charge of a column of shot that it throws forbids calculation. But these are technicalities you need not be concerned with.

As I have cause to explain, in many places in this book, most game-gun shooting is carried out well within the potential striking range of the gun. As any loss in the velocity of the charge between short-barreled and long-barreled guns is quite insignificant, the matter is a purely theoretical one for ballisticians and firearms experts. You can take it from me that the speed at which you can bring a short-barreled gun to a target far, far outweighs any theoretical loss of striking range.

It was tentatively suggested, many years ago, that short barrels are more difficult to align and that the sportsman using them missed the guidance afforded by the extra barrel length. This argument, even if it were true, would only hold good in the case of those very rare shots who actually aim their guns as a rifle is aimed; who shoot, in fact, in the very manner which I advocate that the shooting man should avoid. But even people who "aim" their guns are not so much influenced by barrel length as by "apparent barrel length"; they are victims of an optical illusion.

When the controversy about short-barreled guns was at its height, shortly after the First World War, Major Hugh B. C. Pollard summed up the situation about barrel length in an article in *Country Life*. I cannot do better than to quote him here:

"The most effective ground for criticism of a short barrel is that the eye, accustomed to guidance along the top rib to the foresight, so to speak, misses the customary extra five inch of barrel, and that the short gun gives 'a sense of something missing.' This is very plausible, but I am not altogether certain whether it really means anything.

"The game shot is seldom conscious of his foresight at all. His eye is on the bird, and it is only after discharge that the muzzles lift momentarily and give him a glimpse of half a foot of barrel. He certainly 'sees' the barrels as they come up to the line of sight, but he should not have them in focus.

"I am inclined to believe that the 'sense of something missing' is purely psychological and entirely illusory. Whether it is visual illusion is open to doubt, for, if a large foresight, improvised out of a bead of sealing wax, is applied to a standard game-gun of twenty-eight- or thirty-inch barrels, the barrel appears short, and a twenty-five-inch barrel with a small foresight appears comparatively longer than the other.

"It follows that if a 'sense of something missing' is due to an optical illusion, a small foresight to a short gun compensates for it. If, on the other hand, it is, as I suspect, psychological rather than actual, and due to the unanticipated swiftness of response of the shotgun, it will vanish as soon as the new gun is used in the field or at practice at clays, and is a testimony of the handiness of the new type. After all, driving a different kind of car for the first time often produces a feeling of strangeness, but it has never been suggested that progress in car development should be restricted because of this transient feeling of difference."

This elucidation by Major Pollard not only explains the point at issue but will interest many of the earlier users of short-barreled guns. These, as originally built, have the usual wide shotgun rib with the ordinary foresight, and, in consequence, gave a noticeable impression of shortness until the eye became accustomed to them.

Today the later short-barreled guns are made with a special form of rib and sights in strict proportion. The rib taper is specially designed to harmonize with the perspective effect of the barrels, as seen by the eye, when the gun is mounted to the shoulder. The result is astonishingly effective, for a twenty-five-inch barreled gun is thus made to convey to the eye the effect of a full thirty inches. It can easily be made to appear longer.

The optical illusion is so complete that, if a man mounts one of my own twenty-five-inch guns to his shoulder with his eyes closed and then opens them to look along the rib, he will find it impossible, except as guesswork, to measure the barrel length with his eye.

But, although the modern short-barreled gun is now an accepted improvement, many sportsmen who read this book will themselves be using guns of an older and, in many cases, more cumbersome pattern.

What I teach in this book about gun-handling applies equally to any sportsmen whatever weapon he uses; but I want to emphasize that I hope all who can will, sooner or later, adopt the more modern type of short-barreled gun. The many years of my life that I have devoted to giving instruction in shooting have clearly shown that it takes approximately four times as much ammunition and four times as many hours of practice to enable the average individual to attain a modern standard of efficiency with the long barrel as to reach the same stage with the twenty-five-inch barreled gun.

Years are necessary to learn the really perfect handling of the old long gun. Today the short gun, with its far, far better balance, becomes "part of yourself" in a quarter, or less, of the time. The first season or so with the old guns was always a matter of "chance it." With the new type, "sense of direction" is quickly achieved; success with it is not empirical but logical. The twenty-five-inch gun is easier to shoot with—best of all, to shoot really well with—and not less effective in pattern and penetration than any of the old long-barreled types. Essentially modern in its adaptation to the modern cartridge it dismisses the obsolete parts.

Just as we now find it more convenient to live in smaller houses and use lighter and shorter fishing rods, so in the matter of guns the most convenient gun is the modern lightweight twenty-five-inch. It has been redesigned in every detail, rebalanced, fined down, and perfected during forty years of careful, critical, and invariably progressive work. It is harmonious within itself and in tune with its partner, the modern cartridge.

To the gun-maker who knows no better than to supply his customer with the old standard fowling piece, having barrels shortened to twenty-five inches is bound to meet with disappointment; and I must warn any sportsman who, reading this, thinks that, by carving a few inches off his own barrel, he can bring his gun into line with modern practice, that that policy won't work. Apart from the fact that he will interfere with the choke of his existing gun, he will also be using a weapon which isn't designed overall for the shorter barrel length.

My short-barreled guns are not a wedding of old and new, they are something quite new altogether. I claim for them that they handle like a 20-bore, shoot as hard as a 10-bore, look as long as thirty inches when aligned on a bird and, most important of all, that they quicken the faculties of the shooter and reduce fatigue because they are twice as comfortable as the old heavy guns to carry. Lighter weight and increased strength, better functional design and better handling qualities are the chief characteristics of the best modern shotgun.

I suppose that practically all guns made in London and Birmingham today are in fact 12-bores of one kind or another. The popularity of 16-bores, 20-bores, and 10-bores all date back to a time when the larger caliber guns were much too heavy for many people, and the smaller caliber guns suited sportsmen who through physical disability or personal taste preferred not to carry a gun weighing 7 pounds or more.

Today the modern 12 weighs as little as the 20- or 16-bore of half a century ago. The 16 and 20 have been replaced by the light 12-bore chambered for 2-inch cartridges.

At the other end of the scale, the 10-bore wild-fowling gun of our forefathers has been succeeded by the more heavily built 12-bore wild-fowling guns made to take 3-inch and 2¾-inch cartridge cases.

There is, of course, every reason why sportsmen should take advantage of the change whenever they can. First, the variation of cartridge sizes is an inconvenience. Second, the 20-bore is always a dangerous gun to keep in the same house as the 12-bore, because the 20-bore cartridges just stick in the top of a chamber cone of a 12 gun. In the event of a 20-bore cartridge being accidentally loaded in front of a 12-bore, a burst, or perhaps a serious accident, is almost unavoidable. The same danger exists in the case in which a 28-bore is kept in the same house as a 20-bore. The answer these days, if you want to have a range of guns, is to have a very light 12-bore chambered for 2-inch cartridges; a medium-weight gun which, these days, shouldn't weigh more than 6 pounds for the standard game-gun cartridge; and, finally, a magnum short-barreled gun, full choke if you like, for wild fowling.

All I need add to these comments on the development of the game-gun, as it exists today, is to excuse myself for not referring to the modern automatic or pump gun. These are admirable and cheap weapons for a man who wants to use his gun to keep down vermin or to make an occasional expedition to collect a bird for the pot. But any man who tries to shoot with an automatic shotgun under the test conditions of driven game will never be able to compete with a first-class shot with a properly measured and properly balanced double-barreled game-gun in his hand. For that reason automatic guns have never been popular and, in many places, are actively unwelcome in the English shooting field.

I know that some men can use them with considerable efficiency; but I often wonder how much better they would shoot if they had a gun of lesser weight, better balanced, and of more pedigreed construction in their hands.

This textbook is directed to the sportsman who wants to get the best out of himself under test conditions. Even the idea that the automatic gun, pumping up to five cartridges into the breech one after another, is more deadly than the ordinary double-barreled shotgun is an illusion. It might be advantageous for pumping lead into a cloud of pigeons on a wheat field but, in ordinary sporting conditions, it is a slow-action, ill-balanced, and ugly weapon.

So far as the actual range of the charge is concerned, the effective punch of any gun, even the cheapest mass-produced object, is just the same as the range of the best shotgun that money can buy. In spite of the fact that sportsmen persist in speaking of their own guns as particularly hard-hitting guns, the truth of the matter is that all guns hit more or less the same. All that the gun does is to explode the propellant inside the cartridge and the shot travels just as far as the propellant pushes it. Why you should buy the best gun that you can possibly afford is because:

1. The boring of a best London gun will present the charge in a pattern which is, on average, 30 per cent better than the pattern you will get from a mass-produced weapon.

2. The difference between a good gun and an inferior one is the difference between a thoroughbred horse and an old nag. Both will go; but the way a thoroughbred handles is a pleasure and a source of pride to the owner in itself.

3. An inferior gun has a comparatively short life, in some cases limited to a few hundred days of hard shooting. A good gun will fire hundreds of thousands of rounds, and like it; and will last not for one lifetime but for several generations.

4. You can never get the balance and the tailoring in a cheap gun which a gun built for you will give you. In consequence you can never hope to shoot so well with a gun "off the peg" as with one that has been bespoken for you.

Those are the reasons for buying the best gun you can afford; and now I will give a warning. Just because a gun has a famous maker's name on the barrel it doesn't follow that it is just as good as it used to be. Even the best built guns in the world wear out some day and, although it may look in good condition, an expert will be able to tell you that the barrels are paper thin and completely shot out. The moral, when you buy a gun, is to go to the maker. If he sells you a second-hand one, he will still pass it over to you with the hallmark of his judgment and the pride of his reputation, which is the best guarantee that you will be well cared for.

CHAPTER II

The Components of a Gun

EVEN grandmothers know that this means "Lock, stock, and barrel." I have no intention of explaining in detail how a gun is built or, least of all, encouraging the average sportsman to pull his own to pieces. Leave that job to the gun-maker. He will do it far better than you ever will.

But there are aspects of the "Mystery of Gun-Making," as it is called, which shouldn't be a mystery to any shooting man who is really keen on his sport. Gun know-how can be an assistance in good shooting in the same way that a study of natural history is not only one of the greatest charms of the shooting field but a positive aid to good marksmanship. Know the habits of the game you are hunting, know the animal's ways, and you will be more successful in pursuing it. Know also the subtleties of the arm you are handling, and, in consequence, you will undoubtedly handle your weapon with greater skill.

I am dealing with the stocking of the gun in the next chapter, rather than this, only because the shape of the stock is the most important factor in gun measurement. Gun measurement is a subject sufficiently important to be treated on its own.

THE BARRELS

The barrels of a gun are simply smooth tubes which are roughly measured for size by the number of lead balls made to the diameter of the barrel which will add up to a pound weight. So, in general, a 12-bore barrel is one in which twelve lead balls of the same diameter will add up to a pound; a 20-bore, one that will take twenty lead balls to the pound; a 16-bore, sixteen balls to the pound, and so on.

What distinguishes the barrel of one gun from another is the degree of choke. Choke is simply a restriction in the metal at the muzzle end of the barrel to hold the charge of shot together more tightly as it leaves the gun. The degree of choke in the individual barrels of every gun should be a matter of considerable personal concern to its owner. Very many shooting men have only the vaguest notion of the effect of choke in actual practice.

Here is a table, based on a 12-bore gun with a standard cartridge, to assist:

Super choke should put 75 per cent, or 225 pellets, of a 300 pellet charge within a 30-inch circle at 40 yards.

Full choke should put 70 per cent, or 210 pellets, within a 30-inch circle at forty yards.

Three-quarter choke should put 65 per cent, or 195 pellets, within a 30-inch circle at 40 yards.

Half choke should put 60 per cent, or 180 pellets, within a 30-inch circle at 40 yards.

Quarter choke, better known as Improved Cylinder, should put 50 per cent, or 150 pellets, into a 30-inch circle at 40 yards.

One-eighth choke should put 45 per cent, or 135 pellets, into a 30-inch circle at 40 yards.

True cylinder should put 40 per cent, or 120 pellets, into a 30-inch circle at 40 yards.

After studying this table, don't jump to the conclusion that the super choke, which puts the greatest number of pellets into a 30-inch circle, is the most satisfactory barrel for you.

It is very unlikely indeed that it is. But, as a general rule, if you are ordering a new gun and deciding how much choke you think you will need, it is just as well, if you have the slightest doubt, to err by having too much choke rather than too little. If you want to reduce your choke later, it can very simply be bored to a larger size; but if once the choke is taken out and you have got a true-cylinder gun, you can't put it back again into the barrels. Apart from that, my general advice to you is not to handicap yourself with too close a pattern. The correct boring for you is the one which will enable you to put the largest majority of the shots onto the target.

The following table gives the diameter of the spread of shot with normal loads to the nearest *inch*.

DISTANCES IN YARDS

BORING	5	10	15	20	25	30	35	40
	In.	In.	In.	In.	In.	In.	In.	In.
True cylinder	8¾	19	26	32	38	44	51	57
One-eighth choke	7¾	17	23	29	35	41	47	54
Quarter choke	6¾	15	20	26	32	38	44	51
Half choke	5¾	12	16	20	26	32	38	46
Three-quarter choke	5⅛	10½	14	18	23½	29	35	43
Full choke	4½	9	12	16	21	26	32	40

Having given you those figures, it is worth noting that, in the shooting of driven birds, you will shoot in the ordinary way nearer with the second barrel than the first. For that reason, guns bored both barrels one-eighth choke are most likely to give satisfaction. Remember that it is a tall tree in Britain which is fifteen yards high, and very many driven birds are shot at that distance. The shooter using a full choke, with a correspondingly smaller spread, would need to be very accurate indeed and, even then, there would be a serious possibility that he would badly damage his game.

For walking up game, a second barrel bored one-quarter choke would give an almost identical pattern of spread at five yards greater distance if the first barrel were bored one-eighth choke. The man who is slow with his second barrel would get a similar pattern at ten yards greater distance by having half choke in the second barrel. For rough shooting at all distances, the combinations may be quarter and half choke; quarter choke and three-quarters; or half and full choke for long-distance shooting.

The ideal killing spread is between thirty-five inches and forty inches. If all shooting were at forty yards, then full choke would be the ideal choice. As it is, a great deal of shooting is well within the forty yards range. For that reason, modified choke will suit the vast majority of sportsmen and the greatest variety of shooting. And the modifications for individuals, who are characteristically slow or characteristically fast on their targets, should only be decided after a good deal of practice either at the shooting school or in the field. So, if you are ordering a new gun for yourself, err on the side of too much choke, but have no hesitation in having it reduced if you are not getting the best performance.

Apart from the control which choke exerts over the pattern of the shot, it also serves the very useful purpose of checking the wads from scattering the shot. Some form of choke in a modern game-gun is clearly desirable.

The Body or Action

Apart from the action of fully automatic guns, all game-guns are built either with what is called the sidelock action or the box lock.

Years ago, it was truly said that the sidelock action handled more sweetly than the box lock, then more generally known as the Anson and Deeley, after the two great craftsmen who designed it. But it must be remembered that, in those days, all best quality guns were sidelocks and all cheap quality ones were box locks. The best sidelocks, at that time, were better than the cheaper box locks.

The box lock has always been a cheaper action to make because it is simpler to work and contains fewer parts. The sidelock has a larger body and is the heavier of the two actions. The box lock not only has the lightest possible body but, further, the triggers are nearer to the breech of the gun, thus saving woodwork and, in consequence, saving also the weight in the gunstock. Indeed, it is probably true to say that, if there had never been any hammer guns, there wouldn't be any sidelock guns at all made today; for, in fact, the sidelock is purely the old hammer lock with an internal tumbler instead of an external hammer.

In fact, some sidelock ejectors should be treated with even greater suspicion than some box locks. There is the type of sidelock which has an overdraft on the ejectors, causing the gun to run back after ejection. The barrels have to be pulled down again against the weight of the spring whilst fresh cartridges are inserted. A gun should always stay wide open after ejection. Then again, we have the action which does all this but is very hard to close, a further handicap to quick shooting. The trouble is often due to bad positioning of the limbs and the excessive strain of main and ejector springs. All these actions I am talking about are of nineteenth-century vintage; but, unfortunately, some of them are still turned out by conservative gun-makers. Sportsmen should be on the lookout against them.

In spite of what I have said about sidelocks—that the best sidelocks are more expensive to make and, in some ways, more reliable—I admit to a personal prejudice in the matter myself. Personally, I normally shoot with sidelocks and so do most other sportsmen who use "best" guns. But, in fact, the matter is one of personal taste and prejudice; and no sportsman will go wrong, whichever action he uses, provided he buys the best.

Whichever action you choose, the important thing is to settle on a gun that is easy to open and easy to close. In most of the normal game-guns the opening of the breach cocks the locks and the closing of the gun cocks the ejectors.

[96]

The ejector springs should not be of such strength that they throw the fired cases great distances. All that is needed is an ejector which is certain in action. With a good gun, the ejector hammer gives a direct blow, instead of a glancing one, and springs of mild strength are quite sufficient and, in handling, much easier to compress.

You will find that there are some "easy-opening models" which are easy to open and hard to close. I personally disagree with this type of gun, as the dropping or throw of the barrels on opening helps this first operation. Further, I find myself, and I think most other sportsmen will, that I can pull far better than I can push, and I would rather have a gun which is easier to close. If a tired loader has one of these guns in his hands, he is inclined to lift the barrels instead of lifting the stock to close the gun.

Of other easy-opening types there are those that fly open at the touch of the lever whilst they remain unfired, but once the trigger is pulled, the extractors which previously freed the opening are held and the gun is hard to open. Another fault with them is that they all need a lighter spring and shorter rebounding strikers; but that is a technicality.

Today the strikers of some "easy-opening models" have a measure of rebound; a good feature, because a striker which indents the cap of the cartridge and stays there is making a grip on the indentation of the cartridge which is a check to easy opening.

So, on the whole, there is a lot to be said in favor of choosing an easy-opening type of gun. The tension, when the gun is closed, stops vibration and tends to check barrels from shaking loose from the face of the action. Further, when shooting with one gun, you can open and reload without altering or bending the body.

With the old type of breech opening you have to bend down to reload and then stand upright again to fire. That doesn't sound much of an effort, but I estimate that, in a hot corner, you can shoot 25 per cent more game with greater accuracy thanks to the absence of this bodily effort.

THE FORE-END

To a sportsman who only handles guns casually it may seem surprising that the mere choice of a fore-end offers such a tremendous variety, from the American beaver-tail, as it is called, to the humpbacked and raised fore-end which some trap shots prefer. Actually, it is my opinion that this is a part of the modern game-gun which has not yet been perfected. Let me do no more than put down what is needed in a well-designed fore-end in the hope that some clever gun craftsman can solve the problem.

In the first place, when we are shooting, we are constantly varying our forward grip on the fore-end of the gun; not only in accordance with our build and the length of the gunstock, but also according to whether we are shooting ground game, grouse, or pheasants. I should like to have a fore-end which was adjustable for all three conditions, or long enough to allow me to trombone my hand up and down it at will.

Second, the ideal fore-end should not be too smooth of surface. It is very important that the hand should grip the fore-end and not slip. On the other hand, the checkering must not be so rough as to injure or bruise the hand on recoil.

The third requirement of a fore-end is that it ought to be of sufficient size to fill the hand and yet prevent the fingers of a large hand encroaching over the rib. In addition, it ought to be a non-conductor of heat so that we can shoot a great number of rounds very quickly without discomfort.

On æsthetic grounds, it ought not to be too large or conspicuous and it ought to be at least as light as the standard fore-end which is in use on game-guns now. It is very important that we should not start adding to the overweight of a gun.

So much for the ideal. Here, for the interest of sportsmen, are a few of the many notions which have already been tried out towards the achievement of the objective:

The "Colley" fore-end is simply a deepened one which certainly has the merit that it keeps the fingers off the barrel; but I dislike it because it encourages the left or forward arm to lift the gun upwards instead of to point it forwards.

The humpbacked fore-end also keeps the fingers off the barrel, but the humpback encourages the shooter to pull in with the forward hand instead of pushing out and, as you will remember from the drill, that is bad style.

The beaver-tail is a great favorite with Americans, and, to my mind, it most nearly fills the bill; but it is just too much of a handful and adds rather too much to the weight of the gun for an ordinary shot.

On balance, the nearest we have got to the solution of the problem so far is the leather hand guard with fastener. The ordinary hand guard, which is a metal sheath encased in leather, is a most beneficial accessory which can be fitted onto the barrels of any gun. It has the three advantages that (1) it improves the variability of the handgrip on the fore-end considerably, (2) it effectively protects the hand from heated barrels when a great many rounds have been shot off in succession, and (3) it provides a warm and pleasant grip in hard weather when the metal of the barrels becomes almost as uncomfortably cold as in hard shooting it becomes uncomfortably hot. The objection to the hand guard, if it is merely sprung over the existing fore-end and not fastened with a catch to the barrel itself, is that it has a dangerous habit of slipping forward in shooting, unless the spring steel is squeezed really tight onto the barrel. So, if you use a hand guard, either have an attachment put on by your gun-maker to hold it in position or squeeze it on as tightly as you can. If you don't, you will find that, one day, you will pick up your gun by the hand guard and have it slip through and fall to the ground with frightening results. Further, you will find that it is not very pleasant when it shifts its position as recoil is taken.

As a substitute for the hand guard, the ordinary glove is no protection from a heated barrel, and I am still looking for the ideal glove, one that buttons up the back. The objection to the ordinary glove is that it exposes the disc of the palm just where it touches the barrel. The glove I want would be thin and flexible, with fingertips and ball of thumb reinforced with some material which would protect the side of the thumb and the first finger which touches the barrel, in addition to the other three fingertips. In fact, the hand actually touches a very small area of the barrel. As an experiment, wipe the barrel dry and then grasp it in normal fashion. The thumb and fingerprints that are left behind will show you just how small is the area of surface which is touched.

TRIGGERS

If you are not a very keen shooting man indeed, it is possible that it has never occurred to you that trigger pulls, or the shape of triggers and trigger guards, should be a matter of any significant importance at all. I can only tell you that first-class shots can become so sensitive about the trigger pulls of their guns that they can notice a difference of half a pound or less. They won't be satisfied with their guns until the maker has adjusted them exactly to the comfortable pressure.

The weight of trigger pull depends on the weight of the gun. For instance, if you are one of those sensitive shots accustomed to putting on exactly the same amount of pressure every time you fire, you will probably require that your $6\frac{1}{2}$-pound guns should have pulls of 3 pounds right trigger and $3\frac{3}{4}$ pounds left trigger. But if you use a lighter 12-bore, or even a 20-bore weighing perhaps only $5\frac{1}{2}$ pounds, you will find that, although the lighter weapon may have exactly the same measurements as your heavier gun, the pull you require will have to be altered.

As a rough guide, the weight of the first, or right, trigger pull should be approximately one-half of the weight of the gun. A 6-pound pull on a 13-pound 8-bore feels just as light as a 3-pound pull on a 12-bore of 6½ pounds or a 2½-pound pull on a 20-bore weighing 5 pounds.

Generally speaking, the left pull should always be about 25 per cent heavier than the right because the greater leverage makes it feel proportionately lighter. Of course, the man with only one gun is not likely to be such a sensitive judge of trigger pulls as the man who uses a pair of guns. The latter always has the comparative pulls between number one and number two to contrast, and he can immediately detect differences between his two guns; for instance, that one responds instantly and that the other drags and causes him to pull on his birds. The man with fingers as sensitive as that must use "best" guns with locks which are less likely to vary. But for the general sportsman, it is just as well not to worry very much about trigger pulls. If you are having trouble with your trigger pulls, you can probably overcome it pretty quickly by going back to the drill. Practice gun-mounting with a slightly relaxed grip. If you do that, all the little troubles of varying pull will inevitably disappear. If you are throwing your shoulder forward and making your trigger pull with a rigid finger, a light pull isn't really necessary; and, in the interests of safety, a pull on the heavy side is even desirable.

Many years ago I used to have a pigeon gun with a 1¾-pounds right pull. As there was no safety catch on the gun, I had to be very careful indeed not to jar it as I closed it, because that alone was enough to make it go off. I now use a 2½-pound pull on a 6-pound gun; but I cannot even recommend this pull to anyone who has not a very sensitive touch, or who wears gloves, or who shoots in a very cold climate. In fact, gamekeepers and other shooting men with strong muscles who are accustomed to hard exercise or hard manual labor are more often inclined to put on a pound or so of pressure on their triggers before being aware of it. If you are a strong man, accustom yourself to a heavy pull.

The basic disadvantage of a heavy pull is that it causes one to drag off the target. On the other hand, the danger of too light a pull is that the gun goes off before you are "on." Don't be ashamed to have a heavy pull yourself. Many good shots prefer it. One of them, for example, was Frank Troeh, undoubtedly the greatest trap shot ever born.

The American trap-shooting records show that he started shooting in 1912 and, in registered shoots, broke between the years 1912 and 1938 the huge total of 129,603 targets for the expenditure of 132,970 cartridges for a lifetime average of .9746 in all sorts of weather. He is also an all-round game shot. I remember him asking me to try his gun, a graceful compliment I eagerly accepted. But, on calling my target, I could not fire it. I examined the breech for the safety catch whilst he looked on with amusement. There was no safety catch. I tried again without success and then discovered that he used a pull on his gun of over 8 pounds weight.

The expert is not only concerned with the weight of pull but also with its crispness. Here again, the best lock (another argument for the best gun) can alone give a never varying safe, crisp, and light pull. The cheap lock, owing to the irregularities of its component parts, cannot fail to vary; further, the shaping of the sears and the bent of the tumblers is cruder and only too often the pull is a long drag.

More sportsmen are troubled by the fact that when they make a bad trigger pull they imagine that the trigger pulls themselves are at fault. Sometimes the consequences can be blamed on the shape of the trigger itself, but more often the trouble is that the shooter has taken an uncomfortable grip.

Basically the trigger is the lever which raises the sear nose and thus releases the tumbler. If it is so shaped that the fingers slide upwards during the effort to pull it backwards, then the nearer the finger moves towards the point of axis the more effort will be required. On the other hand, of course, the greatest leverage is obtained near the extreme tip.

Assume we have a gun with one of those small grips which allows the hand to get anywhere. When our hand is on the top of the grip and the shortened finger can reach only the top of the trigger, the weight of the pull is apparently much harder than when we try again with the hand placed more firmly underneath the stock. The extra reach allows us to pull at a lower angle with the first joint instead of the fingertip. As a matter of fact, there are not so many bad triggers about today as there used to be; but there are still bad trigger guards.

In choosing a gun you should look for a trigger guard which is sloped to allow sufficient escapement for the finger. It was how the great nineteenth-century gun-maker, Joe Manton, solved the problem over a hundred years ago.

Finally, very large hands need large trigger guards and a greater width between the triggers. The super-sensitive shot, who requires a very light trigger pull, should have his trigger blades checkered to prevent his finger slipping.

THE FORESIGHT

Some shooting men will tell you that they never see their foresight, others doubt whether it is of any importance, and the great majority, I suppose, agree that a foresight is necessary.

The expert shot is at all times most particular as regards its composition, color, and shape. At various times foresights have been made of gold, silver, and other metals, porcelain, and ivory. When I was a boy, the pigeon shots of the period generally favored an ivory sight because, against the dark background, it showed up white, and, against a light background, it showed up dark. But they were all undecided as to the best size and shape. I remember that one well-known shot had a wide flattened blob on the end of his gun and argued that the fine pinhead sight he had discarded caused him to look at his gun too long, whereas his "billiard ball" sight was always in vision and helped him to focus his eyes on the bird instead of on the gun. There was something in what he said.

The Hon. Seton Robert Beresford, who, in his book *Beresford's Monte Carlo*, tells many interesting tales of the old days when Englishmen went out to shoot live pigeons from traps there, records that he himself used different foresights for different occasions.

As regards color composition, I prefer a white metal to ivory on my gun because the latter can be so easily broken. As regards shape and size, I think it is important not to have so fine a sight that it is difficult to find without looking. Again, the sight should not be so large that it distracts the eye. Let it be a medium spherical sight such as is normally fitted today.

True, most of us only use the sight, or rather I hope that most of us only use the sight, for sitters and target shooting. But it does help to show where we have been pointing after we have missed.

THE TOP RIB

The top rib of a side-by-side double-barreled gun may be concave or flat in varying widths at the breech and the muzzle end of the gun; also it may be plain or engraved, file cut or engine turned, and so on, in endless variety. In my opinion, the worst rib of the lot is the concave or half hollow rib which is unengraved. It reflects the sunlight and, when swamped in the center, it acts not so much as a guide to the eye as a distraction for it. A perfectly flat and wide rib, although file cut or engraved, still occasionally catches the eye and looks humped up in the center.

[104]

Long experience has convinced me that the ideal rib is one that is narrow and flat and is also cut up by file or engraver to show a dead black surface. The narrower a rib is made, the longer it seems. When I was working on the development of my twenty-five-inch gun, I also evolved a special rib for it, which is now known as the "Churchill quick-sighting rib." This rib, when properly fitted and file cut to show a thin dead black line, is an enormous aid to shooting. Of course, it decieves the eye and makes the barrels look much longer than they really are. But that's the purpose of it. As I have said so often now, I don't want you to see the gun-barrels but to look at your bird, and I don't want the rib on the top of the gun to distract your eye either. My quick-sighting rib appears as a dead black line which never has to be looked for because it is in the shooter's field of vision just before a gun reaches his shoulder. It encourages him to do the right thing. Second, the rib shows up clearly in the shooter's eyes as the gun kicks backwards on the recoil. In other words, it helps him to see where he has been pointing.

On all short-barreled guns, the Churchill quick-sighting rib is really a necessity; on barrels of any length it has material advantages.

SHAPE OF THE BUTT

We have now covered all the components of a gun except the stock, which I shall deal with in greater detail in the next chapter. The butt, of course, is the further extension of the stock; but it calls for some general comments which are outside the major consideration of the stock itself.

The expert always demands that the butt of his gun should fit the shoulder perfectly. The very tall thin man may need a prominent toe to check too high a gun-mounting and to prevent the gun turning or canting. But any fully-chested person needs a normal toe, which means a stand or drop of two inches from the upright.

Personally, in my own workshops, I have always concerned myself very deeply with the matter of settling the width of the butt. I have learned how important it is through shooting guns in their rough state with huge blocks of wood for butt ends; and I have learned that, if a stock is narrow enough, it can be bedded into the fleshy part of the shoulder; but if it is too wide, then it comes onto the bone.

A well-rounded recoil pad is my own preference; not so much for saving recoil as for the purpose of fitting the shoulder perfectly and holding there at the instant of recoil. A square and wide wooden butt is inclined to slide instead of to give. When this happens, the second barrel is fired with the butt on the shoulder bone instead of against the flesh.

Automatically, the vein which carries blood down to the arm runs in front of the shoulder bone. When this vein is sandwiched between bone and butt, then a bruise extends far down the arm and leads the unfortunate shooter to believe that he has been firing with the butt on the muscle of his arm. The normal depth of the butt should be five-and-a-half inches. The normal stand in gun measurement is two inches off the upright.

The Measurements of a Gun

THE SHAPE of stock which fits one man is not necessarily the best for another man of similar build. A great many factors influence the selection of the best shape of stock for the individual.

The tendency of many modern guns has been towards a grip which is too straight for practical mounting. The line is graceful and looks well in an illustration, but it is a handicap in use. (See Illustration 1.)

The natural stock developed in my short-barreled guns is the same in bend and general measurements as the last named, but with very material alterations to the grip. The tang of the action and trigger plate curve down so that the hand moves naturally parallel to the line of sight without enforcing a strained position to the right arm. (See Illustration 2.)

The third model is a return to a pattern over a century old. This is the keeled or "roach-bellied" shape shown in Illustration 3. It was copied from an old muzzle-loader and possesses a pe-

culiarly pleasant balance, as well as proving not only a pleasant contour but a comfortable grip.

Trap-shooting guns for competition experts need special adaptation to the needs of their specialized shooting position. The Monte Carlo (Illustration 4) is the basic model. It is also very

valuable for game shots with long necks or those who find difficulty in mounting an ordinary stock to the face without the butt rising half above the shoulder.

Illustration 5 represents the old flintlock stock which is oc-

casionally preferred but presents a return to a gun shape not particularly practical for modern shooting conditions, driven game in particular. The hand and grip is small and comfortable but is likely to slip through the hand on recoil of stock.

Illustration 6 shows a full left-eyed gunstock which is occasionally necessary.

Illustrations 7, 8, and 9 represent the development of the pistol grip in its various degrees of quarter, half, and full. The most appropriate form for the individual depends not only on arm length, width of body, and size of hand, but also particularly on the type of gun and its special use.

Full pistol and half-pistol grips are more suitable for single-trigger guns than for double triggers, as with the latter there is always a slightly different position of grip with each barrel. A pistol grip also checks overhead swing. The full pistol grip, therefore, is more suitable on the special trap gun or for walking up game and it is seldom seen on the modern game gun.

The half-pistol grip is more common. It is preferred to the straight stock (Illustration 1), but the special stock (Illustration 2) has all the advantages of the low-curved hand of the half-pistol grip without any of its disadvantages and would be more likely to suit the majority of sportsmen.

Illustration 10 represents a gun with deepened fore-end. This hardly concerns stocks, but, with certain individuals, is a palliative for bad gun-mounting. Except in the case of a man who is disabled or limited in his freedom of physical movement, the need for this amendment suggests that the gun is either badly balanced or does not fit.

The fitting of the stock of a gun to an individual is one of the highest arts of gun-making. The length of stock necessary depends not only on the length of the shooter's arms, the breadth of his body, and the length of his neck, it also depends on the position of the left hand, the position of stance, and finally the weight of the gun.

Weight of gun. The general rule is that the heavier the gun the shorter the stock, and vice versa. To go to extremes, the man who shoots well with a 12-bore weighing 6 pounds with a fourteen-and-a-half-inch stock would probably need a fifteen-inch stock if he was shooting with a .410 and a stock as short as fourteen inches if he was shooting with an 8-bore wildfowl gun. The reason for this is that the shooter hugs the heavier weight and extends his arms with the lighter one.

Position of Stance. If the body is turned too much sideways, the shooter needs a longer stock than if he normally stands squarely to the target and puts his shoulder forward into the butt of the gun as he fires.

Position of Left Hand. If the left hand is held too far back, the result is that the shooter can handle a much longer stock. In reverse, if he overreaches with the left hand, the tendency is that any stock will become too long.

To the many keen sportsmen who read this book and who have not the means or the opportunity to have a gun specially made to measure for them—and to those, too, who on occasion have to shoot with any odd gun they can lay their hands on—it is worth emphasizing this point that the shooter can, to a certain degree, control the length of the stock by regulating his grip on the gun. It is by no means an ideal state of affairs and, in driven-game shooting, with really fast, well-presented birds, no sportsman with a gun which doesn't fit him can hope to put up his best performance. But, if you are using a borrowed gun, or you have got a gun which is too long or too short in the stock for you, you can overcome, to a large extent, the problem of fit by drawing your hand back on the forehand if the stock is too long and extending it, if necessary, right up to the barrels if the stock is too short. In fact, His Late Majesty, King George V, was one of those who adopted what is called the straight-arm stance. He invariably moved his left hand forward during gun-mounting until the left arm was fully extended up the barrels. I don't recommend the practice to the majority of shooters, but George V, as is well known, was in his prime one of the greatest shots of his day, and the straight-arm grip on the barrel may be an unusual style, but, assuming that everything else is all right, it is still good style.

The man who is away from civilization may feel doubtful about the fit of his gun and wish to test it. To do this, he should cut a finely pointed piece of paper and shove it in the breech absolutely central with the rib, so that the point stands up about three eighths of an inch above the barrels. This point is the temporary backsight. Next, with equal care, fasten a precisely similar point at the muzzle end to serve as a foresight.

Then, with both eyes open, and holding the gun in the ready position, look at an object and mount the gun at it.

Close both eyes a fraction of a second *before* the gun is home to the shoulder. Then, *before* you pull the trigger, open the eyes and observe where your sights are really pointing.

Practice this at various objects or points of aim and you may find that, though you may be "dead-on" for straight-away shots, and, say, shots to your left, you will yet find that you aim over or behind in the case of shots to your right or overhead.

In order to avoid false stance, move the feet after each shot and, above all, avoid adjusting yourself to an artificial and temporary fit to the gun, the idea being to take these snap shots as naturally as possible. The information to be gained from this experiment is limited to the discovery that your failure of certain shots is, in all probability, due rather to the poor fit of your gun than to any other cause.

For a more critical analysis, an outdoor shooting test can be made without the paper sights. If a whitewashed steel or iron target, about three feet square, is available, this is best; but if it is not, you can extemporize an adequate test by sticking double sheets of newspaper on a wood frame or on a hedge. See that the print is the right way up so that you will know afterwards which is the top or bottom of the pattern.

In the center of the target make a big ink aiming spot; then measure off—do not pace it but measure it exactly—a firing point at sixteen yards.

Assuming the eye is thirty-six inches from the gun-muzzle, also that the gun shoots with true elevation and that the two barrels are in the same line, then errors in bend and castoff will be magnified sixteen times on the target.

Fire several snap shots at the target with your normal stance, then take the center of your composite pattern as the average. If your charge is centered two inches *below* the point of aim, the stock certainly needs straightening one eighth of an inch. A group two inches high represents a nicely placed pattern. If higher, for every two inches surplus elevation the stock should be bent down one eighth of an inch. A group one inch to the left would involve an increase of castoff of one sixteenth of an inch, while three inches to the right would involve reduction of castoff by three sixteenths of an inch.

There is always the possibility, of course, that the shooter rather than the gun is at fault; hence any consistent error should be further tested not only in terms of the gun but in terms of gun-mounting as well. The following rules apply:

POSITION OF THE SHOTS ON THE TARGET AND EXPLANATION

Shooting on the right. Causes may be: (*a*) too much castoff; (*b*) head too far forward with eye too far over the stock; (*c*) stock too short; (*d*) incorrect stance.

Shooting on the left. Causes may be: (*a*) not enough castoff; (*b*) stock too long; (*c*) pulling in of the left hand; (*d*) stock on the arm instead of into the shoulder.

Shooting low. Causes may be: (*a*) too much bend of stock; (*b*) too heavy a pull; (*c*) flinching; (*d*) left hand not far enough forward or a badly balanced gun that is heavy forward and shoots low.

Shooting high. Causes may be: (*a*) stock too straight at the bump; (*b*) too light a pull; (*c*) too long a stock; (*d*) too much "toe" to stock.

If you want to make a quite simple experiment to test whether the length of stock on your gun suits you, the overhead shot is the best test. For the going-away shot, whatever the size of the gun, the shooter can extend or shorten the reach of the left hand to make the gun fit. But in the overhead shot, if the gun doesn't fit really well, you will recognize that something is wrong. If the stock is too long, you may well find that your swing is checked. You may indeed find that you can shoot more easily by using the second trigger. If the stock is too short, you will notice that you have to push your left hand up the barrel to make a smooth and natural follow-through.

If the stock is finally proved to be at fault, it should be altered by an expert who has seen you shoot. Self-gun-fitting is very much like self-doctoring; not by any means a certain cure. Nevertheless, to suspect a malady is the first step in locating it and putting yourself in the way of a cure.

ꝗ CHAPTER IV ꝗ

Cartridges

Don't blame your shell if you miss. Once in a thousand times it might happen that you mounted your gun correctly, placed the charge correctly, and the column of shot misbehaved itself to the extent that the bird slipped through the gap in a bad pattern. But, for practical purposes, you can assume, if you miss, that it was your fault.

Don't become a "size of shot" fanatic either. Fifty years ago, shot was either as soft as putty or as hard as steel; there was no happy medium. Cartridges were not of the quality that they are today and guns did not shoot such regular patterns. For that reason, No. 5 shot was the most popular size. But, as cartridge manufacture improved, the 5½ or "medium game" (often labeled M.G.) ousted No. 5, and, lately, Nos. 6, 6½, and 7 have gained popularity.

Today, if you have never shot with anything else in inland game shooting except No. 6, it wouldn't make any material difference to the results.

In fact, I know that many sportsmen like to use No. 6 at the beginning of the season and change to No. 5 at the end of it. Others, when they are shooting on the marshes, put No. 8 in the right barrel to deal with snipe and No. 4 in the left barrel against the chance of a possible duck. What so often happens, in practice, is that they miss the duck with the No. 4 and bring him down, to their surprise, with the No. 8 and vice versa.

On this subject—size of shot, types of powders, various loads —I probably know as much as anyone. A well-known writer, many years ago, used to call himself the "twenty-thousand shot man," which was the number of rounds he claimed to have fired at testing plates. I wouldn't like to estimate how many tens of thousands of rounds I myself have loaded and shot at plates. I am still at it. And, after a lifetime with a gun in my hand, I assure you that I can quote you figures to prove pretty well anything.

It is self-evident that big shot has greater energy, at a given range, than small shot; but, when it comes to penetration, we know that the fine-pointed gimlet penetrates better than the blunt-pointed one. Generally speaking, the more pellets there are in a cartridge, the better chance there is of hitting a vital spot and bringing the game down. A No. 7 in the head is much more likely to kill a bird than a No. 5 in the body, although pellet energy is less.

In the days of muzzle-loaders, when the argument about shot sizes was even more clamorous than it is among shooting men now, experts like General Hangar recommended 2 ounces of No. 2 shot over a charge of little more than a dram of powder for all forms of inland shooting. At the same time there were other shooting men who preferred to put in a couple of drams, or more, of powder with about ¾ ounce of No. 6 shot. In those days there was some reason for the variation of opinion, because the shot was soft and the powder was not as efficient as it is now. In our own time cartridges are so standardized and patterns are so regular that it won't help anybody to shoot straighter to worry about cartridges, powder, and shot at all; except perhaps over the price of them.

Nevertheless, I am quite aware that nothing I say will stop keen shooting men from regarding the matter as of major importance. I remember one renowned shot who always used to insist that his cartridges should be loaded with No. 4, but marked with No. 6 top wads. Another sportsman swore by 5½ shot and, if circumstances necessitated his using shot of another size, such was his conviction that, by a natural reflex, he never shot so well. So, if you have a taste for different types and different sizes of shot in different loads for different game at different seasons, I certainly don't want to persuade you to change. You will always shoot best with the cartridge you trust best and, if you feel happier with a pink cartridge than a brown one, you *will* be happier —and shoot better accordingly.

The only circumstances in which the size of shot can be a matter of importance is in shooting heavy fowl like geese, where No. 3 is probably the best size. And, if you happen to be shooting driven snipe or on a marsh where snipe represent the larger proportion of the game, I would recommend you to use cartridges loaded with No. 7, or even No. 8, shot.

But, for all general shooting purposes, you won't improve on No. 6.

If you want to satisfy yourself with a personal test, and nothing will satisfy you so completely as a personal test, get a piece of old sheet iron and wash it over with white distemper or whitewash. Then, at the standard distance of forty yards, which should give you a thirty- to forty-inch pattern on the plate, fire a number of test rounds with different sizes of shot; remembering, after each shot, to wash over the plate again with whitewash so that you get a clear silhouette of each individual pattern.

Experts, when they are testing cartridges without the aid of a proof gun and a chronograph, distinguish by ear the quick cartridge from the slow one. By looking at the cap indentation and the case expansion, they can judge pressure and, by studying the pellet marks on the plate, they can gauge whether the charge is hitting hard or not. In your own case, you may find this more difficult. But, if you examine the pellet marks on a steel plate after they are fired, you can judge by the size of the marks whether the pellets were hitting hard or not. Make a close examination and you will discover that the marks on the plate vary in size. If you find pinhead marks, it means that the pellets that made them were useless so far as penetration was concerned. But a strong bruising mark on the plate indicates that your shot was hitting well. Alternatively, if you want to test penetration, there is no better subject than a telephone directory. You can simply measure penetration by the different letters to which different parts of your shot charge have penetrated.

If you make this experiment carefully, with all the different sizes of shot, you will find at the end of it that you have learned precisely nothing at all except that modern cartridges have a standard steady performance and that, if you hold your gun straight and pull the triggers at the right time at the right range, anything you shoot at must be killed. This applies, whatever modern smokeless powders you use, whatever fancy loads within reason that you adopt.

If you simply use standard cartridges, or you have cartridges especially loaded for you by your gun-maker, in the end it comes to much the same thing. Hand-loaded cartridges are more pleasant to use and a fraction more reliable. It is satisfying to shoot with a special load and a special charge boxed up for you by your own gun-maker. But although, as a gun-maker, I would like to tell you otherwise, the greatest advantage between a high-priced cartridge and a low-priced cartridge is that the cases of higher-priced cartridges are waterproof and, as a consequence, you can use them without the annoyance of finding that the paper tubes have swollen and stuck in the chambers of the gun. For wild fowling and for shooting in wet weather that can be a very important consideration indeed. But, on economical grounds, I am bound to say that what I would recommend any sportsman to do is to use the ordinary standard cartridge in fine weather and comfortable conditions and to have a reserve of cartridges with top-quality waterproofed metal-lined cases for those occasions when he is using two guns and doesn't want to put up with the irritation of a hold-up with a case stuck in the breech, or in weather in which the cheaper papered cases will swell.

Apart from these general comments, I don't want to leave you with the impression that the modern cartridge is an ideal one. In many ways it leaves a very great deal to be desired. In the first place, the composition in the cap is still made in many cases of the ancient priming mixture, containing potassium chlorate, which has already rusted millions of gun-barrels. The Sinoxoid, and other types of non-rusting primers, should be universal. In fact, it isn't available, at the time of writing, in Britain at all. Nowadays, too, the excellent bulk powders E.C. No. 3 and Smokeless Diamond are no longer manufactured. We have to put up with new powders, which are certainly efficient and more economic to produce, but which, to my mind, don't compare with the old stuff. On economical grounds, too, the soft center felt wad, greased to wipe the barrels, has been replaced by a patent cardboard wad which nobody pretends is equal to the old.

For my part, too, I find objections to the British crimped case. Crimping the cartridge means that it needs an extra three sixteenths inch of case over and above the ordinary turnover. This extra length enters the bore of a 2½-inch chambered gun. Sportsmen, using what are known as "new crimp" cartridges, really should have their chambers lengthened accordingly, but, in that event, this would necessitate, under English law, re-proof; a rather risky proceeding, as a proof charge is said to be approximately treble the service charge, which would shake up many a gun safe enough under normal pressures.

If I had my own way, the paper-cased cartridge would be a thing of the past. The all-metal case is the ideal. A metal-cased cartridge, which is obviously completely waterproof, with a non-rusting primer, will, in my opinion, be the cartridge of the future.

But these are matters for the experts. I repeat to you, once again, that this chapter, from the point of view of the average shooting man, is the most unimportant chapter in this book. Worrying about your cartridges won't help you to shoot a fraction straighter. If you master the drill, you will kill your birds with anything in the way of powder and shot you can buy at the gun-makers today.

True, you will occasionally come across a bad cartridge. The usual trouble is that, in manufacture, the turnover hasn't been made strong enough. Just as a squib will fizzle off ineffectively if you don't put your foot on it and the harder you tread on it the better the bang, so the turnover of a cartridge builds up pressure according to its strength.

A good tight turnover holds until the cap ignites the powder and the powder combustion forms the propelling gases. You can test turnover yourself by the very simple method of taking a cartridge in your hand with your index finger pressed on the top wad. Tap the brass end of the cartridge sharply on the table. If you can move the top wad with the pressure of your index finger, it means that the cartridge isn't packed strongly enough.

Even so, it will probably shoot well enough to kill your bird at normal ranges. It is a very bad cartridge indeed, and a very rare one, which won't kill at twenty yards.

But I realize that everything I am saying is militating against one of the favorite discussions at a shooting lunch. Every keen shooting man likes to believe that his cartridges make a difference. In an attempt to co-operate, on pages 121–3 I give tables, if only for the record, of the bores of gun and the number of pellets in game-gun cartridges.

Just to emphasize the relative unimportance of these tables to the average shooting man, let me reveal to you that many years ago I built some double-barreled weapons which were designed to fire only one pellet at a time. They were constructed with the same care and precision, and attention to the shooter's measurement, as a first-class gun. But they weren't shotguns. They were double-barreled .22 rifles.

With these guns, in the hands of a good shot, it was possible, again and again, to smash a clay pigeon. Subsequently, I supplied some of them to American sportsmen who were keen to pull off long shots at duck. In practice, what we found was that these .22 rifles, tailored to fit the user, had an effectiveness comparable to about 33 per cent of a shotgun in the hands of the same man, but, of course, they were killing game well outside the extreme ranges of a smooth-bored gun.

One very fine American shot who had one told me that, on several occasions, he had succeeded in pulling off a right and a left at mallard at over a hundred yards.

The moral is simply that, if you are using a gun properly, time and time again you would hit your bird if you only had a single bullet in your gun. In fact, the shooter who is on his day is doing this consistently. And, if you hit a bird with any size of shot from BB to No. 8, in the center of the pattern, you will kill him as certainly as if you had hit him with a .22 bullet, because the concentration of the pattern is always at its greatest in the dead center of the charge.

By all means use the cartridge as a convenient excuse to explain your misses. Surprisingly, it is an excuse which is often accepted by even experienced shooting hosts. But, privately, don't believe a word of it. When you get home, go through the gun drill again. Practice, if you can get the opportunity, on clay pigeons. Practice, practice, practice . . . and you will never have a dud cartridge again.

In fact, you may get so good that your shooting friends will ask you what cartridges you use with the notion of adopting the same brand of straight powder that you yourself favor.

Bores of Gun

DESCRIPTION	APPROXIMATE SHOT CHARGE Oz.	APPROXIMATE WEIGHT OF GUN Lbs.
4-bore 4 in.	3–4	$14\frac{1}{2}$–$18\frac{1}{2}$
8-bore $3\frac{1}{4}$ in.	2–$2\frac{1}{2}$	$10\frac{1}{2}$–$12\frac{1}{2}$
10-bore $2\frac{7}{8}$ in.	$1\frac{7}{16}$–$1\frac{5}{8}$	8–9
10-bore $2\frac{5}{8}$ in.	$1\frac{1}{4}$–$1\frac{3}{8}$	$7\frac{1}{2}$–8
12-bore 3 in.[1]	$1\frac{3}{8}$–$1\frac{1}{2}$	$7\frac{3}{4}$–$8\frac{1}{2}$
12-bore $2\frac{3}{4}$ in.[1]	$1\frac{1}{4}$	$7\frac{1}{2}$–$7\frac{3}{4}$
12-bore $2\frac{1}{2}$ in.[1]	1–$1\frac{1}{8}$	$6\frac{1}{2}$–7
16-bore $2\frac{3}{4}$ in.	1–$1\frac{1}{16}$	$6\frac{1}{2}$
16-bore $2\frac{1}{2}$ in.	$\frac{7}{8}$–$\frac{15}{16}$	$5\frac{3}{4}$–6
20-bore $2\frac{3}{4}$ in.	$\frac{7}{8}$–$\frac{15}{16}$	$5\frac{3}{4}$–6
20-bore $2\frac{1}{2}$ in.	$\frac{3}{4}$–$\frac{13}{16}$	$5\frac{1}{2}$
24-bore $2\frac{1}{2}$ in.	$\frac{11}{16}$	5
28-bore $2\frac{1}{2}$ in.	$\frac{5}{8}$	$4\frac{3}{4}$
32-bore $2\frac{1}{2}$ in.	$\frac{1}{2}$	4
.410-bore $2\frac{1}{2}$ in.	$\frac{7}{16}$	$3\frac{3}{4}$

[1] Churchill "XXV" guns with 25-in. barrels are built approximately 8 oz. lighter.

Pellets in Game Charges

OZ. OF SHOT	SIZE OF SHOT			
	4	5	6	7
$1\frac{1}{2}$	255	330	408	510
$1\frac{7}{16}$	244	316	391	489
$1\frac{3}{8}$	234	303	374	468
$1\frac{5}{16}$	223	289	357	446
$1\frac{1}{4}$	213	275	340	425
$1\frac{3}{16}$	202	261	323	404
$1\frac{1}{8}$	191	248	306	383
$1\frac{1}{16}$	181	234	289	361
1	170	220	272	340
$\frac{15}{16}$	159	206	255	319
$\frac{7}{8}$	149	193	238	298
$1\frac{3}{16}$	138	179	221	276
$\frac{3}{4}$	128	165	204	255
$\frac{11}{16}$	117	151	187	234
$\frac{5}{8}$	106	138	170	212
$\frac{9}{16}$	96	124	153	191
$\frac{1}{2}$	85	110	136	170

TRUE CYLINDER (=40 PER CENT) PATTERNS

OZ. OF SHOT	PELLETS IN 30-IN. CIRCLE AT 40 YARDS FOR DIFFERENT SIZES OF SHOT			
	4	5	6	7
$1\frac{1}{2}$	102	132	163	204
$1\frac{3}{8}$	94	121	150	187
$1\frac{1}{4}$	85	110	136	170
$1\frac{1}{8}$	76	99	122	153
$1\frac{1}{16}$	72	94	116	144
I	68	88	109	136
$\frac{7}{8}$	60	77	95	119
$\frac{3}{4}$	51	66	82	102
$1\frac{1}{16}$	47	60	75	94
$\frac{5}{8}$	42	55	68	85
$\frac{9}{16}$	38	50	61	76
$\frac{1}{2}$	34	44	54	68

IMPROVED CYLINDER (=50 PER CENT) PATTERNS

OZ. OF SHOT	PELLETS IN 30-IN. CIRCLE AT 40 YARDS FOR DIFFERENT SIZES OF SHOT			
	4	5	6	7
$1\frac{1}{2}$	128	165	204	255
$1\frac{7}{16}$	122	158	196	245
$1\frac{3}{8}$	117	152	187	234
$1\frac{5}{16}$	111	145	179	223
$1\frac{1}{4}$	107	138	170	213
$1\frac{3}{16}$	101	131	162	202
$1\frac{1}{8}$	96	124	153	192
$1\frac{1}{16}$	91	117	145	181
I	85	110	136	170
$1\frac{5}{16}$	80	103	128	160
$\frac{7}{8}$	75	97	119	149
$1\frac{3}{16}$	69	90	111	138
$\frac{3}{4}$	64	83	102	128
$1\frac{1}{16}$	59	76	94	117
$\frac{5}{8}$	53	69	85	106
$\frac{9}{16}$	48	62	77	96
$\frac{1}{2}$	43	55	68	85

Half Choke (= 60 Per Cent) Patterns

OZ. OF SHOT	PELLETS IN 30-IN. CIRCLE AT 40 YARDS FOR DIFFERENT SIZES OF SHOT			
	4	5	6	7
$1\frac{1}{2}$	153	198	244	306
$1\frac{7}{16}$	146	190	235	293
$1\frac{3}{8}$	140	182	224	280
$1\frac{5}{16}$	134	174	214	267
$1\frac{1}{4}$	128	165	204	255
$1\frac{3}{16}$	121	157	194	242
$1\frac{1}{8}$	115	148	184	230
$1\frac{1}{16}$	109	140	173	217
1	102	132	163	204
$\frac{15}{16}$	95	124	153	191
$\frac{7}{8}$	89	116	143	179
$\frac{13}{16}$	83	108	133	166
$\frac{3}{4}$	77	99	122	153
$\frac{11}{16}$	70	91	112	140
$\frac{5}{8}$	64	82	102	127
$\frac{9}{16}$	58	74	92	115
$\frac{1}{2}$	51	66	81	102

Full Choke (= 70 Per Cent) Patterns

OZ. OF SHOT	PELLETS IN 30-IN. CIRCLE AT 40 YARDS FOR DIFFERENT SIZES OF SHOT			
	4	5	6	7
$1\frac{1}{2}$	178	231	285	357
$1\frac{7}{16}$	170	221	274	342
$1\frac{3}{8}$	163	212	261	328
$1\frac{5}{16}$	156	202	249	312
$1\frac{1}{4}$	149	192	238	298
$1\frac{3}{16}$	142	183	226	283
$1\frac{1}{8}$	134	174	214	268
$1\frac{1}{16}$	127	164	202	253
1	119	154	190	238
$\frac{15}{16}$	112	144	179	223
$\frac{7}{8}$	105	135	167	209
$\frac{13}{16}$	97	125	155	194
$\frac{3}{4}$	90	115	143	179
$\frac{11}{16}$	82	106	131	163
$\frac{5}{8}$	75	97	119	148
$\frac{9}{16}$	67	86	107	134
$\frac{1}{2}$	59	77	95	119

CHAPTER V

The Care of a Gun

THE MODERN game-gun, as made by a first-class gunsmith, is an arm with an almost indeterminable lease of life. Properly looked after, it will endure year after year without deterioration; but only the very few take the proper amount of care.

The vast majority of sportsmen have indeed never learned how to assemble a gun properly when they take it out of its case; or how to dismount it when they put it away again. Most second-hand guns carry the scars of brutal ill-treatment. It is to the credit of their makers that, in spite of it, they are still sound, if battered, weapons.

A gun is normally put away in its case in two pieces: the barrels with the fore-end attached and the stock and actions. Take down your gun case and, without reading further, put one of your own guns together in your usual way.

Unless you have a very exceptional knowledge of gunmanship, I fancy that you began by lifting out the barrels, removing the fore-end, and placing it on the table beside you. After that, you lifted out the stock and action and then fiddled about for a few seconds while you hooked the lumps on the barrels into the action of the gun. I shouldn't be surprised if you bruised the metal even slightly as you did so. Subsequently, you picked up the fore-end again and clamped it under the barrels of the gun.

First, the chances are that you did not hold the barrels at the correct angle to the action when you tried to join the two to-gether. Second, you took a considerable risk of denting the barrels, or dropping them, by handling them without the firm grip that the fore-end normally gives you. Third, as you at-tempted to hook the barrels into the action, the probability is that you hadn't pressed the lever completely home.

Let me now describe to you, in detail, how you should have assembled the gun. Taking the barrels out of the case, you should have removed the fore-end and, instead of putting it down, placed it loosely beyond the fore-end loop which nor-mally holds it to the barrels. Then, with a firm grip round fore-end and barrels, you should have taken the stock of your gun under your left arm, forced the lever well back with the point of your thumb and then, holding the barrels at right angles to the action, smoothly slipped the lumps into their seating. It should have been a movement as oily as the movement of a limb. When the barrel was locked onto the gun, you should have then grasped the weapon by the small of the butt and, only then, re-leased your grip on the fore-end and adjusted it in its proper position.

Dismounting the gun, you should go through the process in reverse. First, remove the fore-end and place it loosely above the catch on the barrels. Grasp fore-end and barrels with your right hand, give yourself a comfortable grip, and then, pressing back the lever of the gun to its full traverse, break the weapon in your hand. Subsequently, the fore-end is clicked on in its proper place.

Many shooting men, when they dismount their guns, still be-lieve that they rest the mainsprings by releasing the cocking levers. Don't do it. First of all, the action of a shotgun, unlike a rifle, can be severely damaged if you release the pins on an empty chamber. If you must do it, make sure that you have got snap caps in the barrels. But, apart from that, releasing the main-spring is quite unnecessary. Whatever you do, the mainsprings in a gun are always under tension and, in fact, the difference in the pressure on the springs between a gun cocked and uncocked is a matter of not more than a quarter of an inch. Put your gun away fully cocked. The springs won't mind and, further, when you come to mount the gun, it will come together that much more easily.

When you buy a new gun, you will notice that the gun-maker supplies a cleaning rod, a mop, and a wire brush—and little else. The equipment is not really adequate to clean a gun properly or to keep it in the order you should. In fact, any keen shooting man should keep in his gun-cupboard not one cleaning rod but two or three all fully assembled. The wool mop, which every gun-maker supplies, is not really an essential, although it is useful for wiping out the barrels with light oil before the gun is put away. The essentials of gun cleaning are a jag, with patches cut to size to fit it, a wire brush, and some excellent gun oil. In addition, you can treat yourself to all sorts of accessories which are useful but not essential, such as a toothbrush which is really very valuable for brushing mud out of the checkering of the stock; a chamber brush designed for cleaning out the chambers which are larger than the barrel of the gun beyond; some wax polish to keep a shine on the stock; an oily rag and a clean rag for polishing up the stock itself.

Properly speaking, every shooting man, unless he is one of those fortunate individuals, these days, who has a manservant, and a manservant, too, whom he can really trust, should clean his own gun. However tired you are at the end of the day, it is foolish to delegate the cleaning of a weapon, which costs as much as a piano, to a keeper or somebody else who "couldn't care less." And, if you clean your gun yourself, clean it properly.

I see so many shooting men whose idea of cleaning their guns is to insert a rod into the barrel, scrub the top fifteen inches diligently, and ignore the first ten or fifteen inches of the barrel (which most needs cleaning) altogether, except as they push the brush in or pull it out. They put away their guns with fouling under the extractors and in the recesses of the action. Usually there is wet which will cause rust in the gutters on each side of the rib. There is mud in the checkering and, probably, they have made a dent in the barrel which, through putting the gun away dirty, they have failed to observe.

Perhaps the most important thing to remember about the necessity of cleaning guns is that the firing of *one* cartridge creates just as much fouling and leaves just as much chemical which can do damage as five hundred cartridges. That wasn't true in the old days when sportsmen used black-powder flintlocks. Black powder was comparatively harmless to the metal and the necessity for cleaning the gun was determined rather by the need that, after forty or fifty rounds, the barrels became so fouled with the residue of the powder that they had to be cleaned in rather the same way that a pipe has to be scraped out at intervals to remove the carbon. But the principal disadvantage of modern cartridges in Britain is that the chemical composition in the cap corrodes the barrels. It is very foolish indeed to put away any gun at the end of the day without cleaning it with very great care.

Different shooting men have their own different ways of cleaning a gun, and different accessories. But the principle never varies. When you bring home your gun at the end of a day's shooting, dismount it, not forgetting to replace the fore-end on the barrels; and, if it has been raining during the day, take the stock and action in your hands by the small of the butt and shake it thoroughly. It is surprising the amount of water that can collect in the striker holes in the face of the action. You will do a great deal to keep rust down if you remember to do this after a wet day's shooting. Next, wipe over the action and the barrels and set the barrels up in a safe place to enable any water which has collected in the gutters on each side of the ribs to drip away and dry off.

To clean the barrels, begin by pushing through an old rag to get out the worst of the fouling. A good trick is to roll up a tiny ball of newspaper and push that, with the point of the jag, through the two barrels. The idea of getting rid of the worst of the fouling before you start cleaning is to keep the rest of your cleaning gear clean and in decent order. Subsequently, using Three-in-One, or better still, an oil solvent with three parts of water(because oil alone will not eliminate the chloride), clean the gun thoroughly with a linen patch wrapped round the jag. When I say thoroughly, I mean work the cleaning rod up and down, with pushes of about three or four inches at a time, from the chambers to the muzzle and back again.

Make a really thorough job of it and put some elbow grease into the effort. Subsequently, hold up the barrels to the electric light and look at them carefully, from both ends, to satisfy yourself that there are no revealing streaks of leading showing. The leading is something to look for. The barrel should be absolutely moon-bright when you have finished with it. If it isn't bright, go over it again with a wire brush, also soaked in oil. Use the wire or bronze brush as enthusiastically as you like. You won't do any harm to the barrel. Go on with the brush and the rag until your barrels are absolutely bright examined from the chamber *and* the muzzle end.

After making sure that the barrels are quite clean, raise the extractors and poke around to clean out any residue of powder which has got underneath them or in the ridge of the chamber which takes the rim of the cartridge. This is a fiddling job but a very important one. Next, with a piece of oily rag, wipe out the gutters on each side of the rib very carefully. Subsequently, wipe the barrels over to remove any blood marks or finger marks which you have left on it.

Then pass on to the stock. Wipe over the metal work carefully with an oily rag. Then, with a matchstick, put the very smallest drop of oil into the cracks where the trigger blades extend through from the action into the two pinholes on the face of the action, on to the safety catch, and under the lever of the gun.

If the gun is muddy, clean the checkering gently with an old toothbrush. When it is quite clean, if you are particular about the appearance of your stock, rub it with a little oil; or, better still, polish it up like a piece of furniture with a good quality wax polish.

Treat the fore-end in the same way that you treat the stock of the gun. Rub the mud out of the checkering and administer a smear of oil to the ejector springs, the joined catch, and the flats and face of the action. After that you can put your gun away.

I want to emphasize that it is unwise to use too much oil. Heavy oiling of ejectors and cocking limbs, strikers and trigger blades, is not to be recommended. When a gun is overhauled by the maker—as every gun should be at regular intervals—fine oil is put on the working parts which is sufficient to last the season. Excessive oiling causes the woodwork to swell, locks to get "gummy," and pulls to behave irregularly. Oil you must, but the tiniest touch of oil is adequate. Much more important to remember is not to put the gun away wet, with drops of water under the cocking levers or water where it will create rust hanging about in the gutters under the ribs.

If you can possibly arrange it so, it is much better to keep your guns fully assembled in a case, or a rack, than to put them away in their cases. If the only place you have got to keep your guns is in their cases, never leave them there for more than a few months without taking them out to have a look at them and wipe them over. If you *must* put them away for a long period, either send them to the gun-maker to look after them for you or, alternatively, coat the barrels and the actions with the jelly called "safety paste." It is a very excellent preservative. Whatever you do, don't use one of those old-fashioned rods covered with baize inside the barrels. They don't do any good at all and, in fact, encourage rusting.

It is always a good thing to treat your baize-lined gun cases with D.D.T. or some other effective moth spray. Many a sportsman has had an ugly shock when he has opened a beautiful new gun case which he hasn't looked at since the season before to find that the clothes moths have cut it to pieces.

If you get interested in taking care of your guns, you will get nearly as much joy out of that as out of using them. I have only given you the bare essentials of gun cleaning here. You will find, if you get interested, that you can buy the most intriguing box of tackle and complete gun-cleaning outfits containing detailed and adequate instructions on cleaning a gun properly.

It is a wise and economical policy to send in your gun or guns for overhaul and thorough cleaning at the end of every season. The owner's cleaning, however thorough, is necessarily limited to externals. The gunsmith strips the locks and action and makes a general overhaul besides cleaning and lubricating all moving parts. In the process, wear and tear are noted and corrected and the gun properly tightened up for the next shooting season. This is much more important than is generally realized, for if there is any undue free play or movement about the action of a gun, and the weapon is fired repeatedly in that state, the hammer action of the firing is likely to exaggerate this small element of wear and tear into a serious looseness.

Further, a great many sportsmen never realize the extent to which, in the season, they bruise, dent, or cut the barrels of their guns. A dropped gun, a hasty scramble into a car, or any of the casual bumps of a day's shooting may account for it. There is only one thing to do: never entrust your gun to a man who may, or may not be, a master of his craft, but send it back to the maker or to a gun-maker known to be reliable. Barrels are sensitive things and, if any accident occurs which dents or bruises them at all seriously, DO NOT ATTEMPT TO FIRE CARTRIDGES THROUGH THE INJURED TUBE. Rather give up sport for the day than run risks with an expensive gun. The primary causes of burst barrels are as follows: first, the barrel is indented; second, a hard tight-fitting wad meets the obstruction and turns it into a bulge; finally, the smallest obstruction to the damaged muzzle will burst the barrel, for the strain flies to the weakest part and that part is already strained to its limits.

Repeated use of a dented barrel tends to wear the internal bulge thin. In extreme cases, it may push it out and so turn the dent into a bulge. Both render the subsequent repair more difficult and involve the removal of important metal in polishing.

There is another reason why you should always send your gun to the maker for an annual overhaul. Apart from protecting the gun for a very small charge, it also does a very great deal to improve it. In fact, it takes much longer to "run in a gun" than a car. This periodical overhaul and polishing of all the mechanism gradually converts a solid medium-priced article into a better quality machine, whilst the best gun, after a few overhauls, gets even better in its sweetness of opening and closing, its crispness of pull and behavior under fire. Apart from this, you are neglecting a valuable article by putting it away and allowing the mechanism to rust, as it certainly will.

There are one or two minor mishaps which may occur in the field. A loose-fitting fore-end may drop off the gun while it is being closed. If the ejector hammers are down, it may be difficult to replace. In the fore-end can be seen the projecting hammers of the ejectors. If the fore-end cannot be replaced with the gun in a partly open position (as it was when it fell off), these ejector hammers should be pressed back into the fore-end until they cock. This should not be done except with a blunt tool such as the end of a hard-wood cleaning rod. Best of all is to fit the fore-end onto the barrels and push the protruding extractor or extractors back by using a firm pressure against a wooden bench, or its equivalent in the nearest fence or gatepost.

When a single trigger gun jams and the top lever refuses to operate, push the trigger forward and pull the safety catch back.

The cause of a gun jamming is often to be found in a striker sticking in a cap. The speediest solution of this problem is, if the other barrel is loaded, to fire into the air, trusting to the jar of recoil to dislodge the errant striker. Then hold the lever open with the thumb and give the gun a sharp jerk. This usually puts matters right and, at all events, it cannot damage anything except the striker point.

If the lever refuses to open under ordinary pressure, hold the gun sideways; put both thumbs, one over the other, against the lever and the fingers of both hands against the right lock. The amount of pressure from such a squeeze is ever so much more than can be made with one finger and thumb; after opening, look for and remove the cause, which may be either a burst rim or powder residue between barrels and action.

Another embarrassment occurs when a cartridge slips behind the extractor. This is a case when force should not be applied. There is a danger of "making things worse." First, dismount the barrels, put the extractor out to its limit, and, if the case cannot be manœuvred into position for extraction, it will be necessary to remove the screw holding the extractors; pull them bodily out, remove the case, and replace them. If the arm is an ejector, the ejector hammers may need re-cocking in the manner previously explained.

The irregular functioning of ejectors may be caused either by lack of oil and friction from rust or by use of wrong kinds of oil which gum the cocking and ejector limbs. If a washout with paraffin and a relubrication with good gun oil of the limbs protruding from the action fail to remedy the trouble, the gun should be sent for adjustment.

Sometimes the gun action cannot be easily closed. This may be due to an unusually thick-rimmed cartridge, a rare but, nevertheless, not unavoidable fault in machine-made, factory-loaded cases; or, more often, to a slight deposit of fired powder, fouling, or dirt getting between the barrels and the action, either on the flats of the action, the flats of the barrels, or in the slots of the action. Clean out any accumulation and see that the extractor screw is right home; if this is loose and projecting, it will prevent the gun closing properly.

When assembling the gun, note that, should the barrels refuse to close long before they are in contact with the action, the trouble is usually due to a projecting striker catching on the base of the extractor. If the latter is pressed back with the finger, the gun will probably close.

But, no doubt, the commonest mishap you will have in the shooting field is to find that a cartridge sticks in the chamber and the pressure of the ejector spring is not strong enough to throw it out. This very often happens with cheap cartridges which have got damp or odd rounds which, for one reason or another, are misshapen. The best thing is always to carry one of the finger-ring cartridge extractors in your pocket. Alternatively, an equally effective method is to carry in your pocket— or see to it that a keeper carries in his pocket—a sausage-shaped piece of lead about an inch long (an elongated fishing sinker is ideal). If a spent cartridge case gets stuck in the chambers, take out the loaded case and then, with the breech open, drop a piece of lead down the muzzles. Even a fisherman's weight of about an ounce will, in the fall, gather sufficient momentum to remove the most obstinate obstruction.

The sportsman, going abroad, is sometimes induced to take cheap, or machine-made, guns on the assurance that these are quite good enough for the rigors of an expedition where rough usage will be the rule. This is the most fatal of false economies. Generally, it can be said that the better the gun the worst usage it will stand. The metal of which cheap and most foreign guns are made is remarkably soft. As a result, the guns shoot and wear loose with astonishing speed. They are not constructed to last and, though sold at a low price, are not cheap in terms of a serviceable life. They are seldom worth repairing, for they will give out in a fresh place almost as soon as the first source of trouble has been mended. The man who is away from civilization of any kind can, however, effect temporary repairs if one of these arms "shoots loose" by simply center punching the metal at the sides of the front lump beneath the barrel to bring the metal of the hook nearer to the cross-pin or hinge-bar, and thus close the breech of the barrel towards the action face; or, if the bolt is loose, a light hammering up to the back lump will enable the bolt to pull the barrel tighter down to the action. There is, however, neither economy nor reliability in cheap guns. They may not, perhaps, be actively dangerous—they carry proof marks—but they are invariably inefficient and unreliable and always provocative of small delays and embarrassments in the field. Any sportsman who is going abroad should take expert advice from his gun-maker on the care of his weapon in the country to which he is going. In tropical countries especially extra precautions are necessary to protect the woodwork and the action. These are best explained by the gun-maker when he knows the particular country to which the sportsman is going. Alternatively, he should find somebody who really knows what he is talking about on the spot.

CHAPTER VI

The Shooting School

IF ANYONE asked the ordinary shooting man if he could see shot in the air, his reply would probably take the form of an impolite negative. Yet it is quite easy to see shot in the air once you get the knack of it. It is the trade secret of most shooting school coaches. They can *see* where you are shooting.

During the war it was fairly commonplace for people behind a big howitzer to see the shell in the air and trace its track. A howitzer shell is a big object and its initial velocity is not very much higher than a shotgun charge. Airmen have reported that they have seen artillery projectiles from the cockpit, and there is every reason to suppose that their claim is sound.

It is not yet established what degree of perception the human eye can undertake in terms of time. Some people take a long time to focus their vision on an object; others see it and recognize it as quick as thought; far quicker than speech. It is largely a question of knowing what you are looking for. The mind may be slow to interpret the unexpected, but as swift as the eye to mark an object once the strong factor of personal disbelief is removed.

You think you cannot see shot in the air because you have always been told that you cannot. You can. And, with a very little practice, you can pick up the trick. I don't suggest that you will see the shot charge as a swarm of individual pellets; but what you *will* see is a sort of "aerial disturbance."

At 25 yards range the human eye cannot discern differences if these are less than a certain minute of angle. Two bullet holes on a .22 range target are not visible as separate holes unless the difference of centers exceeds one tenth of an inch. A double is only visible without glasses, as a double, if the degree of separation exceeds this. In the same way a definitive line on a landscape target, shot at 25 yards, has to be one tenth of an inch or over before it is effective, and it is not effective then with thin shading lines near it. In fact, the behavior of our eyes is something which it is very difficult to calculate exactly.

Although we think of our cartridges as smokeless and flameless, there is actually a fair amount of smoke and quite a big handful of flame at every discharge. If you are shooting at dusk, you will see the flame. If you are shooting on a still day, with a damp stagnant atmosphere, you will see the smoke. As the shooter, you may not notice it; but, if you look down the line of guns as a spectator, you will.

The shooter himself cannot see his own shot because the flame, smoke, and hot gasses get in the way; but any ordinary individual, having been told where to look, will soon pick up shot in flight and follow them to the target. At first, what you will see is only the wad; but, very soon, you will learn to disregard the wad altogether.

I need hardly say what a valuable asset a well-trained loader who has been taught that trick can be to any sportsman. The loader can say *where* you are shooting and with that information you can, or you ought to be able, immediately to correct your shooting instead of getting flurried and blundering about in your anxiety to discover what you are doing wrong.

Muzzle blast means a flame of two or three inches and a gas disturbance nearly as big as an orange. It is because of this that the shooter cannot see the shot that he fires himself. If you can imagine an air gun firing a 12-bore load with equivalent velocity it is possible that one could see the effect; but with powder it is impossible for anyone, except an observer behind the gun who looks not at the gun-muzzle, but at a point in the air on the line of shot and forward of the gun.

The observer should stand behind the gun and his eye level should be about three inches above the gun-muzzles. To begin with, it is wise to stand on something like a soapbox which gives adequate elevation; but, once the trick has been acquired, this additional height is not necessary.

This is the way to make a practical experiment. Choose a safe level site. The shooter kneels down and shoots parallel with the ground. The observer stands a foot or two behind the shooter's shoulder. Unless the observer is a very quick learner, it is quite possible that he won't see anything at all for the first dozen rounds or so; but if he studies the matter carefully and sets about it in the knowledge that he will see the shot if he concentrates, he will pick up the trick in well under 60 rounds. There are, however, several requisites which are necessary.

Most people are inclined to jump, start, or flinch at the report of a gun. Even experienced rifle shots sometimes find adjoining rifle fire disconcerting. It is only with practice that they become almost unaware of it. Shooting school coaches, of course, never notice gunfire at all, but the shock of constant explosions can be a little trying to an individual who is not at it all day and every day. A plug of cotton wool, or better still cotton wool kneaded up with a pinch of plasticine, forms a very good "shock stopper" even if it checks conversational exchange. Make no mistake that this is an important requisite of learning to see shots in the air. "Observer's jump" has to be overcome. But once the shooting becomes monotonous, "observer's jump" vanishes and you can employ your ears to be as dead to the gun as many listeners seem to be dead to the background of sound provided by the radio.

The kneeling position is a very good one for the shooter to adopt. In the learning stage, it gives an observer altogether better angle of vision. In fact, proof guns are normally mounted about two feet from the ground and fired over open country; and most proof attendants can see the shot charge every time on its way to the twenty-yard target. Indeed, background is very important and even the expert coach and gun-fitter prefer certain weather conditions, such as a slightly overcast to a cloudless sky, or the glare of brilliant sunshine. But, even so, the expert coach can still see the shot in the air and tell from it where the gun-muzzles are pointing at the instant of discharge. That is something which comes from experience; yet, once the loader has got the knack of seeing the shot in the air, he is able to tell the shooter exactly where he is shooting even though he may not be able to locate the error.

But the trained coach sees a great deal more than merely the flight of the swarm of projectiles. He sees the flight of the charge with the center of his eye, but he is also aware of the gun-muzzles on the outer edge of his field of view. He is looking ahead to the shot pattern and he is literally watching the gun-muzzles "out of the corner of his eye." He sees how the gun comes up, whether steadily or jerkily, whether it checks or wavers, how true the alignment on the target is, and whether the barrels are level or canted to the right or left. He is also able to detect, from the muzzle movement, errors of gun-mounting. Some people, for example, tend to bring up their gun out of parallel with the axis of vision; that is to say, the barrels are dipped or pointed. The barrels come up before the stock, or the stock comes up with the lift of the right hand quicker than the left hand, and the fore hand pushes out the barrels.

From this the trained coach can also judge whether the gun comes up in front or behind the bird. From the level of the muzzle he can gauge whether the left-hand grip was correct, or over-stressed, or whether the right elbow was properly kept down. "Lifting the elbow" is not a gesture which makes for clean shooting. Lastly, in that fraction of a second when the skilled coach sees the barrels at the same time that he sees the shot in flight, he gets an impression of the shooter's behavior at the instant of firing. He can tell if the trigger has been snatched, or pulled with too great anxiety, or whether, as he hopes, properly and automatically pressed as a sort of reflex of gun-mounting.

Every shot makes occasional errors; otherwise none of us would ever miss. But the coach is not dealing with an occasional fault. He is searching out and trying to remedy a consistent one.

I think it very unlikely that an amateur, or even a regular loader, can be trained to make the all-round assessments of shooting as a professional can; but anybody who shoots with one man regularly would be well advised to have him taught to see shot in the air. It may well be that, if he gets to know his master well, he can even help him to diagnose his errors. But, even if he can't do that, he can very quickly learn to explain where the charge went.

What the layman can do, as distinct from the coach, depends a great deal on personal intelligence. There is probably a limit to the groom-chauffeur-loader-handyman's capacity; but, if *two* sportsmen get together to practice gun drill and to help each other by marking shot in the air, they will be able to do a great deal to help each other's shooting.

The preliminary instructions are simple. Plug your ears if you jump at a charge. Stand behind your fellow shooter's right shoulder as he kneels and look in line with whatever stationary target you have erected. Incidentally, it is a good idea to test patterns on sheets of paper at the same time. When you are observing, fix your eye in the first place about a couple of yards in front of the barrels. If you don't see anything, increase the distance, shot by shot, a yard at a time. The distance that accommodates itself most easily varies with different individuals. You can only find out what personally suits you best by experiment.

Your first impression, on seeing the shot, will be a kind of "flicker" as a ghost of a shadow passes. In a few more shots you will be able to pick up the line and follow its course to the target. Actually, it is doubtful if we really see the shots themselves; but the turbulence is enough. When a few pellets are very close together you *may* see them but only as a part of the general disturbance. What you see is perhaps closer to a heat effect, but it is nevertheless a substantial visible entity. In a very short time the knack is acquired and you can follow shot from gun to target as easily as you can a golf ball from tee to green.

All good shooting is really synchronization in timing. Most good shots say frankly that they "do not know how they shot." This is true: but if we use the slow-motion cine-camera we find that, quite unconsciously, arms, body, and gun move at the same speed whilst picking up the bird. The gun is for the time a rigid member of the body, not a movable projection free to move in arcs of the body as center or pivotal axis. In a word, a good shot doesn't move his gun onto a bird; he turns the whole body and head, the gun moving rhythmically *with*, not independently *of*, the body. In fact the secret of good shooting is to point yourself, not the gun, at the bird.

When shooting clay pigeons, some indication of imperfections in shooting can be inferred from the way the pieces fly. A perfectly centered hit usually means a cloud of dust and no big pieces; but a clay hit at nine o'clock will usually throw off its bigger pieces in a direction opposite to the point of fracture. That is to say that, if you hit a clay at nine o'clock, or on the edge, the bigger bits will fly towards three o'clock. The rule is that where you hit the clays will be revealed because the larger pieces will take the opposite direction to the side hit by the charge. Clays which are hit, but not broken, are an indication that you are shooting too high.

I can imagine a keen shooting man thinking, as he reads this, that it might be much simpler to use tracer cartridges. Tracer cartridges have been in existence in various forms for nearly half a century, but they fail in their object because, in nine cases out of ten, the shooter cannot see the trace until too late, owing to muzzle blast. It is visible to others and may cause interest and hilarity; but it also distracts them from the job of looking after their own shooting. In practice, tracer cartridges are little used, but I understand that the latest examples are non-poisonous and not likely to start moor fires. If you kill a bird with a modern tracer, it will still be edible.

But there are other objections to its use. The unskilled observer can see where the trace goes, but he sights it rather late and only after recovery from blast dazzle and recoil. He cannot gauge where it is in respect of range, and the apparent tracer line may be sixty yards high. As the bird (at thirty yards) has gone on, the impression is that the shot was behind. An individual observer might have seen it pass in front of the bird, whereas the gunner himself, seeing it later in relation to a bird which has gone on, sees it behind. It is a misleading affair and even well-skilled and well-placed observers can tell little from a single tracer shot. In brief, tracer cartridges are on the whole best avoided. Much better to learn to see the shot in the air and to use ordinary shooting school methods rather than spectacular but misleading pyrotechnics.

Let's assume that you have now mastered how to see shot in the air. And that, with the aid of a friend, you are beginning to learn where you are with your shooting—right or left, high or low. But, so far, you don't know the reasons which lead to the misses. You know that you are shooting in front or behind, too far to the right, too far to the left, but you don't know why.

Years of coaching lead me to some useful and helpful generalizations. Admittedly, what I can tell you is not a complete explanation of every shooter's behavior with a gun; but, for practical purposes, the advice I can give you is likely to be correct in the case of ninety-nine people out of a hundred. So let's diagnose the symptoms of the most common disorders among shooting men.

I think you can learn from what I tell you. But I do want to remind you again that the advice of the written word, however invaluable as a record or a foundation, does not replace, and never can replace, the personal contact. You can get help from this book, for it will show you where you are wrong; but, even if you can diagnose your own faults and perhaps partly cure them, it is still better to go to a specialist for treatment, for self-diagnosis often overlooks other faults in its eagerness to cure one. Doctors, in the ordinary way, don't try to physic themselves. But I realize that this book is likely to be read by many people who are denied the opportunity of being able to go to shooting schools where there are first-class coaches. For them, the written word from me will have to be enough. For the rest, they will have to do what they can to experiment with the means available.

Perhaps you are reading this in a place where there isn't a clay-pigeon trap within hundreds of miles; but you can devise a moving target which is better than nothing at all. All you need is an old inner tube out of a bicycle tire and a supply of empty tin cans or other projectile. If two strong tall stakes are driven into the ground and the inner tube used as a simple catapult, you will find that you will be able to throw empty food cans, or even some easily obtained local produce like a gourd, or a melon, with considerable effect. Alternatively, of course, you can get a strong-armed human being to pitch for you, but you will be well advised to see to it that he is standing behind a protective sheet of metal or an earth butt. Now, with an experienced friend who has learned to see shot in the air, start shooting.

My advice now is to the observer:

The most puzzling shooter to help is the really *inconsistent* shot who seems to miss birds sometimes in front, sometimes behind, sometimes to the right and sometimes to the left. Watching him shoot you fail to find any rhyme or reason in what he is up to. In that event you can be practically certain that, in ninety-nine cases out of a hundred, he is letting his eye leave the bird and shooting at some point in front where he thinks his shot will intercept it. This is not always a conscious process; it is a sort of half memory of loose advice about "shooting in front" and "forward allowances." What is really happening is that he is not firing at the bird at all but at a vague point on space somewhere on the bird's line. Even if he judges it fairly well, in terms of relative speed and range, a quick snap shot sometimes puts him ahead of the bird, but more often he momentarily pauses with the idea of letting the bird get to the place that he expects to meet it and, in consequence, shoots behind. This is a very common type of error, typical of the man with quick reactions who tends to anticipate the bird rather than travel with it.

In fact, you can learn a great deal about a man's shooting without looking at the target he is shooting at. Look out for the case of the man who is so hypnotized by the appearance of the bird that he mounts his gun slightly behind it and then has to make a terrific heave with his arms and body to try to recapture the line of flight. The fault of this type is that he always looks at the muzzles of his gun instead of concentrating on the bird.

These, of course, are fundamental errors. They overtake a man who has shot fairly well in an untutored sort of way all his life, and they are responsible for half the disappointments of middle age and nearly all the disillusionments of the youthful shooter.

In both these cases the remedy is that the offender must be taught the only sound basic method of shooting. He must master the gun drill and be trained to look at the bird, pick it up with his eyes, body, and hands, and mount the gun without any special effort. It is a matter of controlled rhythm.

If you want to help a man who is making the sort of mistakes that I have described, it is paradoxical, but true, that if you tell him to "try to fire behind the bird" he thinks to himself that that will be rather easier than trying to hit it in the beak. At once he relaxes and unconsciously falls into the correct rhythm of movement of body, gun, and eye. It does not follow that he will begin to hit his bird; but he will begin to shoot with the same degree of relaxation and he will begin to *shoot* consistently. Consistency is the hardest thing to attain in shooting; consistency in performance, even if the performance is in error. Once you have nailed an error, and the man keeps on making it, it is relatively easy to put him on the straight road. It is invariably the emotional man, with his quicker reactions and inconsistent stresses, who is the most difficult to train.

It would be easy, indeed, if every error of shooting behind or in front of a bird could always be related to human emotions, but we must also look for physical bad habits.

A common error among many shots is to "trombone" the left hand up and down the fore-end. Sometimes the shooter grips the fore-end at one point and sometimes another. If his hand is too far forward, he will tend to shoot to the left (i.e., behind a right-hand crossing bird), and when the hand is back towards the breech, he shoots to the right (i.e., behind a bird crossing right to left).

A hand guard is usually an immediate cure. It tends to place the grip.

Once you have overcome some of the commoner errors in shooting you will still find that there are some angles of shot that you can take successfully every time and others which continually beat you. Normally speaking, it is easier for a right-handed man to take a crossing bird moving from right to left than it is for him to take a crossing bird left to right. The reason is simply that the body movement in taking the right to left bird comes naturally and he does not usually swing as well in the reverse direction. There is also a very great difference between low birds on the left or high birds on the left; and, in the same way, low and high birds on the right.

A man who is fairly good at pheasants, however they come, may find himself shooting high and over low birds such as grouse and partridge. The reason appears to be that, for the low shot, he bends his neck too much and gets his eye down to below his *normal* for his gun rib.

He will also shoot to the left if his left eye takes mastery. In other words, the shooter who, through poor mounting or head movement, gives more work to his right eye (which is normally dormant as the stock is held to the right shoulder) lowers his vision to a point where half the eye only sees the gun. The left eye, unobscured by the gun, unduly balances the effect. It sees too much. The cure for this kind of missing is to keep the head well up in the normal position, in which you take average pheasants, and to be careful not to bend the neck or "stoop" to shoot.

If you are shooting with a friend, arrange it, if you can, so that you get the largest variety of shots possible. It is only in that way that you will find out your weakness. The same on-coming bird presented to you again and again may become so easy that shooting is automatic. You will know its place in the air before it reaches you. In the actual shooting field you never know what is coming or at what angle it is going to approach you. We have a phase in the shooting school where we shout out to the boy in the trap: "Vary them." There is no surer way of finding out a sportsman who is feeling a little above himself; and there is no better way either of really shaping him up into a first-class shot.

Don't be content, when you are shooting clay pigeons, to shoot them somehow or another. Concentrate on style and the finesse of gun-mounting and anticipation. Try, too, if you are taking the same shot again and again, to improve your performance by killing your bird earlier and earlier. Within a few rounds at the shooting school we can tell the difference between a first-class shot and a good average performer by the fact that the first-class shot will always break his clay, or almost always, ten yards ahead of the middlingly good man.

In the case of a man in good physical condition, a natural flare for athletics, and the keenness that goes with it, what I have said in this book can scarcely fail to benefit him if he follows my advice carefully. But, in the course of a lifetime of intensive work as a gun-fitter and coach, I have learned that there are many cases where special treatment is called for. Many of them are related to physical handicaps of one kind or another; and many of them are cases of an almost melancholic loss of confidence.

The most usual symptom is when a man comes to see me, who, after many years' shooting, complains that he has completely lost confidence in his gun, that there is something the matter with it, and it won't do what he wants it to. Usually it isn't the fault of the gun at all. Usually what we find is that we are dealing with a case of nerves, brought on either by ill health or through over-anxiety to do well. The man who is sick dwells on his trigger and the over-anxious man snatches and fires before his left hand can get to the bird. The result, of course, is always the same: a clean miss.

To shoot well it is extremely important to feel complete confidence in your gun and your cartridge. You must make up your mind that, if you miss, it isn't the gun's fault; once in a thousand times you may pick on a bad cartridge and, once in a lifetime, something may go wrong with the mechanism of your gun. Normally, if you miss, it is your fault. You must believe that. Second, you must count the bird dead before you pull the trigger. I know several good shots who would be really wonderful shots if they could only master themselves and concentrate on the one shot they have to make instead of worrying about the bird they missed or wondering what people will say about them if they don't put up a better show later in the day.

I remember one man who was, I think, one of the worst shots I have ever seen; yet he was by no means a novice. At his first lesson he did everything but kill the bird. He was so slow, even in starting his gun-mounting, that the target would move yards ahead of his gun before he got up to it; and, even then, in many cases, he wouldn't fire at all. He explained that his trouble was lack of co-ordination and that a specialist was treating him for this complaint. It was evident that eye and hand were not working together. I treated it as just another case of nerves.

At the second lesson, I took out the try-gun and a pair of snap caps for practice at ordinary incoming targets. For the first dozen birds or so I also held the gun with my right hand round the action, immediately in front of the trigger guard. As soon as the bird appeared I helped mount the gun to the shooter's shoulder whilst keeping the muzzle on the bird. After a bit of practice he was doing fairly well and I knew I had taught his left hand what to do. As I had also called "pull" and the trigger *had* been pulled each time fairly consistently, I went on to the next job of teaching his eye where to look. I told the shooter that he was now ready to do some actual shooting, but that all I wanted him to do, at first, was to shoot behind the bird and not to bother about hitting it at all. All I was concerned with was to polish up his style. To his surprise he began smashing the birds at once and whereas, on the previous occasion he had come to the shooting school, the bird was over his head before he could get his gun up, now he was doing much steadier work and banging his gun in front. A little later I was able to fit him and to coach him into being quite a reasonable shot.

There was another case of a man who was suffering from severe war wounds which completely paralyzed both his legs. He could shuffle along with the aid of a walking-stick and could stand without its aid; but the recoil of a 12-bore gun would disturb his balance and knock him over. As he was still keen to shoot, he wanted me to supply him with a .410-bore gun. I saw that he was helpless without his stick; he had no body swing. So, rather boldly, because I had never come across a case like his before, I suggested that he should hold his stick at his back with his left hand, using it in effect to help support his legs in the form of a tripod. Then I taught him to shoot with one arm only. He is still using a 12-bore gun.

I had another pupil who couldn't stand at all, but sat on a cushion on the ground. He had no need to turn round as he could lie back and shoot birds that passed well overhead. I remember this very well as he nearly singed my hair off on one occasion when I knelt at the back of him.

The worst case of flinching I have ever come across was a man who, when he fired, would close both his eyes tight, hang on with both hands, and fail to pull the trigger. I decided that this was a case in which the only thing to do was to do the shooting myself and let him watch me. Sportsmen so rarely get the chance of watching anyone else shoot that it is sometimes a lesson in itself just to let them see the instructor polishing off a few clays. At first my pupil even flinched at the noise of my shooting; but, a little later, he wanted to try again. I told him to keep his head and neck very stiff, to sink it in fact, as if he were shrugging his shoulders. I hoped that that device would cure him of flinching. It worked, and he, too, became ultimately quite a reasonable shot.

Another case of a physical disability was a tall man who came to me with such a long neck that, although his stock was sixteen and a half inches, he had to put his head down to meet it. The consequence was that his neck muscles were loosened and his head was jarred back every time he fired a shot. He flinched badly and suffered from gun headache. I built him a stock on the Monte Carlo style (*see page* 104) which would come up to his face instead of him having to put his face down to the stock. By getting him to put his shoulder well into the gun his trouble was cured.

Troubles with the right hand are comparatively rare. But I remember one case of a man whose trigger finger was in good order, but whose middle finger was slightly bent and the other two fingers completely doubled up and useless. There was no grip at all in the hand and, on recoil, the gun jumped back and bruised his fingers. After several experiments he found that, first, by pointing the left hand at the bird (in other words, by keeping it firm and not pulling), a certain amount of recoil was taken bodily by this left arm. Secondly, by pushing the right shoulder forward and altering the stance, there was less injury to the right hand. But all was by no means well. I made him a very curved pistol grip, somewhat on the lines of my one-arm grip, but very narrow. It was an improvement, but still the shooter could only hold the gun between middle finger and thumb. Finally, I discovered that, although the other two fingers were doubled up and weak at the top joints, yet they could pinch my finger when I forced it between the two knuckle joints. This gave me the idea to fit a small rubber peg on the left side of the grip to fit between these fingers. Finally, this shooter, too, was able to carry on without discomfort.

I wouldn't like to tell you how many people have come to see me who have introduced themselves quite cheerily by saying: "You have probably met the worst shot in Britain; now you are meeting the worst shot in the world." There was one man who came to me to confess that he had been shooting ever since the shooting season had begun and that he had not killed one single bird. I am never worried by cases like that very much. In fact, I maintain that the very bad shot is a much easier task to pull together than the ordinary shot. The very bad shot is usually doing something consistently wrong and can be speedily put back on the mark. The ordinary shot is usually so inconsistent that he fills the air full of lead and misleads himself and everybody else by the fact that some head of game occasionally runs into the charge he throws up.

Often, when a man finds his shooting going off, he starts worrying because one off-day leads to another and the whole is put down usually to increasing years. I am not sure that this is the cause at all. As a man grows older, muscles contract and slight modifications in a lighter gun, refitted for these physical changes, will allow him to enjoy his sport more than ever before.

To demonstrate how little old age and bad sight is a bar to good shooting, I remember one man whose sight was so poor that he couldn't see a bird in front. Yet he was still very keen to go on shooting. I decided that the only way to deal with him was to tell him that he must rely on his loader's eyes entirely and rest what was left of his own by looking at nothing until his loader said "Mark" for an overhead bird, "Left" for a left-hander, and "Right" for a right-hander. He was then to "look into the blue" at an angle of about forty-five degrees. If the bird came at all into his vision, he was to snap at it, but otherwise he wasn't to look for it. As he only shot pheasants, we had no low shots to cater for. The improvement was noticeable immediately. An onlooker said that his sight had improved 100 per cent; but what had really happened was that he had stopped staring about, looking here, there, and everywhere and so forcing his eyes out of focus. Now he was concentrating on letting the birds come to his eyes.

Whatever your physical disability, I want to emphasize that, if you are keen to shoot, there is usually something that can be done to help you. The one-arm gun, for example, is intended primarily for those who have lost an arm, but men with artificial legs, men who are weak on their legs, and men who have a weak left arm might all be better and safer shots for its use.

The late Lord Gough was classed, not as one of our best one-armed shots, but as one of the best shots in Britain—so great a distinction that a sporting magazine once published a full-page article entitled "Are Two Arms Necessary for Shooting?" With the right tools and proper technique a man using a one-arm gun can easily hold his own on the field.

Of course a special gun is needed. The gun I designed is based on the fact that, for the one-armed shot, the ordinary gun is too top-heavy. The weight of it causes head movement in gun-mounting and a poking aim which may look dangerous even if it is not so in reality. By twisting the lever and fitting triggers and safety work in a forward position much nearer the breech, the gun balances in one hand. The lever, safety catch, and triggers can all be manipulated without shifting the hand or relaxing grip. The technique is to shoot, right foot slightly forward, and to keep the gun under the armpit in ready position until 99 per cent of the body swing has been completed. Plenty of indoor drill until a smooth effortless action is obtained will allow a man using a one-arm gun to be as quick as anybody on the fast driven partridge and steady on the high pheasant.

TRAP SHOOTING

How to Shoot Clays

THERE is a great difference between trap shooting and pigeon shooting. Trap shooting or, as it was originally called, clay-bird shooting, is the direct descendant of the old practice of pigeon shooting. This, in its turn, is a direct descendant of the pastime of popinjay shooting, still practiced in Flanders and of such antiquity that it is mentioned in the *Iliad*. The popinjay was a pigeon tethered by a short length of cord to the top of a tall mast and capable of restricted flight. With bow and arrow a material amount of skill was needed to hit such a small moving target.

The development of the art of shooting on the wing, subsequent to 1760, and the gaming tendencies of the Waterloo period led to matches between sportsmen in which live pigeons thrown by hand from a pit or from behind a wall furnished the target. Towards the middle of the nineteenth century, rules regulating pigeon-shooting contests and the guns and loads to be used were more or less codified, and collapsible boxes known as traps were introduced.

During the late Victorian era live pigeon shooting enjoyed a certain social recognition; but during the present century it passed out of keeping with social taste in this country and is now no longer legal in Britain, though it is still very popular abroad.

Modern trap shooting employs discs made of a mixture of pitch and pulverized limestone and known as clay targets to distinguish them from live birds. Primitive traps, or throwers, designed to eject either clays, or hollow glass balls stuffed with feathers, were introduced during the eighties of the last century. These early devices were not very good. Largely owing to their mechanical imperfection in use, these did not achieve immediate popularity. During the past generation very important developments have taken place and the modern automatic clay target trap has brought about an astonishing change in the sport. Clay-bird shooting clubs are increasing rapidly, the number of local clubs being a noteworthy feature.

Independently of their value as one of the most pleasant of summer pastimes and the opportunity they afford for keeping in shooting practice during the close season, they are excellent schools for the novice who wishes to learn how to handle a gun. Clay-bird shooting is the most valuable approach to the senior sport. Its educational value is so great that it was adopted during both wars as part of the essential training of the fighting services.

Game shots ask: "Are the conditions of clay bird shooting any use to me as practice for actual game shooting?" The answer is that they certainly are.

Good shooting depends on a co-ordination of muscular effort, correct stance, correct movement, and automatic adherence to certain rules. Trap shooting gives you this practice in a very close approximation to natural conditions. The double rise events, particularly, afford excellent training, whilst the string of successful shots at clays gives one a thrill closely allied to a fine pickup after a drive. The two are not strictly comparable in all respects but one may safely say that the "quantity" element in scoring hits on clays is almost as exciting as the "quality" element in game shooting. In addition, there is the spur of the competitive element and the pleasure of outdoor recreation in company with those of kindred interests.

Though a shooting man may have ever so much sport of a

regular kind, he would do well to take part in trap shooting meetings when he can conveniently attend them. I have often seen really excellent shots seriously perturbed by the presence of a stranger, perhaps a friend of one of the farmers who has come out to see the sport and, in all innocence, has placed himself behind the one member of the party who is easily put off. Public shooting contests help you to overcome the nervousness of being watched. You learn that you can't shoot your best unless you concentrate. And, having once adopted this attitude, you can obliterate the onlookers from your mind.

Trap shooting differs from game shooting because game rises slowly, gains velocity rapidly, and maintains or accelerates speed until out of range. Trap shooting reverses this sequence, the clay being projected at a high velocity which gradually lessens as it reaches the crest of its rise. In practice, we remedy this difference by adopting a different technique which meets the conditions inseparable from artificial targets.

THE POSITION IN WHICH THE GUN IS HELD IS DIFFERENT

Indeed this section might just as well be entitled "How to shoot at moving objects with the gun at the shoulder," because this position—with the gun ready mounted to the shoulder—is now universally adopted by the best competition shots. It is quicker, and quickness is the essence of modern trap shooting.

Stance, grip, and the technique of gun-mounting are exactly as previously outlined in the drill section—with the difference that you mount your gun AND POINT IT AT THE TRAP. You do not shoot at the trap and you do not keep your head down to the stock. You remain aiming at the trap. The trap is about to throw a target to a known height but at an unknown angle and projection. Thus, if your head is down to the stock, you will not have adequate freedom of movement for the eye to follow the

[157]

bird, and the gun to follow the eye, with accurate alignment in the time.

A close study of the best European and American trap shots reveals systematic head movement as the basis of their skill. If their procedure were analyzed by a slow-motion film we should see: (1) the gun is mounted to the shoulder and aimed at the trap; (2) the head is then very slightly eased off the stock; (3) on the appearance of the target the head moves to it first; (4) the gun remains pointed at the trap almost until this head movement is completed and is then raised rapidly to the target which it rapidly overtakes. Discharge occurs on the instant that alignment is obtained.

The whole art of trap shooting is comprised in the ability to take instant aim and pull the trigger practically without visible swing. Speed is all essential. The quick shot has a very marked advantage over the slow shot where clays are concerned, for his speed gives him what is for the moment an apparently stationary target.

If we examine the flight of a clay target we find that it is thrown off the trap to the distance of fifty to fifty-five yards. At about fifteen or twenty yards from the trap it reaches the zenith of its curve. For the next ten yards or so it travels a practically horizontal course. Viewed from the gun stand it appears to be hovering although, in point of fact, it is still moving rapidly away from the shooter. This is the position in which the quick shot takes the target. At the end of its horizontal flight it loses momentum and begins to fall earthward with a pronounced dip. The slower shot, who only comes into action at this stage, has thus a more difficult target to tackle than that of his swifter competitor, independent of the fact that targets that have lost their spin are harder to break; also, at the increased range, a target may pass unbroken through the gaps in the pattern, by now become wide.

The quick shot has the choice of any relative point during the transit of the target over the latter portion of its curve of flight. An expert selects the precise point where he knows his gun will give its best killing pattern.

When you are shooting clays, remember everything in the instructions regarding stance, grip, and gun-handling.

Don't put your left hand too far up the barrel, because this makes you shoot behind your right-hand target.

The eye must never be brought down to the rib; the rib should be brought up to the eye.

When mounting a gun at the trap, bed the butt in the right part of the shoulder and do not shift it again.

See that the trigger pull of your gun is both quick and sweet. It must respond instantly. For most people, a bad trigger pull is fatal to good trap shooting.

Apart from practice shooting at clays in the shooting school, the game of trap shooting takes the form of either what is called "Down the Line" shooting or Skeet.

"Down the Line" trap shooting is the earliest form of clay-target shooting. It used to be much more popular than it is today when there were many clubs around London. The reason that it has decreased, rather than increased, in popularity in recent years is, I think, largely because the best performers of "Down the Line" shooting became so monotonously consistent that the novices gave up all hope of trying to compete. This in spite of the fact that in "Down the Line" shooting a system of handicap is normally employed. The fact is that a man, equipped with a gun specially made for the job and keeping in constant practice, can give the average game shot twenty-five in one hundred and beat him at "Down the Line"; although the same trick shooter at clays probably wouldn't do much better than the next man at a shoot in which live game were the targets.

The trouble with trap shooting is that it is largely trick shooting. And, although it is great fun when you can hold your own, it is essential that you should study the very special technique which is required. The man who is keen should first get himself a gun which fits him and preferably with a raised ventilated rib. The reason is that trap shooting is so fast that, on a hot day, a mist can form along the rib of an ordinary gun and so obscure the target. Further, a special trap-shooting gun should be laid to shoot level, or even slightly below the mark.

In shooting, the weight is always on the left foot and the eyes should not be focused on the trap house but just over the top of it, ready to pick up and snap the target as it rises whether right, left, or center.

Many years ago I was a very keen trap shot myself, and it was in competition with me that Frank Troeh, the American champion, first shot "a hundred straight." The second "hundred straight" was made in similar fashion by Alec Maunder. And, subsequently, astonishingly long runs have been made over automatic traps. A few of my American friends have each made runs of over five hundred. And one of them never missed for a week, breaking 1,500 clays straight. I mention that to emphasize how important it is to master the trick of trap shooting. If you want to excel at it, it is essential that you perfect your style until you can break the clays with mechanical precision, something that you can never hope to do, however fine a shot you are, in the real shooting field.

The champions at "Down the Line" shooting adopt many and varying methods. One will hold his muzzles high, another drop them below the traphouse; one keeps his head erect and snaps as the gun touches his cheek, another "rides" his target; but all follow the essentials of successful shooting at inanimate targets. They don't look for the bird until they see it. When they see it, they keep their eye on it. And then they make a smooth swing and a snap finish.

The clay target can be likened to a windowpane. Fire a high velocity bullet through a window and it leaves a neat hole. But take the bullet and throw it with your hand and you will shatter the window. Therefore pattern and not penetration is what is required of the trap-shooting cartridge. You should use one with a smaller charge of powder and a heavier charge of shot. If your cartridge has too high a velocity, the pellet can actually go through the target without breaking it.

SKEET

In 1927, I myself introduced the game of Skeet to England. I had seen it at the Western Plant at East Alton in Illinois and was immediately attracted by its possibilities. I still think that Skeet is the best form of competitive clay-target shooting for the ordinary game shot. A special gun is not required for it. It lends itself to many variations and it provides far better practice for live game shooting than "Down the Line" events.

The technique of shooting at Skeet has been developed by American experts. The basis of their method is that they "point out" their target; that is, they hold their guns ahead of them in almost the position they intend killing, and, with a barely perceptible movement, yet perfect timing, snap their birds. But I wouldn't advise a beginner to try and begin that way. Here is a description of the various targets and the methods to get good results and good practice (*see diagram on page* 164):

THE FIRST BIRD AT NO. 1 STAND. You are alongside the High Trap and, from the diagram, you will appreciate that the target is coming from overhead and is going away; but, to your eye, it is flattening out and beating down whilst your gun is coming up in a contrary direction. For this bird only you should hold your muzzle high, put plenty of weight on your left foot, look well ahead, and take care not to shoot over the top of it.

THE SECOND BIRD FROM NO. 1 STAND. This is an easy left incomer from the Low Traphouse. Keep your eye on it and put a little of your weight on your left foot, don't try and shoot too quickly, yet at the same time don't let it get too close. That sounds a difficult instruction, but if you get the opportunity to shoot at Skeet you will very quickly realize what I am getting at.

THE FIRST BIRD FROM NO. 2 STAND is an away bird from the High Traphouse. Put your right foot forward and put most of your weight on it. Don't look at the Traphouse. Look midway between the Traphouse and the center and shoot off his "front leg."

THE SECOND BIRD FROM NO. 2 STAND needs another change of stance. Draw back the right foot slightly, put a fraction more weight on the left foot, face the center but swing the body back towards the Low Trap. As with every other bird at Skeet, take care to make a snap finish.

AT NOS. 3, 4, AND 5 STANDS, as you can see from the diagram, we have wider crossing shots. A change of stance is necessary. Put your weight on the right foot for the High Trap bird, on the left foot for the Low Trap one. Don't look at the Traphouse but look at the center. If you find that you are shooting behind your bird, turn your body a little more towards the particular Traphouse that individual birds are coming from to encourage you to make more body swing.

AT NO. 6 STAND we have what is a fairly easy incoming bird from the High Trap, but it is a really tricky target from the Low Traphouse which is often missed by the slow shot because he is deceived by its direction. If you watch the bird leave the Trap, you can easily be fooled into believing that it will eventually cross your front and end by overshooting it. In fact it doesn't cross your front but rather fades away to your right. You can turn this otherwise difficult target into one of your easiest by putting all your weight on your left foot, looking towards the center, and making a very very fast shot AT THE BIRD'S TAIL. Don't worry to shoot in front of him; your natural overthrow will give you all the necessary lead.

AT NO. 7 STAND we have a couple of easy targets. Put all your weight on your right foot and raise your left heel slightly to the income. Reverse the process for the away bird.

NO. 8 STAND which is situated between the Traphouses can be a difficult one if you don't know how. Both High and Low Trap birds are trick shots which make knowing how to look and how to stand a matter of the utmost importance. If you look at the Traphouse, the bird will come at you like greased lightning and will pass overhead before you can get your gun up. Yet, if you will only look well into the blue, putting your weight on the right foot, and raise your left heel, bending the body back for a direct overhead shot, you will find the bird climbs into vision and becomes a quick, but nevertheless a simple, shot.

THE LAYING OUT OF SHOOTING GROUND

It is possible today for anyone to make his own shooting ground at very little expense. If it happens that you have only got one trap, a single stand can be erected to match either the low or high Skeet tower and pegs put all over the place exactly as if it were a clock-golf layout.

Hitherto it has been customary to stand alongside a single rise trap and blaze away at targets thrown at a known speed, height, and angle. This isn't bad practice for the novice but, as soon as possible, he should get more variety into the shots he presents himself. The following diagram is one of many of possible variations:

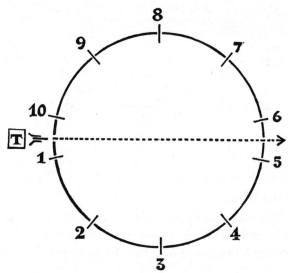

T represents the Trap. The dotted line is the fixed line of flight. The circle is a 30-yard one drawn 15 yards from the trap.

[163]

In the diagram, ten different stands are shown. The shooter must always face the Trap; therefore the Trap itself must be shielded. No. 1 Stand is alongside the Trap and gives the straight-away bird. No. 2, ten yards to the left of No. 1, gives the wide left-hander. No. 3 may be released whilst on the walk from No. 2 and gives the shooter an away bird flying slightly to his left. No. 4 is a wide left crossing shot. No. 5 is a fast bird over the left shoulder that needs a quick turn to be killed behind. Nos. 6–10 Stands are the reverse to the above.

The rules should be that all competitors and spectators should always stand at the rear of Nos. 2 and 4 Stands when the shooter is on that side, or at the rear of Nos. 7 and 9 Stands when shooting for the right field.

Above is a double Skeet layout to enable the shooter to practice for the whole of the Skeet round. T1 and T2 represent the Traps, B the Blinders.

These layouts are only suitable for sites three hundred yards from tracks and buildings. In other, more restricted, conditions, the Trap must be removed or set to throw targets in a safe direction.

An ideal sporting ground can be made out of a disused chalk-pit, as these are generally cut out of the hillside and I have seen many where a single Trap can give a variety of incoming high-driven birds from stands in the "basin" and difficult crossing shots while walking up and around the edges.

If the cost of cartridges is a serious item, competitions may be at five or even at three birds and handicaps may be by distance. The automatic Trap needs at least twenty shooters to form four teams and so give each other a rest, but with the single Trap a party of four can have a most enjoyable meeting, shooting three, five, eight, or ten bird competitions and taking turns in pulling, scoring, or refereeing.

You may put your Trap to throw its targets in the best direction. You may make your own plan of layout to give you the practice you need for your particular sport of rough shooting or for driven partridges, grouse, and pheasants. But the rule should be that you must move to another stand for the next shot. The last point is most important, as in game shooting you are not allowed a second chance.

HOW TO SET UP A CLAY PIGEON TRAP
Dig a hole 3 feet deep and wide enough for standing room. A wooden seat with a backboard should be provided for the trapper. Fix the Trap firmly onto a heavy plank to prevent vibration and broken targets. In front of all this, build a protective earthwork low enough to clear the target and high enough to hide the trapper from view.

[165]

The single Trap can be adapted for driven birds by placing the Trap the other side of a low hedge for driven partridges; in a tree for overhead pheasants; or, firmly secured to a sort of "hobby horse," it can be carried anywhere you wish. The "hobby horse" is a tripod mount with two short front legs and one long back one. The Trap is mounted and the trapper sits on the back leg to steady it.

In my own shooting grounds I have set some morning, afternoon, and evening stands so that, in summertime, we can always keep our backs to the sun. The "hobby horse" has a great advantage in that it can also be moved about to suit the state of the light.

PART FOUR

FIELD NOTES

*Shotgun Shooting in Britain Described from the
Standpoint of Its Practical Application to
Shotgun Work Everywhere*

Shotgun Work in America

EVERYTHING that I have said so far about the handling of a game-gun is global, to use the current phrase, in its application. Whether you are shooting guinea fowl in Central Africa, snipe in India, wood-duck in the swamps of Arkansas, or birds' nests in China, the drill is the same.

Unless you use your hands and your feet properly, hold your head steady, and swing your gun with your body smoothly onto the object you are aiming to hit, you will miss whether it's a quail—or a flying saucer.

But now we come to the practical work of shooting in the field. Since this book is addressed to gunners everywhere, it would be quite impossible—and, I hope I shall demonstrate to you, even undesirable—to deal with all the local variations in sporting environment and game-bird shooting in different areas of the world.

In offering this instruction book to you, I am of course aware that the code and the conditions of hunting in North America are *outwardly* different from those ruling in Britain and on the European continent.

In Britain, and throughout most of Europe, the emphasis is on what is called driven game: that is, birds rounded up and driven as fast and tall as they will fly over a line of guns. In this style of shooting—the most difficult and interesting style with a smooth-bore gun—hundreds, sometimes thousands, of head of fur and feather are killed in a day.

The type of hunting which is the common form in America is called in Britain "rough shooting"; and every shooting man in Britain will wish me to say to you that it's none the worse for that. In fact, even in Britain rough shooting is the sport of the average shooting man. The shooting of driven game, often with two guns and a loader, is a luxury sport. But the technique of shooting practice and the code of shooting manners in Britain has been evolved in the field of driven game.

Driven-game shooting is a comparatively recent innovation, but so, in fact, is most shotgun practice. Prior to the nineteenth century it was unusual for a gunner with his muzzle-loader to attempt a flying shot at all. The father of it all was probably the great nineteenth-century sportsman, Colonel Peter Hawker, who wrote a classic book called *Instructions to Young Sportsmen* and who himself, using flintlock guns and subsequently the first percussion-fired weapons, was probably one of the greatest rough shooters of all time.

It was in Hawker's day during the nineteenth century that the great gun makers of London—men like Joseph and John Manton—created the masterpieces of the gunsmith's art of which the weapon you hold in your hand today is the lineal descendant.

It was in Britain too, with the development of the breech-loader, that, after Hawker's death, the art of shooting driven game was practiced for the first time. Before that, shooting in the English countryside had very much the same pattern that it has in America now, with, of course, the notable difference that in Britain the sporting rights belonged to the riparian landlords whereas in America the sport is the property of every citizen who takes out a hunting license.

I don't want you to count that a mark against the system in England. The fact of the matter is that England is a very small country and but for the existence of the landowners to preserve the game England might now have no game at all. In fact, because game has been closely preserved for hundreds of years, England, with her tightly packed population, has nevertheless a head of fur and feather of one kind or another which compares favorably with an equal acreage almost anywhere in the world.

So, in asking you now to take your instruction in scatter-gun shooting on the basis of conditions in the British shooting field, I am inviting you to learn from the classic school. Britain is the place in which the shotgun is the natural sporting weapon of the countryside.

If this were a book on rifle shooting, based on practice in the English shires, it wouldn't be worth a ten-cent cigar to you. Rifle shooting in Britain itself is confined to range practice, miniature rifle shooting at vermin like rooks and grey squirrels, and the unique sport of stalking the Highland stag. But for every bullet fired from a rifle barrel in Britain there must be tens of thousands fired through smooth-bore game-guns.

From a shotgun country, I want to show you, in a rifleman's country, how to use smooth-bore weapons to the maximum advantage. My advice to you is that you will learn best if you learn the English way.

You may never shoot from a Scottish grouse butt or an English covertside. It doesn't matter. But you should never take a shotgun in your hand unless you are sure that you would be safe enough not to blot your copybook from a numbered stand in Britain in the company of a party of experienced driven-game shots. You will never be the shotgun performer you would like to be until you can feel in your bones that you can pick your birds with the skill and courtesy of a top shot in Europe.

To begin with, make up your mind not to play about with rifles and shotguns at the same time.

Apart from the danger of taking out rifles and shotguns on the same hunting expedition, I doubt if little Annie Oakley herself could have put up a good show using a rifle and a scatter-gun at the same time. I said at the beginning of this book, and I say it again now, that if you are in form with a rifle, your muscle memory will instinctively be making you do all the things, such as looking down the barrel and hanging onto the trigger, which are fatal when you are using a shotgun. Alternatively, if you are in form with a shotgun, the temptation to make a dangerous swing with the rifle may be well-nigh irresistible.

Anyhow, it is quite unnecessary to take a rifle to deal with a possible chance at a deer. In the big-game country of Africa, some men I know actually prefer to use a 12-bore shotgun to deal with leopards and lions. In the hands of a man who knows how to use it, a 12-bore is a far safer and more effective weapon against small deer, especially in close country, than any rifle. The secret is to see to it that you are loaded with mold shot such as S.S.G. If you want to be prepared for a chance to deal with winged game as well, my suggestion is that, on a hunting expedition in which almost anything is likely to turn up, you should load No. 6 into your right barrel and S.S.G. into your left. If you cannot kill a small buck, or even a bear, with S.S.G., you ought not to have a gun in your hands at all.

So make up your mind which weapon you are going to specialize in. I hope you will decide that, in the everyday hunting that you enjoy so fully in the States, a smooth bore is good enough. Save up the rifle for the big occasion. And when you are using the rifle, concentrate on the rifle and put away the scatter-gun.

I have a suspicion that when I am talking about shooting driven partridges, grouse, and pheasants in the chapters that follow, you will be tempted to skip them. Please don't. There is something there for you on every page.

And I beg you, don't get a notion into your head that because I am talking about driven game rounded up by a line of beaters that that's a sport that cannot come your way. If you are out with a party of friends after ruffed grouse, or quail, pheasant in the prairies, or any bird you like to mention, there is not the slightest reason why you should not organize your day between yourselves so that you can see driven birds as well.

Even if you advance in a straight line, if you go up wind some of your best birds should break back over the guns. But, ideally, you would do well to contrive your day so that you are driving your birds towards each other; providing, that is, that you feel reasonably confident that the men you are out with are safe shots.

Personally, I have often wished that I could organize one of those shoots in the prairies when the pheasant shooting season is open for a couple of days for cock pheasants. On a properly organized shoot, those ringnecks could be put up high enough to call for some pretty shooting. But I confess that I would like to know before I started that the friends who were with me knew how to use their guns in a way in which I wasn't actively endangered myself.

Alas, I am afraid it is true that many American gunners, owing to the system which allows anybody to have a go in the proper season, are not trained as shooters are before they are allowed to make an appearance at the English covertside. I only hope that the study of this book will do something to reduce the appalling number of fatal accidents which occur in the United States every year.

In practice, I don't think that it will ever come to an end until an altogether stricter code of conduct is enforced by hunters themselves. The established tradition of the English shooting field—that if a man offends the rules of safe shooting, he can expect to be publicly rebuked and, in grave cases, ordered off the field—is no more than a simple precaution for the safety of everybody concerned. If this book does anything to bring about a similar state of affairs in America, I shall feel that it was worth while irrespective of whether I am able to teach anybody to put up a more consistent performance with a gun.

Now read on. Accept what I tell you as if I were your grandfather. Suck eggs my way and apply the lessons that follow, which are written largely from the standpoint of the British shooting field, to your own hunting days. If you do as I tell you, you cannot possibly go wrong on a hunting expedition in any company anywhere from Central Park to Timbuctoo.

The Rules of Shooting

THE RULES of shooting, which is a sport not a game, are unwritten. The interpretation of the code varies in different company, in different countries, and at different times.

In some company, and the individual is the only judge of that, it may be counted part of the game to kill a bird before the next man can raise his gun to it. In rough shoots, where the chief anxiety of the host is the hope that enough game will be killed to give everybody something to take home, it is permissible to take every chance that offers. On occasion it may be regarded as reprehensible to pass by the opportunity of adding to the bag. On rough shoots the simple rule is to ask your host what the form is.

"Are we standing on ceremony today or not?" "Do you want us to shoot hen pheasants?" If your host says, as he probably will, that we are shooting everything today we can catch up with and it is up to you fellows to make a bag, then of course you are entitled to do your best to drop everything that comes into view. But if it is a big day in the coverts or on the stubbles with numbered stands carefully organized, you can very easily blot your copybook by being over-zealous, as surely as you can, in your own estimation, by missing your birds.

The rules of shooting are unwritten because they vary from shoot to shoot. In one shoot the rule may be "cock pheasants only" and only to the man they fly to; but everything else free for all. On another shoot the etiquette may be strict on game but it may be the custom to have a sweepstake on the head of vermin shot. In that event you are fully entitled to try and kill jays, crows, and squirrels before your near neighbor can get his gun to them. But, if in doubt, don't take a chance.

In many ways it was easier in the old days when the host of the shoot exerted a discipline as strict as a Master of Foxhounds. Before the First World War, in the heyday of driven game shooting, a gun could expect to be publicly rebuked, if not ordered home, if he made the slightest mistake in etiquette. On the great shoots the people who were invited were not even supposed to have their "off days."

The standard of etiquette in shooting in the nineteenth century is exemplified in the story of two great sportsmen, counted among the finest shots of their day, who were surprised by a covey of eight partridges which swept overhead of them in the middle of a pheasant drive. Immediately the two men fired two barrels, changed guns, and fired another two barrels into the covey. Between them they shot the lot. The story was quoted in their own time, not for the brilliance of their feat in bringing down four birds each out of the covey, but for the fact that they were so experienced and knew the etiquette of shooting so perfectly that neither of them shot at what might have been counted the other man's bird.

I have instanced these stories not in the hope that any average gun can achieve that combined perfection of manners and marksmanship, but to indicate the ideal that every shooting man should endeavor to attain. If it was true in the old days that a man was likely to be ordered off the field if he offended the code, it is no less true today that, although shooting hosts are more reluctant to speak their minds out loud, they think much the same way as their forebears.

For the man who offends, the situation is rather worse today because, very often, when he finds he is not invited out shooting again, he doesn't know what he has done wrong.

Further, it is useless to pretend that, however safe a shot a man may be, he will ever be as welcome as a shooting guest as one who shoots really well. Nothing is more exasperating to a host, who has gone to considerable trouble and expense to present game as effectively as he can over the guns, than somebody who is unable to make his fair contribution to the making of the bag. But, while a poor shot will obviously never get the invitations to shoot that a really brilliant shot invariably does, it is well to re-member that the most brilliant shooting will never make up in the eyes of your host and your fellow guns for a breach of the rules of safe shooting.

You may feel that I have already said enough about the im-portance of safe shooting in the earlier parts of this book. But, as a gun expert, I am consulted continually by the police and by the insurance assessors about shooting accidents, and for that reason alone I am more conscious of the dangers than an ordi-nary shooting man who has probably never had personal experi-ence of a serious gun accident in his days and who, I hope, never will. But I can assure you that shooting accidents are far com-moner and far more surprising than any member of the ordinary public would think possible.

There is always an element of danger in shooting which, from long experience, I am inclined to believe is inevitable; but it can be reduced with care and experience to a negligible factor. On the whole, there is a far greater risk of an accident driving in your car to join a shooting party than in using a gun in the field, but, just as we seek road safety, we should seek gun safety too.

I can think of no better way of emphasizing the dangers than to relate to you details of some of the accidents that have come my way. It is surprising how many of them reveal a quite singu-lar succession of circumstances.

There was the case of a keeper, an exceptionally careful man, who, while standing by a five-barred gate, cautiously lowered the hammers of his gun and rested the butt on one of the top bars of the gate while he lifted his knee to tighten a button or strap on his leggings. The way he stood, the barrels were on his shoulder and the butt on the gate; but, by some accidental movement, the butt slid off the rail and the gun slipped down between the bars of the gate until it was arrested by the heads of the hammers. The impact was sufficient to fire one of the cartridges. As the barrels had now slid off his shoulder, the keeper was shot just beneath his shoulder blade. Fortunately, it was not a fatal wound; but it was an accident which most people would say was not only improbable but impossible.

This accident would, of course, not have occurred if the keeper had been using a hammerless gun. In very many hammer guns with rebounding locks, the hammer can be pushed forward into contact with the striker without using a great deal of pressure. A doubtful advantage with the majority of hammer guns is that the gun cannot be opened until the right hammer is lowered from full cock position. In winter, I should prefer to open the gun and then lower the hammers as it is so perilously easy to let one of them slip under the thumb. By my method, it does allow one to follow the strict rule: always take cartridges out before you do anything.

In another case I remember, a man who was ferreting for rabbits lay down his gun fully loaded whilst he knelt down to listen at the bury for the sound of his ferrets working. His companion accidentally kicked the gun and the man who had his ear to the hole was shot.

The all too common accident is that caused by a man crawling through a low gap in the hedge and dragging his gun after him by the barrels. A bramble, wire, or unseen stump catches the triggers and there is another inquest to which I am called in as an expert witness.

Today fencing is not kept up as it ought to be. One cannot blame the farmers who use wire because it is the cheapest form of fencing; but wire is almost as dangerous to the shooting man as it is to the fox-hunting man. And the danger isn't only wire. On an average day's shoot we all encounter gates so rickety on their hinges that they won't open; stiles in advanced decay, rotten rails, and untrimmed barely practicable gaps, not to mention very slippery mud and awkward ditches. Never, never, never leave a cartridge in your gun, especially when you are alone, if you have to negotiate any sort of obstacle at all. Never mind how agile or confident you are. I know.

But what you do by yourself is your own business. What I am principally concerned with is to advise you how to behave in company, because, if you are shooting regularly, you will find that you are usually shooting in the company of other people.

There is no question that the greatest responsibility which falls to anybody in the shooting field falls to the host. If the host doesn't belong to the old-fashioned school which said what it thought in a loud voice and with decorative expletives, he nonetheless has a very large responsibility. If the host has the misfortune to have a guest who is, for example, shooting dangerously, one formula is for him to approach the offender, and other likely offenders, and say: "Sorry, old man, but one of the guns —I won't tell you which—recently had a nervous breakdown and, as a consequence, he is very jumpy. Would you mind making a point of it today to open your gun immediately after we finish each drive and keep it open until you are in position for the next drive? Show it to the other guns if you will, not ostentatiously of course, but show it to them just to prove it is empty. And if you notice anything, let me know as soon as you conveniently can."

If a delicate hint of that kind produces no improvement, the host must decide whether to order the guest home or, if he prefers to avoid that unpleasant responsibility, at least wrangle the numbers so that the offender is kept on the flank and can then hazard only one neighbor.

Incidentally, drawing for place and maintaining a routine movement is a device which might well be done away with in the shooting field. On many of the best shoots today it is no longer practiced. The host selects the guns for each beat. It is not, of course, a working principle for syndicate shoots; but, even on a syndicate shoot, the captain can seed the draw by putting all the odd numbers to one side of his case and the even numbers on the other side, giving the best shots all even numbers and moderate shots the odd ones. This device at least ensures that the good shots don't get bunched together but are placed in positions in which they are able to assist their less accurate neighbors.

If you shoot with a party of country gentlemen, you will notice that they never take low pheasants down a ride. They never shoot a rabbit in front unless it is against a bank and dead safe, and they seldom shoot hares in flat country until they are through and behind the lines. The sport is a commonplace to them and they have a true sense of proportion. They never take a shot which might pepper a beater, or a dog, which they can't see, but who might be there.

The novice, perhaps a townsman, who shoots irregularly is usually keener than the countryman and must always watch out lest in the excitement he falls into an error of judgment. A very good rule for the novice in his first season as a game shot is never to shoot at anything on the ground. Afterwards he will learn never to shoot at ground game at all until past the line or in a place where experience tells him that to shoot is safe. Remember that beaters are usually near when rabbits are flushed. Every gun should know exactly where the other guns and the beaters are placed before he raises his own. Rather let a hundred rabbits go by than risk a ground shot in which you don't know where the charge will finish.

It is on record that on one occasion a sportsman shot a rabbit at forty yards in a grass field. The rabbit was central between two beaters over thirty yards apart. The rabbit was killed but *both* beaters were peppered. An accident of this kind is not so abnormal as one might imagine; but what appears quite credible to people like me, who know a great deal about guns, is often received sceptically by those who only think they know about guns.

Take the possible reasons for the foregoing accident. It is possible, though it is more possible than probable, that the wads blew through the charge and so dispersed it over a wide area. This is the phenomenon which accounts for so-called "cartwheel" patterns we occasionally get when plating guns, when only half the pellets can be accounted for on the steel plate. No one knows how wide the other pellets have flown.

In practice there is a risk in shooting ground game, or birds below the ten-foot level from the ground, not only to those in line with the gun, but to those parallel to the target and within twenty yards of it on either side.

The ordinary sportsman may well say that for years he has shot rabbits ferreting and never known a ricochet. This is probably true; but most rabbiting is close-range work and it must be remembered that at ranges of ten or twelve yards pellet energy is so high that the pellets are either smashed to fragments or penetrate and lodge in the earth. At ranges of forty yards pellet energy is much reduced and contact may turn them rather than destroy them. They can glance off a stone or other hard surface and proceed with their mass unreduced yet with sufficient velocity to penetrate. At low velocity and longer ranges the danger is rather more from the wide dispersal of pellets than from ricocheted ones, the pellets having lost energy being almost killed on contact.

I have fired many thousands of experimental rounds and have brought pellets back to within a couple of yards of my feet at

twenty yards' range. By an arrangement of plates I have succeeded in getting double and treble ricochet pellets zigzag to
almost any direction of the original target. The basic safety of
shotgun shooting is that nature has provided targets which fly
in the air, but though the patter of shots falling about one from
somebody else's gun is normally harmless there are conditions
when it can be very dangerous indeed.

The effective range of 6½-size shot has been calculated by one
"pen shooter" as fifty-four yards. Even if he clothed his back in
a pound of newspapers, I feel sure he would be uncomfortably
reminded of his schooldays if he put his theory to the proof. The
real range of a shotgun on a windless day is at least two hundred
yards. The maximum for No. 6-shot is three hundred yards. Of
course, at two hundred yards the shots have little potentiality of
penetration, but it must never be forgotten that a pellet which
would not penetrate tough and resilient skin can yet blind at one
hundred and fifty yards.

These figures only relate to a normal charge. In some cases
cheap cartridges mean cheap methods of production and cheap
materials. In that event, high pressures and badly fitting wads
can permit a condition to occur known as "balling," or the fusion
of a few pellets. This condition may be produced by tilting wads
or through the gases from the powder touching the sides of the
shot column which fuses a few pellets together, and it can also
be caused by undue pressure pressing very soft lead pellets into
close adhesion.

However, balling is possible and three or four pellets may join
together and fly in a compact projectile mass. I have cut holes in
a mild steel plate at thirty yards, and although extreme range is
unknown, yet it is at least five hundred yards. According to its
mass it would of course be capable of causing a serious wound
at very long range.

The law takes a very odd view of these strange cases and there
are far too many people going about with no notion of how

deadly a shotgun can be beyond fifty-four yards. As the majority of accidents arising out of balling, and other circumstances, are settled out of court without report, the emphasis of danger isn't rubbed home as much as it ought to be.

But the main consideration is not how to settle, or account for, accidents, but how to prevent them. You may not be a very good shot, but never let anybody say that you are not a careful one. Never fire at anything you cannot clearly see and, more important, see beyond. Know that a hedge may have anything on the other side of it, from a couple of rustic lovers to blackberrying or mushroom-gathering villagers or their children.

Remember, too, that the fact that you didn't know they were there, or that they had no business to be there, doesn't free you from your liability in civil law.

Because it *can* happen to any man using a gun that he may be indirectly, even excusably, responsible for an accident to somebody else, I'd say that it was a prerequisite of going into the shooting field that every man who carries a gun should take out an insurance against accidents. Sportsmen's premiums are very low indeed and they can cover you for third-party risks as well as risks to yourself and your guns for a few dollars.

Never make light of those far too common incidents when people get "peppered" or "tickled up" in the course of a shooting season. For the person who is hit, even at long ranges, it isn't funny. To be hit with a few shotgun pellets with only enough energy left in them to penetrate the skin is like being hit hard with a baseball bat. The shock is considerable. That it should happen at all always means that somebody has taken a risky shot which shouldn't have been fired and which he is very lucky has ended without more serious accident.

In the old days, at the beginning of the present century, and in the latter years of a past, a great deal of attention was given to seeing to it that the guns stood in a true line. That was a wise precaution. Today there is a tendency to place guns not in relation to their neighbors, but to the best advantage to the bag. As an axiom of safety the line should always be as straight as possible. The guns who are walking up with the beaters are usually in unknown territory and the keeper who posts them has duties elsewhere, but it is best that they stop at a safe distance before reaching the "all out" end of the beat. The keeper should delegate this duty to an experienced beater who knows the ground. The beater can tell the "back" gun when and where to stop.

As I said in the beginning of this chapter, there are no general rules of safe shooting; but it is possible to lay down a code of proper conduct:

(1) Always unload after a drive. Always unload before passing a hedge, gate, stile, or other obstacle.

(2) Never shoot ground game in front of the line unless you know exactly where everybody else is and unless you can see beyond the quarry. Be very careful of shooting into the ground if it is in a stony place which might cause ricochets.

(3) Keep the safety catch always back at "SAFE" and practice until it is a habit to push it on as the gunstock leaves the ready position under the arm and the forward hand is raising the gun to eye level and pointing at the bird. Many shots can acquire this routine easily, using the side of the first joint of the thumb instead of the ball of the thumb and thus retaining correct right-hand grip. But, regardless of how distracting this effort may be at first, it is a very necessary precaution.

(4) When using a pair of guns, be sure that your loader is really well trained. He must be drilled parade-ground style. Don't use a second gun at all if the only loader you can find is a borrowed gardener or a chauffeur who may blow your toes off or cause an even worse calamity in his anxious effort to please. If ever you are given a bad loader, put one gun down and shoot

with the other, letting your man hand you the cartridges. It is not worth risking an accident. If, on the contrary, you are shooting with a man regularly you will be advised to have him properly trained which won't take longer than three or four hours' tuition on a shooting ground. If you are determined to take risks with an untrained man, quadruple your accident insurance policy.

(5) If you shoot with a hand guard on the barrels, make sure that it fits tightly. Hand guards can usually be squeezed tight by hand if the fit is loose. Remember that, when using a pair of guns, you take the second gun in the left hand while passing the fired gun back with the right hand. If the hand guard is loose, the gun may slip through it to the ground with most serious consequences. As a matter of technical detail, a stud catch can be fitted by a gun-maker which will save this particular annoyance and danger.

(6) Always carry your gun safely. When there is any doubt about the going, open it. The loss of time—closing your gun again and bringing it to your shoulder to shoot—is infinitesimal. The man who makes a habit of always opening his gun and unloading at any stop or obstacle, allowing it to remain open until a fresh start is made, then loading and closing his gun in readiness, will never shoot as the careless ones often do with an empty gun.

(7) Train yourself so that your forefinger never touches the trigger until the gun is up to eye level, otherwise a slight insensitiveness in cold weather or a stumble may apply pressure before you realize it. If you wear gloves in cold weather, always have the trigger finger cut off. In practice, a woollen mitten gives greater warmth and far better grip.

(8) One shoots many days and no game is really very important. Don't try to kill everything and never shoot when there is the slightest doubt of human safety. No one will ever blame you

for not shooting. You are much more likely to get the blame for killing a bird which isn't properly coming to your gun.

Many shooting accidents happen at the end of the day when guns get tired and rather casual. The novice is usually more of a danger with his left barrel swinging down the line after he has missed with his right barrel. It is in order to avoid this that coaches often take out the left mainspring of a double gun until a novice learns his job. Actually he learns quicker and, further, it encourages him to use his first barrel effectively instead of letting it off as an explosive gesture.

The mechanical side of really good guns is seldom likely to be the cause of accidents. Design is very stabilized and, always provided guns are kept in good order, mechanical danger is a very rare hazard.

If by any chance the cartridge misfires, don't bring the gun down from the shoulder until you have pulled again. Then pull back the safety catch and lower it carefully, taking care that the muzzles are kept pointing to the ground. In some cases of mechanical fault the gun may go off with the movement of the safety catch whilst it is being opened.

There will always be fatal accidents which are difficult to understand. It is often reported how people get shot cleaning their weapons in circumstances which leave no real explanation as to why the victims, who alone could have told, got into the positions they did. Some accidents happen with most unusual weapons. I knew a keeper who was seriously wounded by an alarm gun which was loaded with a shot cartridge inserted in a barrel block at the base of a rod. At the top of the rod was a heavy weight secured by a pin. When the pin was drawn, the weight was released and fell on the striker of the barrel block, thus firing the cartridge. The keeper was careful to secure the falling weight, but he picked up the gun and turned it upside down allowing the barrel block which held the cartridge to slide down the rod and back on to the fixed weight which fired the shot. The result was that the keeper was wounded. The moral is that with this type of alarm gun, a very common model in wide use today, all bottom blocks should be fixed.

Once in a while cases are reported of weapons which have not been used for a generation being found still loaded. It is not uncommon for firearms collectors to find old muzzle-loaders in which the charge has been left in the gun and which they at once boil out and draw. The action of all magazine and automatic self-loading weapons causes a fresh cartridge to be carried from the magazine to the barrel every time a fired or "unfired" cartridge is extracted from the barrel. Many accidents have happened owing to forgetfulness or the belief that the ejection of the live round from the barrel has unloaded the gun.

If, having read as far as this, you feel that the risks and the dangers of game-gun shooting are so great that it seems almost impossible to believe that you won't get into trouble, let me comfort you by saying that, although I have probably fired as many, if not more, cartridges than anybody else living today, I have only been badly shot once and tickled up not more than a few times, although I have had many bad scares. Neither have I ever been present when a serious accident has happened, although I have been called in so often after the event. But there have been many occasions when I have had to take a deep breath.

Once, when I was loading for a very important personage, I said "No" and stopped him just in time from shooting at a rabbit which ran in front along the hedgerow. As we later left the stand to pick up the game which had been shot, two children crawled out from under the very bush where the gun was pointed to shoot the rabbit and raced to our stand to gather up the cartridge cases as mementos of the world-famous personage who had left them behind.

The discipline of a shoot is probably the most important factor to its safety. The better the manners, the safer the shoot. Guns must keep to their stands and never move to pickup until the drive is over. Beaters must beat slowly and make a noise, lightly tapping with a stick or a couple of pebbles. The absolutely silent beater, who uses his stick to walk with and moves like a ghost, is a danger. It is best for all concerned that a beater within range should be visible and audible.

The correct handling of a gun in company is largely a matter of good habit, and the drill should be inculcated into every young man using a gun for the first time. It is proper for a gun walking with the beaters to fire in the air to signal the start of a beat. (Incidentally, it also helps to get birds on the move.) And, normally speaking, especially at the end of the drive he should not shoot at birds going forward. During one pheasant drive, where there were a lot of birds, I remember seeing a flanking gun shooting low and medium pheasants. He seemed to have no idea that he was dropping his shot not only on the beaters but on his fellow guns standing in the front line. If you are on the flank, or, indeed, wherever you are standing in a drive, your first responsibility is to identify precisely the direction from which the beaters are advancing and the position of all the other guns. Experienced guns, when they take their stand at the beginning of a drive, make a practice of carefully identifying their position to the man on either side of them by waving a handkerchief or their hat.

Whatever you do, never change your position in the course of a drive. For better or worse, stay where you are. If, in quite exceptional circumstances, you do decide to change your position, make sure that both the adjoining guns know exactly where you are going. But on the whole, that's a matter which should always be decided before the drive begins. In practice, if you do try to improve your position, you'll generally find that you are not much better off. The bird that draws you forward, or to the left or the right, won't be typical of the way the birds will fly in the greater part of the drive. Generally speaking, you can depend on it that the keeper knows what are likely to be the best stands. It is very much in his interest to see that you get as much good shooting as possible.

The only circumstances in which, in an organized shoot, it may be advisable to move from the numbered stands is in exceptional weather conditions. If the wind has suddenly changed to an unexpected direction, if the weather is bad, it may well be that the guns can take up better positions than those already laid down. But normally speaking that is the responsibility of the host. Every gun should be very reticent indeed about changing his place from the numbered stand allotted to him. In rough shooting, in which the guns are probably their own beaters and the day alternates between drives and walking up, it may well be that it is left to the guns themselves to take up what seems to them the most advantageous position. Even then, you are not freed of the responsibility of making sure where your neighbors are standing and establishing exactly your own proper and legitimate field of fire.

Your legitimate field of fire is an angle of 90 degrees immediately in front and immediately behind you. The 90 degrees to your left and right are a danger.

If a covey of partridges or a bouquet of pheasants comes over, it is reasonable for the guns on each flank of them to shoot at the same time; but always remember, in those circumstances, that your natural birds should be the ones which are nearest to you. Remember the story of the two sportsmen who, between them, without poaching each other's birds, killed every partridge in a covey of eight.

On any day when game is abundant there will be many occasions on which you will not be immediately certain whether the bird is rightly yours or not. But every pheasant, from the moment you see him, gives you time to look to your manners before you shoot. In case of doubt, your gun, which should be at the ready position, should be poised ready for mounting. A typical case of doubt is when a pheasant, or very often a woodcock, flies down the line. Hold your hand until the gun next to you has had a fair chance. Don't shoot if he misses until the bird is well in your area. As a matter of good marksmanship, that is the right moment to shoot.

Harking back to the drill, you'll find, if you watch, that the man who swings his body properly whilst his gun is mounting is usually a safe shot. The man who first mounts his gun and then swings onto the bird looks unsafe and usually is. If you have the misfortune to be posted next to a poker, particularly in grouse and partridge driving, it can be disconcerting enough to put you off your own shooting. It can be even worse if he also has the habit, which such people often have, of sitting on his shooting-stick while he is waiting for the drive to begin, with his gun loaded (and his safety catch up) laid across his knees pointing in your direction.

On one occasion, when this happened to me, I elaborately pretended to imitate the offender's example. I made a show of loading my own gun and pushing up my safety catch and then laid my weapon across my knees with the muzzle pointing in *his* direction. He at once lifted his gun and pointed it to the front, and I reversed arms and reloaded. Not a word was spoken.

One old sportsman who used to give me some delightful days shooting used to have a habit of saying "Unload your guns and follow me" when he led us on to the next drive. I remember another who would withdraw a cartridge from an open breech, with the inquiry "What cartridges are you using?" When the man who hadn't unloaded his gun withdrew his own cartridges for comparison, the host looked at them and then handed them back with a quiet "Put them in your pocket, my dear chap."

I hope I have now repeated the safety precautions and illustrated them with anecdote and example with sufficient emphasis to make an impression even on the most negligent of gun-handlers. No shooting man can ever afford to stop thinking about safety. And the moment of greatest danger is when a man forgets for one unforgiving second that he has got a lethal weapon in his hands.

But these basic rules of conduct in the field wouldn't be complete if I confined myself to the responsibility of the man with the gun to his fellow human beings. The second responsibility is to the game which he is shooting. It is a familiar paradox that most sporting men love the thing they kill. Nobody has any right to use a gun against game who isn't trying all he knows to kill clean and who hasn't studied what to do in the unavoidable circumstance when an animal is wounded.

When you are shooting, it is your duty to mark down everything you hit as carefully as possible, with the most particular attention for the head of game which looks like running. The etiquette of the shooting field requires that you must not leave your stand to retrieve wounded game while the drive is on but, immediately it is over, you should send your dog, or call in somebody who has got a dog, to go after wounded game first and foremost. Even if it is personally unpleasant to you to dispatch a "runner" cleanly and humanely, it is your duty to do it whenever necessary. Too many shooting men have only the vaguest idea how to put a wounded animal out of its misery. It is not good form to break a partridge's neck by taking it by the head and spinning its body in the air. Neither is it particularly stylish to pull off a pheasant's head in the effort to break its neck.

The quickest and cleanest way to kill a partridge or a pheasant, if you don't mind doing it, is to crack its skull sharply between your front teeth. Alternatively, you can break its neck cleanly by twisting the head to one side or the other and carrying it back with a sharp pull. The proper way to kill a rabbit is to give it a rabbit punch with the side of the palm of your hand in the back of the neck. You can kill a hare the same way, but I don't recommend it because hares bleed profusely and, if you pick them up by the back legs and strike them behind the ears, you'll probably spatter your clothes with blood. The way to kill a hare

[191]

is to place your boot or shoe across the back of its neck as it lies on the ground. Pressing down the head, quickly pick it up by its back legs and draw its body sharply across the leg which is holding the hare down. This will kill the animal quickly and humanely and will ensure that you haven't got to send your shooting clothes at the end of the day to the cleaners.

However well you think you are shooting, always resist the temptation of boasting about it. The lookers-on see most of the game and nothing irritates a man who may feel that he has had the worst of the luck, or is off his day, than the bumptious gun next door who boasts about the head of game he has killed. Count the game you bring down by all means. In fact, the policy is to be recommended because it's a guide for the pickers-up, but don't talk about it, except in passing, and as modestly as you can to the people who are picking up the birds. And remember never to give yourself credit for any bird which you are doubtful about. Nothing makes a gun more unpopular with the keepers than if he gets the reputation of claiming game which is as diffi- cult to find as the rabbit in the conjurer's hat. If you believe that you yourself are not an offender in this matter of claiming birds which you only think you have killed, I can only tell you that, privately, most shooting men are the victims of this harmless self-deceit. I remember an occasion at a tea at the end of the day's shooting. When the keeper brought in the figures for the total bag, the host for fun asked each of the guns to write down on a piece of paper the total head of game that he guessed that he himself had shot. All the guns, except me, put down what they believed to be their score on a piece of paper. I excused myself saying that I would take what was left over. The result of adding up the scores turned out exactly as I expected. Taking the guns' own reckoning of what they had killed and subtracting it from the total bag, it left me owing many birds on the day's shooting.

Curiously enough, even some of the best and most experienced shots tend to delude themselves about their marksmanship. I have even heard a man claim that over the season for pheasant he had put up an average of 80 per cent of pheasants to cartridges expended. If he had achieved that, he would be one of the greatest game shots that the world has ever seen. In truth, I should be surprised to learn that he put up a better performance than 30 or 40 per cent of the cartridges expended.

If you can kill one bird out of three cartridges expended, you can call yourself a good shot. Of course, there is a great difference between the average of birds fired at and killed as compared with the average of cartridges fired for each bird killed. You would probably put up a better average if you based it on birds killed out of those fired at, but, personally, I prefer to establish it on the basis of the number of cartridges fired to produce the average of birds killed. If at the end of a day on which you know your friends thought you were shooting well you honestly add up the number of the head of game you are *quite certain* you brought to bag and compare it with the number of cartridges that you fired, you may be surprised to discover—although I wouldn't be—that your average was as low as 25 per cent.

It is not my purpose in this book to discuss matters which are outside the actual business of safe, straight shooting. There are many admirable books on game preservation and estate management and the natural history and ecology of the game animals of this country. You can read about correct relations between riparian owner and keeper, and game rearing and game management in relation to agriculture, elsewhere. All I need remind you here, at the end of the first chapter on Field Notes, is that at the end of the shooting day it is customary, and pleasantly so, to tip the keeper as a reward for the sport he has provided. Sometimes shooting men become unnecessarily anxious as to the size of the tip they ought to give. I personally think that tips should not be based wholly on the bag. Much better to tip the keeper on the basis of the quality of the sport he has provided and, in a reasonable proportion, to the capacity of one's own pocket. If in doubt, consult an older shooting man, or a regular guest, at the particular shoot you are attending. Normally speaking, $5.00 is reasonable for a smallish day, and $10.00 for a big day, in the coverts. But far more important than the tip is to remember to thank the keeper and to add, if you can, a personal word of comment on the way he showed his birds. He will appreciate that quite as much as the crinkly note you put in his hand.

Finally, however tired you are and however late you get home, DON'T FORGET TO CLEAN YOUR GUN. So many people do. Remember that, with smokeless ammunition, one round fouls the barrels just as much as a hundred rounds. Remember, too, that the chemical composition in the cap, which is what causes the damage, starts working immediately you lay the gun down. The sooner you clean your gun, the longer you will have a gun with barrels free from pits and moon-bright.

CHAPTER III

Clothes and Accessories

THE EMINENT Victorian sportsman who devised a shooting hat out of a dead hedgehog made, I suppose, the most memorable attempt to resolve a problem which has baffled countrymen since the invention of gunpowder. It was a gesture, magnificent though forlorn, to determine, once and for all, the most suitable attire for a day's shooting.

Although the inventor of the hedgehog hat is now in the happy hunting-grounds, it must be evident, even to the most casual observer of the country scene, that people who go shooting are still doing their outrageous best to keep his memory green. Every other recreation, even golf, seems to have sartorial limit beyond which no self-respecting sportsman is supposed to go. Not so shooting. The right clothes for the shooting party are still anybody's fancy. So much so that I shall never be surprised if, instead of a sweepstake on the bag, the ladies are invited to award prizes for the best fancy dress.

Sartorially, the most amusing shoot I ever attended was one during the war years in England. Half the guests were American officers and the other half were local English sportsmen who, in their knickerbockers and tweed suits, Newmarket boots and check riding breeches, deerstalker hats and Norfolk jackets, labored under the impression that they themselves looked normal. The American hunters in their peaked red caps, checked lumber jackets, and short rubber boots, were convinced that it was the Englishmen who looked extraordinary. We only lacked a Frenchman with a feather in his hat and tassels on his cartridge bag to complete a scene in which every member of the party would have been convinced that the others looked quite ludicrous.

So in this book I am not going to have the temerity to suggest to you, or anybody else, how to look your best for a day's hunting. While I can advise you with every confidence on how to carry a gun, I realize that in the matter of the clothes that a man carries on his back individual taste and national custom are likely to prevail.

But, while you will decide for yourself the clothes in which you feel you *look* your best, I will venture to give you a few leads as to the clothes in which you will *do* your best, because you will find that the choice of your wardrobe can have a direct and noticeable influence on shooting performance.

If you turn out for a big day in a carefully tailored suit, you may look elegant but you won't shoot as well as you will in the loose-fitting battered jacket you customarily wear. Shooting is a sport in which you must feel comfortable, free in your movements, and familiar with the feel of your clothes. Whatever clothes you ultimately insist on wearing, make a policy of settling on the style and sticking to it.

The only unequivocal piece of advice I am going to give you on shooting clothes is to tell you that you *must* wear a jacket which is baggy at the elbows and has, for preference, a raglan-type shoulder with a large armhole. Tailors have a notion that they can make the necessary allowance for freedom of movement by putting a couple of pleats at the back of a shooting coat. The pleats help a little but they don't compare with the freedom which a wide pivot sleeve can give. Most golfers, to whom freedom of arm movement is as essential as it is in shooting, wear what amounts to a blouse. Normally speaking, the blouse or windbreaker isn't the ideal wear for shooting as the butt of the stock rucks up the material.

The best jacket for shooting I myself have evolved, after many failures and half-successes, is one I keep at my shooting grounds to lend to people who arrive, as they often do, in town suits. Although I am a square and stocky man, my old coat fits quite well on six-footers, and I am amused how often my pupils remark that my old jacket seems to fit them better than their own.

Here is the specification: You want an ordinary, well-fitting jacket without inside or outside breast pockets on the right side if you are a right-handed man, or on the left side of you are a left-handed man. There should be no visible shoulder pad but a piece of thick buckram inserted between the lining and the shoulder, stitched criss-cross in the way that buckskin is stitched into the knee of riding breeches, to keep the padding flat and to prevent any ridges of puckering. The pockets should be of extra strong linen. The buttons, strongly threaded, should be of bone or other soft material with rounded edges. Sharp edges scratch the gunstock and metal buttons make bad rucks in the woodwork of the stock.

My jacket has four buttons, instead of the usual three, and a neat lapel so that the gun can come to its place in the shoulder without the heel of the stock tripping up on it. I have also got a storm button under the lapel so that the collar can be turned up and buttoned close round the neck when it rains. The collar is made of the coat material on both sides and not lined in a way which shows up a different color when the collar is turned up.

While you may not care to adopt this device for yourself, my own coat has, within the lining and starting at the front of each pocket, a belt on the same principle as the belt at the back of your waistcoat. This belt (inside of course) has the ordinary buckle for adjustment. This allows the weight of the pocket content to be carried on the waist instead of dragging on the shoulder. The thought is that you'll use your pockets on many occasions to carry cartridges. With a belt such as I recommend, you will be spared the effort of lifting the weight of a pocketful of cartridges every time you lift your gun or raise your arm. As an experiment, put ten cartridges or a pound weight, which is the same thing, in each pocket of an ordinary jacket and you'll find that every time you raise your gun you have to lift the lot. With the inside strap to take the weight and loose pivot sleeves, you can fill your pockets, yet the jacket will not drag down from the shoulders; neither will you have to raise the weight of your cartridges with your arms. The theory of the extra wide sleeve with the wide elbow room is based upon the drill that, in gun-mounting, you stretch the forward arm and bend the other. There is no reason at all, of course, why you shouldn't have storm cuffs fitted for hard weather as well.

The sort of breeches you wear is unlikely to affect your shooting, but it's a sound rule to avoid long and baggy creations such as golfers favor. In wet weather and in wet roots—and in the shooting season roots are usually sopping wet—baggy trousers quickly get saturated and, if you are doing a lot of walking, they will chafe the inside of your leg as well.

But although you can suit yourself what breeches you wear, footgear is important. If you wear the wrong sort, it will definitely have an effect on your shooting performance. Don't cripple yourself with heavy shooting boots at the beginning of the season if you have not been wearing them regularly; much better have a thick sole put on a lighter shoe. I personally prefer boots and anklets to shoes and gaiters. A boot feels lighter than the heavy shoe because of the better support round the ankles and, when walking heavy ground, is much less tiring to lift. The anklet prevents the water from the cabbages and the grass from entering, and the only disadvantage I know about them is that they take longer to put on and take off. Perhaps some enterprising bootmaker will turn out a combination of boot and anklet with a zip fastener.

Nails in the heel and round the edge of the sole of either a shooting boot or shoe are a help on slippery ground, but, if too close together, they collect chunks of dirt. The very sensitive shot will find that he can keep his balance better with low heels because high ones have a tendency to pitch the shooter forward.

Personally I wear a cloth cap when I am shooting. In fine weather you can pull down the peak of the cap if the sun is shining in your eyes or give it a rakish tilt if the sun is hitting you at an angle. You can use it as a waterproof seat if the ground is damp and park it out of the way in your pocket if you don't want to wear a hat at all. The objection to a cap is that, in pouring rain, unless you turn it back to front, you get a soaking down the back of the neck. For that reason a tweed cap with an all-round brim, such as fishermen wear, might be even more suitable.

But I repeat that this is simply the clothing that I wear myself when I am out shooting. The only firm advice I give you, whatever you wear, is to have your shooting jacket made with wide deep sleeves, because that will definitely have an effect for the better on your performance.

Rather than carry a waterproof about with them, a lot of shooting men these days seem to prefer to wear a waterproof gabardine shooting jacket. These jackets have a good deal to commend them. The principal snags are, first, that they tear on the slightest contact with barbed wire and, alas, barbed wire is now a ubiquitous enemy; and, further, they are particularly susceptible to stains, such as blood and oil marks. At the end of a very short season, they can look quite filthy, whereas tweed can still look reasonably respectable, if smelly, after years of hard work. And wool tears much less readily than most materials.

Wild-fowlers and pigeon shooters, who have to take very much more care over their camouflage than the shooter in the coverts or on the stubbles, hardly need any special advice from me. Most of them are masters at concealing themselves in the mud or in the hedgerows. Most of them, too, have learned that you can't do better than to dress yourself as nearly as possible as the modern soldier in the field. When I am laying-up for wild-fowling, I personally wear a set of army surplus laverack clothing: a blouse and waterproof slip-on trousers and a hood at the back which can be pulled over the head. The whole of the nasty mixture of green, khaki, and yellow looks pretty awful, but in a blind it undoubtedly works.

All I need remark about clothes, in addition, is that wild-fowlers who put on a series of sweaters and waistcoats and jackets to keep out the cold of a winter's day should, if possible, try to use a shorter stocked gun than the one they use in ordinary circumstances. Otherwise they will be at a definite disadvantage in their gun-mounting. But more about this later.

The field accessories of the fully equipped game shot can be extended as indefinitely as a fisherman's tackle. Cartridges can be carried in the pocket (which is the best place if you don't require too many); in a pigskin bag; in a belt, bandolier, or a haversack.

The pigskin cartridge bag (cowhide is not so tough or weather resistant) is used almost universally for covert shooting. You can get a bag to hold 50, 100, or 150 12-bore cartridges. The 50 size is rather small to get your hand into quickly for loading; the 150 size is too cumbersome and heavy; the 100 size, with 50 to 75 cartridges in it, is probably ideal.

If you are using a cartridge bag, it is a good idea to wrap a piece of chamois leather round the brass buckles which attach the shoulder strap to the two sides of the bag. This will effectively prevent the buckle from rubbing against the stock of the gun and rutting the wood. Gun-makers can remove these ruts from the stock of the gun, but it is far better to prevent it happening in the first place; especially if you have a best gun with a lovely walnut stock that you don't want to spoil.

It is another wise precaution to soak the leather of a cartridge bag in one of the waterproofing oils. It not only makes the bag last much longer, but the leather becomes increasingly supple and, as a consequence, you can draw out your cartridges more comfortably and more quickly. Remember what I told you in the drill. Before you begin shooting give your cartridge bag a good shake. This will cause the brass end of the cartridge to point upwards and the heavy lead to sink downwards.

Many shooters I know like to carry their cartridges in a belt round their middles or in a patent bandolier across their shoulders. I can't recommend it. It's the slowest possible way of drawing cartridges for the gun. The weight is essentially in the place where it will impede, however slightly, your freedom of movement in gun-mounting, and people who wear cartridge belts either find that the cartridges fit too tight and are a nuisance to pull out or, alternatively, they fit so loosely that, when the wearer crawls through a hedge or bends down, the rounds of ammunition drop into the grass.

If you are shooting in the coverts, a stick seat, unless you are a particularly agile character, is an essential accessory. The only advice I have to give you about stick seats, because you will obviously choose one which suits your own personal backside, is to try and have one in which the metal stop at the base is protected by a ring of rubber. Just as the buckles on cartridge bags are the most common cause of ruts in gunstocks, so shooting-sticks have the chief responsibility for causing dents in barrels. The slightest tap with a metal stick on a gun-barrel is sufficient to make a dent which may be invisible at a casual glance but which, on close examination, will be revealed in the barrel.

If you *must* take a dog shooting with you which isn't rock steady, don't attach him to yourself with a lead. That's the most certain way of making sure you'll be off balance when the game flushes. The proper thing to do, if you are shooting at a stand, is to have one of those patent leads with a peg at the end by which you can plug your irresponsible animal to the ground at your feet.

Cartridge magazines, those great leather boxes with oak linings which used to be dragged about the place by Victorian sportsmen, are now completely out of date, except as a convenient box to store cartridges in the gun room. The most suitable container to use, by way of a refill magazine which you can draw on between stands, is probably one of the very large pigskin bags. Better still, have two bags of the ordinary 100 size.

A cartridge extractor is always worth having and, if you are carrying your own game, the best bags are those with the string front which allow the air to get at the game. But never allow game to remain in a bag longer than you possibly can. Ideally, game should be hung up and allowed to cool immediately it is shot. In the early part of the season, hares, for example, will go rotten in a few hours unless very great care is taken to lay them out in a cool place and keep them free from blowflies. Even later on, pheasants, partridges, and grouse will not hang nearly so well if they have been knocked about. The use of the traditional poacher's pocket is the most certain way of making your own clothes smell and making the game you carry in them inedible.

CHAPTER IV

Grouse Shooting in Britain

GROUSE shooting is unlike any other form of shooting in either Britain or America. It has unique features because red grouse is only indigenous to certain parts of the British Isles where the soil is predominantly acid with a bountiful growth of the proper sort of heather and adequate quartz grit.

Heather is a hard, indigestible food, and quartz is the only grit which suits the grouse's gizzard. Attempts to introduce the red grouse in other parts of the world have not been successful. For practical purposes the limits of grouse shooting are confined to northern Britain, with a slight overflow for rough shooting in Ireland.

Even in Britain the majority of sportsmen only get the opportunity to shoot grouse occasionally, and usually do so in strange surroundings. Outside Britain, and especially in America, the unique quality of the sport which the red grouse offers draws shooting men from all over the world for the traditional opening of the season, which has come to be known as the Glorious Twelfth (August 12).

For the very special reason that every American sportsman who can afford it crosses the Atlantic to shoot grouse, as well as for the fact that in Britain it is the opening of the shooting season, I am going to deal with grouse shooting first. I am going to deal with it in detail because it is a form of shooting in which

[203]

even experienced bird shots can be confused by the novel sur-roundings and conditions. It is also a form of shooting (hence its tremendous international appeal) which exposes weaknesses of temperament and gunmanship more than any other.

So, although you yourself may never get nearer to a grouse butt than a pipe dream, I invite you to come with me to the moors and listen to what I have to tell a man shooting grouse for perhaps the first time.

After you have read this chapter you may be surprised (al-though I won't) to find that something I am advising the sports-man to remember far away on the Scottish hills is going to help you to pick off some completely different sort of bird when you are pottering round your own home ground.

Anyhow, you might be rich one day and you might like to know in advance what is waiting for you.

To begin with, there is a tremendous element of luck in the quality of the sport that the grouse shooter is likely to enjoy. You can rent the most expensive moor and be disappointed. You can be a guest on a moor where normally the bags are small and run into a bumper season. It is nobody's fault that nobody really knows how the grouse have fared until the guns get among them on the Twelfth.

It is only too true that he would be an unwise shooter who ordered his cartridges for the season on the strength of the pre-liminary reports from the moors. There is no mystery why that should be so. For two very good reasons the prospects for the grouse season are almost entirely assessed on guesswork.

The first and most formidable reason is the temperament of the average moorland keeper who, even at the point of a gun, can be relied upon to withhold everything that he knows. Char-acteristic of what any moorland keeper is likely to tell you is what a friend of mine heard when he asked his man for an opin-ion of prospects during the coming season. There was a weighty pause while pipes were primed and dogs called to heel and then the keeper replied: "It might be better than it was last year, and it might be worse. Depends how the grouse move."

Keepers being what they are, the second good reason why grouse-shooting forecasts are so uncertain is because the moors are what they are. There are few prospects more calculated to encourage short cuts and snap decisions than a wilderness of knee-deep bog and knee-high heather, muscle-aching hillsides and ankle-spraining descents. It is my experience that high-hearted forays into the hills to see how the grouse are doing usually degenerate into a sit-down and a cigarette in the car while the dogs are turned out to range round the verges of the moorland roads. If a few barren pairs get up, everybody agrees that the moor has gone to pot. If a covey or two is seen dusting in the road, the landlord returns thankfully to tea and decides to double the shooting rent.

But, apart from human considerations, it is, alas, a fact that grouse can never be relied upon to stay put.

It is never safe to assume that the birds crowding a moor in July will oblige over the butts in middle August. For that reason alone, the non-committal attitude of the upland keeper is justified. Grouse are essentially vagrant in habit; and if you drive a small moor frequently, the birds will leave it until peace and quiet have returned.

In addition, "grouse disease," which is an epidemic either of coccidiosis affecting the young birds, or strongylosis affecting the young and old birds, breaks out in a rough cycle of seven years. All indications suggest that in a favorable year for heather growth and when the moors are not too wet disease falls to its lowest level. But too many birds on a moor, followed by a trying season, invariably mean an outbreak of grouse disease. The law of nature allows a certain head of game to a hundred acres, but if we succeed in developing more stock than the ground will hold, the epidemic of parasitic diseases of game spread more swiftly because the feed and the ground will only maintain a fixed head of birds.

Before the first world war, "partridge disease" was virtually unknown in Great Britain. A few birds with strongylosis had been picked up and the possibility of strongyle disease of partridges was known to a few biologists. After the First World War, many landowners tried to recover their losses on shooting rents by making ten partridges grow where only five grew before. In addition, agriculture had gone back and, as there was less standing corn and more grass, an epidemic of strongylosis (little parasitic worms in the bird gut) broke out and spread everywhere. In plain language, partridge disease, too, is a disease of overcrowding; and every Scots moor manager knows that if he has a heavy head of unshot game left and conditions of feed are bad in the hills, it will probably take five to seven years before he has a season again when bags are over-average or even normal.

The consequence, curiously enough, is that nothing exasperates the Scottish keeper more, when the landlord has made a "let" and when there are a lot of birds on the moor, than visiting guns who shoot badly. The lessee may be entitled to bag, say, 5,000 head of grouse in his "let," but if he and his guests are only capable of shooting 2,000 head by the time they go, it is then too late to get the stock down to the limit which is healthiest for the moor. If the moor is let and half the bag is made, the moor is overstocked and, with the additional hazard of bad weather, goes down with disease. It isn't worth shooting again until careful conservation has restored the balance several years later.

So, in general, although many of the Scottish moors are excellently managed, no system has yet been developed which allows for the vagaries of climate. In some years an adequate area of heather can be burned in order to provide new food in the following seasons. In others, bad weather prevails in the legal time for heather burning, and little can be done. What this all adds up to is that, if you have the good luck to be in a grouse-shooting party on a moor and in a season when there are a lot of birds, there is a responsibility on you not to "fluff" them. The landlord and the keepers require you, in the interests of the shoot, to shoot straight. To accept a grouse-shooting invitation which obviously comes at a time when you are most likely to be out of practice and not to have taken precautions at the shooting school before you go north is bad manners, both to your host and to the landlord on whose land you are shooting. Nevertheless, it's no use pretending that to go straight to the moors and shoot grouse well is easy.

The environment is strange. It is August and it is quite likely that a stiff climb up to hill butts may find you out of condition. There is usually a very long wait before the drive begins (assuming, that is, that the game is to be driven) because the beaters will probably have to bring in an enormous expanse of ground by comparison with the shorter beats in partridge or covert shooting.

A gun having been posted with his loader in the butt is usually "in tension." He scours the undulation of the moors and, in ten or fifteen minutes, although he may be unaware of it, he has "fatigued" his eye. I am not sure that it is strictly accurate to say that the eye *can* be fatigued. An oculist could probably demonstrate that all that happens is that there is a slower reaction time for the pupillary accommodation. Actually, from a shooting point of view, the man who looks for the birds for twenty minutes before there is any chance of seeing them has "tried" his eyes and probably fatigued some of his body muscles to the point of bracing them.

I am going to concentrate on showing you how to shoot driven grouse because, if you can shoot driven grouse, you can almost certainly shoot them when they are walked up over dogs. Apart from the unfamiliar surroundings, and the effort of walking through heather and boggy ground, it is no more difficult to shoot walked-up grouse than walked-up partridges or pheasants. It is, normally speaking, the straight going-away shot that I described so fully in the drill.

In fact, driven grouse at the beginning of the season are not —repeat not—difficult shooting. It is towards the end of the season, when they are very strong and the winds blow high, that they can be such very difficult birds indeed to bring down. But it is not the difficulty of the shooting that usually defeats the novice, who may indeed be a very fair shot at other sorts of game, but the curious problems associated with dealing with driven grouse. Before discussing the actual shooting of the birds, I must once again begin by pointing out the very special dangers attaching to shooting from grouse butts.

A great many grouse butts are sited by a keeper with only an eye for the bag and not much regard for safety; or, perhaps, no conception of how dangerous some of the people from the South may be. Butts are very often damnably dangerous because of their site or because of the way that they are constructed. In general, grouse fly along a line which follows closely the contour lines on the maps, but a shift of five yards back or three yards down the slope could make the butts much safer and without the loss of any birds at all. So, when you step into a grouse butt for the first time, your initial responsibility is to analyze its position in relation to the other butts and the other shooting men inside them.

The custom of sticking "stop sticks" in the butts to warn guns not to swing their barrels beyond a certain point to the right or to the left is to be commended; but all too often you find, when you arrive on the hill in August, that some thrifty shepherd has used these sticks for a fire and possibly the wooden flooring of the butt and anything else that will burn as well. At the beginning of the season, you will often discover that the butts are in most discreditable order. The cure is to send for the keeper at once when you arrive and, if necessary, have him send up two stout lads and a pony load of pioneering material to make good all the butts that are in disrepair. The foraging party can also cut a turf drain and provide some sort of standing place. Keepers dislike doing this, as it encourages the shepherds to revel round illegitimate campfires in the following year. But, if you lease a moor, it is a job that almost certainly needs doing.

No general rule can be laid down about butts, as they depend on local conditions. Some could only be made safe with corrugated iron screens of double thickness.

The most fatal kind of butt is where the shooter looks up a hillside and finds that, exactly in line with the normal height of advancing grouse, he is looking into the next butt. The butt usually has a side entrance too, facing the lower butt, thus allowing the gun or loader to get his legs peppered if an emotional shot "follows on" unduly.

The number of people that do get peppered depends to some extent on the season; but, in a bumper year in the Highlands, slight shooting accidents rate almost second to the figures of local motoring accidents. It is not the experienced shots who get peppered. They are usually wise enough to sit down in the butt until the battue is all over, once they have become aware of the first high velocity swarm of visiting pellets coming in their direction. If you find that you are in a difficult butt, mark your safe limits on either side with either sticks or gun bags and perhaps pile up a few extra turfs on left and right flank.

If you are renting a grouse moor, or going as a guest for the first time, don't count your birds before you see them coming over the guns. Nobody in advance of August the Twelfth really knows the head of game that these high and lonely moors hold, because, in the normal course of events, very few people have visited them, except the keeper on his round; and one man can only cover a small part of the ground. However many times you have been to a grouse moor before, never forget the first time you walk into a new butt to assess the safety measures which are necessary to protect your neighbors from yourself and yourself from your neighbors.

After that, when you have made a careful note of where adjoining butts are situated, don't "tire your eyes" searching the heather. Take it easy and look into the "blue"; or better still, don't look at anything at all, but relax and think about anything else under the sun, except shooting.

Don't anticipate your birds. They'll show themselves to you in their own good time, and, if you are not keyed up waiting for them, when the first covey appears over the skyline (and butts are nearly always sighted below a convenient skyline) you will focus it immediately. If a covey flies low, a few feet over the heather as grouse so often do, you will see it for the first time as a sweeping shadow across the face of the moor; but you will realize it in time and you will have plenty of time to get into focus before the birds come into shot.

You will always be told that the best practice is to kill your first birds well in front. It is excellent advice; but it takes some experience to know when unfamiliar birds like grouse are actually in range. Another school holds to the view that you can kill a bird behind at a far longer range as his feathers will not deflect the shot so much as they will if you shoot at him head-on. These are two rival and opposite schools of thought. The only point on which both agree is that a crossing shot is more vulnerable. It is more vulnerable because you are shooting at the moment when the long axis of the bird is exposed to the shot pattern. When he is coming head-on or going away, he exposes his shorter axis.

On the whole, if you are having your first experience on a grouse moor, I think the best advice I can give you is to tell you to treat your first few birds as ranging shots. If you feel you want a little more time when the first covey comes over, take time by all means and try to pick off, say, a single one of the laggards. Whatever you do, don't shoot all over the place because you feel you must let off a couple of barrels. I know brilliant partridge shots who invariably only fire off one barrel in front when the first birds of the day come over. They want to make sure of their swing and settle their eye on the target before they start killing two in front.

You are sure to be excited when you see your first covey. There is sure to be the temptation to shoot into the "brown." Resist it and endeavor to put into practice one of the pieces of advice that we often give in the shooting school. Try and hit your first bird in the tail. That will make sure that you are keeping your eye on the bird and not "poking" or shooting into the spaces between the covey. People often wonder why it is that when they "brown" at a covey it so seldom happens that any of them fall. In theory, the spread of the shot pattern should be large enough to fill up the gaps and hit a bird as well. In practice, what happens is that the man who shoots into the "brown" deliberately aims into the space between the birds. And because, if the gun-mounting is good and the gun fits, the charge will always go to the place where the shooter is looking, he contrives according to the best rules of shooting to miss his birds altogether.

So don't be ashamed to take one in front and one behind at the beginning of the drive or the day. It is far better style to shoot both barrels in front, but it is better to shoot steadily for a little while than to miss your birds altogether.

In theory, a grouse, or any other game bird, coming with his own velocity takes a harder smash from the pellets than a bird going away at the same velocity. If an indignant cowherd threw a turnip with the velocity of 30 m.p.h. at a car moving at 50 m.p.h. towards him he would possibly make a demonstration; if he chucked a 30 m.p.h. turnip after a 50 m.p.h. car the show would be no more than a futile display of rural spleen. That's the principle.

Actually a bird shot thirty yards in front is killable. One well-known shot used to pace out the distance and pull up some heather to mark the point. I am not certain that this is the best way for most people, but it is a good idea to have a sort of aiming point notion of what forty yards is.

My own advice to the grouse shooter is not to worry so much about measuring distance with his eye as to wait till the bird looks big enough to eat. That may sound rather like telling some-one to take an object "about the size of a bit of wood," but, dis-counting snipe, all edible birds have bulk. On the basis of waiting until the grouse looks big enough to eat you will take oncoming birds at between twenty-five and thirty yards, which is just where the crack shots take them. They probably hustle on and fall behind the butts, but they were killed well over twenty yards away.

Once you have killed your first oncoming birds from a grouse butt you will probably change guns because, in driven grouse shooting, it is customary to shoot with a pair and a loader. It is at this moment that accidents so often happen because, believe it or not, there is no room for the "follow-through" shooter at grouse. The butts are in a line, or what is worse, a curve, and accidents are almost as easy as they are when driving a car.

Why aren't the butts set out straight? The reason is that the flight of grouse is very closely along natural contour lines. If the side of the brae was a tilted plain, the butts could be in a straight line, but the topography of the land does not run to plains and experience has probably shown that butts must be placed in a curve. Not necessarily a curve of sharp radius but one that allows the center butt to tickle up his left and right wing butts with a charge of shot at, say, eighty yards if he doesn't limit his firing angle to a restricted front. At eighty yards you will not kill anyone but you could very easily put somebody's eye out.

The story of the American sportsman shooting on the moors who saw an eminent general, on his right flank, pepper a celebrity on the left and himself finally fired both barrels of both guns at the two of them "to stop them fiddling as they were making the birds rise wild" is probably mythical. On the other hand, all myths have some substance in them, and a lesson. Too little care in the butts is criminal, but I am bound to add that too great care may result in the sportsman missing a lot of shots he would otherwise have secured without danger to anyone or risk of the social observances.

I have mentioned the sticks which are usually erected on the turfs or the crevices of the stone wall in well-organized butts to limit the zone of fire and the swing of the too-anxious follow-through. If the sticks are not there, put out some mark of your own to replace them. Further, remember that a slip on uneven or boggy ground where sheep used the butts may explain an accident but won't excuse it. Butts ought to be properly tidied up; but they often aren't. All too often one is expected to shoot in the middle of a quagmire. Nobody can shoot at his best, or even safely, off a couple of rocking stones in a bog, and bad butts are responsible for a lot of bad shooting. If you find yourself in a bad butt you must do all you can to make it more comfortable before the birds begin to come over, and you need have no feelings about telling the keeper subsequently what you think of his winter work and remind him, in future, to see that his butts are prepared properly.

In any case the occupant of a butt must take careful note of his neighbors and work out, *before shooting*, the safe angle of his field of fire. Assuming that you are in a properly designed butt, you'll notice that you usually enter at the side and the site of this entrance is no help at all in remembering your front. If you are not careful, in the heat of the drive, you will find that you forget your precise position in relation to the other butts. Even if stopping stakes are in position, they are very often too wide apart for some shooters. Don't depend on them. The surest way to shoot safe is to shoot according to the drill in the first part of this book. Any man who completes the whole of his body swing whilst gun-mounting and fires at the precise moment that the gun touches his shoulder, not dwelling on the trigger and not following birds when the gun is already in position, won't make mistakes. It is the man who follows the birds round who can put a charge of shot so easily into the next butt.

In the interests of safety, and in the interest of concealing your presence from the oncoming birds, don't fall into the habit of hiding low in the butt, squinting through the turfs, and popping up like a jack-in-the-box when you think they are in range. Any sudden movement like that of the shooter or the gun, or even a fluttering scarf, will frighten the covey off its course. You may get a shot, but it will be a much more difficult task to kill a bird out of a scattering covey. Don't be afraid to stand in the butt as upright as Nelson on his column, but keep still and don't move your gun until the birds are within range and you are ready to kill them. You will shoot better because you will be nicely balanced and ready, and you won't turn the birds because they fear movement much more than your black outline in the center of the butt.

The cause of accidents on the grouse moors is hurry. The cause that so many birds are missed is hurry. If the gun takes it easy, spots his birds well in front, he'll never be hurried and he will never make a dangerous shot. That rule applies equally to the loader as to the gun himself.

If your loader is trained to carry out the system of loading and changing guns and keeping well down, he won't lose you any birds. Loaders as a rule remember to keep low on grouse moors but they are often much too vigorous. And however still you are, a jack-in-the-box loader can negative your own discipline. Never take an untrained loader into the butt; it is dangerous. If necessary, drill your loader with snap caps and rub it into him to keep his head down.

Many grouse shots find difficulty in killing a bird which is driven against a strong wind and appears to be drifting in front of the butt. This is certainly a trick shot but, once learned, it is

the easiest shot of the lot. Fire very steadily at the legs of the
bird and a little right or left according to the direction of the
wind. If you are meeting fast birds traveling with the wind, all
you have to remember is to shoot straight at them with a rather
quicker gun-mounting. You can always trust your eye, as I told
you in the initial drill, to make the necessary allowances. And
only the case of a bird moving much slower than its normal
speed requires conscious calculation.

In case of a shot behind the butt, a gun who completes the
whole of his body swing relatively leisurely, with a complete
180 per cent turn, will kill his birds behind with his second gun
without effort or risk to his neighbors. Gun-muzzles must be
raised, and kept high, during the turning movement. The turn-
about in fact has to be completed with the gun erect. Only when
it is completed should the gun be mounted to the shoulder. If
you swing through, as many people do with the gun half or fully
mounted, and try to follow-through in a complete motion from
"birds coming" to "birds going away," you are taking a chance
on an accident.

The golden rule is to KEEP YOUR MUZZLES UP almost vertically
WHILST PASSING THE LINE. A complete turn of the feet is essential.
You can't shoot with a twisted body over your shoulder at "go-
ing away" birds. You are wasting cartridges if you do.

Grouse have a habit of jinking in the air and slipping sideways
the moment a barrel is thrown. If you stand still as the birds
come towards you, there is a good chance they won't jink. If you
make a movement, they will. But if you find grouse are jinking
for one reason or another, don't be tempted to adopt the jack-in-
the-box tactics which I have already warned you about. Whatever happens, stand still and MAKE SURE THAT YOUR LOADER IS
NOT DODGING ABOUT BEHIND YOUR BACK.

In theory, grouse are driven straight over the butts. In practice, a single bird or a pair from the covey may traverse the line
of butts and be missed by all the guns. This is particularly true

[215]

if they are flying into a crossing wind. To handle this sort of bird calls for a trick shot. But, once the trick is mastered, it serves. Fire steadily just *underneath* the bird and very little towards the line of progress, right or left as it may be. Don't over-estimate pace.

To deal with very fast birds, borne on a thirty-mile-an-hour wind, the sort of birds you get at the end of the season, there is no remedy except experience. You *must* swing your body in time with the bird and snap at it. If you can shoot that sort of bird consistently, you can shoot anything that flies.

Some birds you meet may be very low-dropping targets because the covey is losing height with the intention of settling in the heather behind. Other coveys may be butt shy and rise and turn as you lead with your gun. A quick snap shot will get this sort of bird, but if you are slow, you will be beaten every time by the speed of grouse tactics. If you feel you have remembered everything else I have told you and you are still missing grouse, you will most likely find that the cause of the trouble is that you are putting your head down to the gun instead of bringing your gun up to the face. This happens so often in grouse shooting because guns get tired with the effort of getting from butt to butt; and I suppose their heads are caught nodding.

Physically, shooting grouse, either walking them up or from the butts, is hard exercise. To shoot consistently well you need to be in first-class condition and first-class practice. You don't want to sit up the night before playing cards or treating yourself too liberally to the local nectar.

CHAPTER V

How to Shoot Partridges

I REMEMBER a well-known sports writer extolling the delights of partridge driving, writing the following sentence: "When the whistle blows, you instinctively take a firm stance, tightly grip your gun and search the skyline."

This lyric comment combines so many things you should *not* do that it should become a classic. If you try to shoot like that, you would shoot very few birds at all. But, in justice to the writer, it must be admitted that his description of his own reaction is an accurate record of what people, who ought to know better, regularly do.

Let us imagine that we are watching a first-class partridge shot at one of the big shoots in open country where the hedges are low and guns, in order to remain under cover, have to stand fairly close to the hedge. The first thing which should strike you is that the practiced shot is *not* in a state of tension. He probably stands quite loosely and unconcerned; but you will also notice that, when he shoots, he is far swifter than the neighboring gun who, in his anxiety, has braced himself and gripped his gun as he comes on the alert. The expert kills his birds so far as he can "in front," while his neighbor lets them come too close and so is presented not with an easier shot, but with a more difficult one.

Partridge coveys do not always come straight. They may swerve or split. But you will notice that the practiced shot snaps an odd bird or so as they show for a second above the hedge before they have a chance of breaking back or flanking. At the end of that drive you will probably find that the experienced man has had 50 per cent more shooting and killed twice as many birds as his apparently more alert and undoubtedly more anxious neighbor.

Now if we analyze what the expert did, we find that in the first place he was completely self-confident; more than that, he was not afraid of missing. I can't emphasize to you enough the importance of not being afraid of missing when you are shooting at partridges. MOST OF THE BIRDS THAT ARE MISSED ARE MISSED BECAUSE PEOPLE ARE SO ANXIOUS NOT TO MISS.

The partridge, by comparison with the grouse or the pheasant, flies comparatively slowly. But, from the flurry that some people get into, you'd think they were moving as fast as jet planes. The trouble, of course, is that a covey of partridges, bursting like shrapnel over a hedge, is in itself a disconcerting experience unless you have trained your eye and your mind to deal with one bird at a time. The most certain way to miss is not to be able to make up your mind which of the covey you are going to shoot at.

Returning to the expert, you will notice that his stance is never a rigid one. He carries himself easily and comfortably in a position which allows him to swing right or left without any constraint of the body. You will probably observe that, before the drive begins, he is practicing his gun swing to make sure that he is all set to move sweetly when the birds come into view. He doesn't grip his gun; he holds it lightly and securely with no muscular tension at all. Above all, his eyes are not all over the place "searching the skyline."

When I was discussing grouse shooting, I warned you of the dangers of searching the heather and wearing yourself out looking for birds long before there is any likelihood of their making an appearance. The rule applies equally in partridge shooting. The partridge shot who knows his business isn't rapidly refocusing his eyes here, there, and everywhere looking for birds in all directions at once. He is gazing steadily into the "blue" at the approximate point in the air not where he thinks the birds might appear, but where he would like to kill them if they do.

Standing there he can see the full field of his zone of fire and consequently he isn't tiring his eyes. Any birds coming into his field of fire are bound to be seen and, not only is the covey more easily picked up by the gun, but he himself is not surprised by the appearance of the birds. The covey climbs into his view rather than his eyes having to climb to meet the covey. Without having to swing more than a few degrees he can select his bird and kill it before it gets too close or before it swerves. The whole process is relatively effortless, relaxed, and easy of timing. The characteristic mark of a good partridge shot is that he never seems to be in a hurry but that he kills his birds yards sooner than the average shot standing next door to him.

The man who is anxiously turning his head to right and left, who is tensed and fiddling his gun with shooting nerves, is asking for trouble. He may even commit the major mistake, and one of the commonest, of being caught watching the next gun just at the unforgiving moment when a covey comes to his own sector. Either he doesn't see it in time or, if by chance his attention is just returning to that point, he is so disconcerted and flustered in his movements that he misses altogether.

Surprise makes some people jump, whilst the effect on others is to "freeze stiff." In either case, the sudden appearance of the birds sets up muscular disturbance; either the shooter is momentarily paralyzed and follows the birds with an exaggerated swing, or he is confused by seeing too many birds at once and finds himself too surprised to select one to shoot at. If he is the type who "jumps" to a surprise rather than "freezes," he is still disorganized and probably blazes away unselectively and far too late.

The shooter who looks into the "blue" is normally able to cover his whole field of fire without movement of the head.

Some look just above the hedge, others look well above it according to where they want to kill their first bird (a matter largely dependent on the distance of the stand from the hedge). With this technique, not only will the covey come into view apparently more steadily and with no element of surprise, but, most important, there will always be one bird which looks larger than the rest.

This is an illusion; but it is the bird the shooter's eye first picked up and focused on which is the easiest bird to "snap" and the eye should never be taken off it to consider the others. The first shot should be an easy snap followed by a continued swing onto a second bird. A poor shot is sometimes in such a hurry to shoot his second bird that, instead of keeping his gun swinging onto the first bird until the trigger is pressed and the bird killed, he subconsciously leaves the first bird and begins his swing to the second before he has covered the first.

The "climbing" effect of driven partridges is largely an optical illusion. If you look at the top of a hedge you are probably centering the pupil of your eye and the hedge itself cuts off half your effective field of "aware vision." If you look well above the hedge into the sky you see the birds just as soon as they appear and they remain in vision longer before you have need to move your body or head to readjust to meet them.

PARTRIDGE SHOOTING

"Looking into the blue."

At my shooting grounds I have a very difficult driven partridge stand where the birds come forward very fast indeed. I find that if a gun looks at the hill over which the first bird shows it is over his head before he can get his gun up; but if he looks well above the hill into the sky, he uses the full field of vision effectively and can manage to kill them in time. The diagram shows what I mean.

There are rules for good partridge shooting which can be easily memorized.

1. Choose a flat place to stand on. Flatten out a position, especially if you are standing in a plowed field.
2. Take things easy and *relax*. If hares come by, it is always safer to wait until they are past the line before shooting.
3. When the whistle blows, remain relaxed. Carry your gun at the ready position, with the barrel uptilted, and look into the sky at the angle which gives you the best view of your field of fire. Do not bother if you cannot comfortably see the extreme flanks. Your concern is with your front, not your neighbor's.
4. Shoot straight at the leading bird, as this may split or turn the covey down the line and give other guns a chance.
5. Count your kills and remember the spot in the air where you killed your bird rather than watch the bird to earth; except, of course, where you have got an obvious runner.

On the other side, here are some "Don'ts":

1. Don't count the covey before you shoot. If you waste time doing that you probably won't touch a feather.
2. Don't shoot low into hedgerows. In partridge shooting especially the beaters are very seldom far away.
3. Don't shoot your neighbor's birds. If a covey passes between you, you are entitled to share the shooting; but you should pick your bird on your side of the covey and he on his.
4. Don't talk or make a noise. Coveys often settle in front and break back because of noise.

In recommending you to train yourself to shoot the bird which looks larger than the rest of the covey and, if possible, to shoot at the leading bird coming towards you (and the biggest bird to your eye should be the leading bird), I am also giving you the advice which your shooting host will be most gratified to see you carrying out. Normally speaking, when a covey comes over it is led by the two old birds. If you can shoot the old ones you will render effective service in breaking up the covey and increasing the chances on future shoots of getting the birds over the guns again. Anyhow, the shooting of the old birds, early in the season, contributes materially to the improvement of the stock on the ground. What happens is that the young birds break up and join other coveys and, when they pair in December or January, there is a greater chance of unrelated birds mating together. The effect of this is to produce a stronger stock and to increase the number of partridges on the ground.

The essential obstacle that the partridge shot must surmount is to overcome the natural tendency to be bewildered by the burst of birds. If you are watching a shoot, notice how very seldom the single "Frenchman" coming over the guns is missed; and how often a barren pair is killed cleanly with a right and a left. Birds that come over in a covey of fourteen aren't traveling any faster or any differently. Inexperienced guns allow themselves to be bemused by sheer numbers and, in consequence, commit all the crimes in the book. They change from one bird to another at the moment of gun-mounting. They hang about "poking" the barrels when the gun is already mounted on the shoulder and, in a sort of panic, they shoot behind with bodies twisted and leaning on one leg. Much, much better to attempt to shoot only one bird out of the covey and to make up your mind which bird it's going to be the moment you sight it than to rely on potluck to shoot two in front and two behind; if you happen to be using two guns.

In fact, to shoot two partridges in front, change guns, and shoot two behind is an achievement which requires such perfect footwork, timing, and gun-handling that it is very nearly comparable to a century in first-class cricket. In practice it is very rarely achieved; and in practice nobody should really attempt to use two guns until they can fairly consistently get two partridges out of a covey with one.

Anybody who can do that will shoot far more efficiently and kill more birds than another shot with two guns who hasn't the discipline to pick one bird cleanly out of a covey.

There are certain rather special partridge stands where, by means of tall belts of trees or the arrangement of shooting sites in old chalk pits or quarries, really high birds are shown. This makes for rather different shooting than ordinary partridge driving over the stubbles or out of roots. All the rules I have mentioned still apply, but the methods to be adopted are more similar to those applying to high pheasants. It is worth remembering that the partridge, though it may seem because of its size faster than a pheasant, is always considerably slower. Also, on crossing a screen of trees, partridges tend to come down rather lower than pheasants in similar circumstances; that is to say that, where pheasants would make a high glide, partridges tend to dip and swerve towards ground level more swiftly. By reducing altitude, and offering not the level or rising shot, they present a rather tricky descending one. In some hill drives on downland the same conditions may be noticed, but in general, birds driven in hill country tend to follow the natural contours to their jugging place or destination, a point which is often useful to remember when new drives are being discussed.

In general, it is not easy to get partridges to any height without some rather abnormal feature of the ground. All drives have to be planned with reference to boundaries and the seasonal changes in the agricultural crops.

No matter how accurately you shoot, or however well the birds are driven, any day's partridge shooting will be a failure unless you remember the two vital rules. Get quickly to your stand and, above all, *don't talk*. Not even in grouse driving, or in pheasant shooting, is it so vitally important to be silent as it is in partridge shooting. In grouse driving, a little quiet conversation is sometimes permissible because the drives are generally spread over such large areas. The pheasant is a more amenable chap altogether; although you won't be popular, even in the coverts, if you talk too loudly or move about restlessly at your stand. But, in partridge shooting, which usually takes place in circumscribed territory, the merest undertone travels enormous distances. On the downs, where sweeps are made over very large areas, I have literally seen partridges beginning to run, with the old birds giving them the warning call, when the guns were half a mile away. The partridges could already hear them talking. Coveys are lost on every shoot because the guns are unable to resist the inclination to gossip between stands or to make a noise when the drive has actually begun. In roots or potatoes, partridges will often far prefer to face the beaters than to fly over ground where they have heard the frightening clatter of the human voice.

In the early part of the season the greater number of partridges are shot by guns walking up rather than by driving. In walking up even more than driving, the shooter has a major responsibility to mark where his birds have fallen and, so far as possible, to help other people to mark and gather their own birds. The majority of partridges are shot when the herbage is very thick on the ground. They are small birds with an excellent natural camouflage in their plumage and it is the easiest thing in the world to lose them because a wounded bird will never lose its skill in finding cover, and even a dying one may have enough strength to travel a few yards to crouch under combined straw or penetrate into a rabbit scratch in the plow. If the shooting party has good dogs the problems of picking-up are simplified. But even dogs are often foxed on the dry, warm, and windless days of early autumn. Many a bird drops so far out of range that it is difficult, to say the least, for questing dogs to find it without help.

Assume a normal happening on a normal day: a small party of four guns is walking up partridges in a field of roots. A covey flushes in front of No. 3 gun who kills with right and left barrels, and he and the other guns watch the remainder of the covey disappear over the hedgerow. Probably all concerned are marking where the covey is going to pitch in the hope of getting a chance of shooting into it again. All that the successful shot remembers, or should remember, is that he had one in front, slightly to the left and perhaps forty yards away, and that the other was rather a long shot, slightly to the right. The line moves on until they reach the spot where the successful gun expects to find his first bird. He tramps around until he has lost the line. Then the other guns join him deciding that it must have been a runner. The second bird is searched for, and again the hunt yields negative results. Birds are scarce and the pair would have been a nice contribution to the bag.

That is the sort of thing which is always happening when guns are without a keeper and good dogs. What is the remedy? Of course, the party should have had a dog, but failing that, a little more help from the other guns might have resulted in the quick gathering of both birds to the mutual satisfaction of the host and the man who shot them as well. The moment No. 3 fired, the line should have stood still. The other guns, who saw one or both birds fall, should have taken the line from some landmark or landmarks. The shooter himself, knowing the spot in the air where he killed the first bird, should note that it was slightly left or right of, say, an oak tree. He should have also noted, if he can, a landmark in his rear; say a church steeple. Having those two landmarks he can always get back to the line if he wanders off it. He now goes forward alone. The birds are not to be seen, so he looks for confirmation from the other guns who are holding their ground. One waves him back. He goes back towards a landmark until the marker signals him to stop, looks around, and finds one bird. He then rejoins the line, takes his marks on the second bird, and the other guns, who saw the bird fall, will take their line, too. The difference may be too far to hold up the line any longer; but one of the other guns may be able to direct the shooter because he took proper marks when the bird fell. The result is that the second bird is found, too. In the unlucky event that, by taking marks, the gun is unsuccessful in finding a lost bird, it is a very good practice to drop a handkerchief or some other easily identifiable object at the place where it was believed the bird fell. This means that, after the drive is over, it is possible to go back and have a thorough look without disturbing the ground while shooting it.

It is worth remembering that distance along the ground is always misleading. The average shooter's guess of what he thinks is forty yards is in practice probably nearer thirty, and his fifty yards is in practice probably nearer thirty-five yards. We are all poor judges of distance between thirty and fifty yards, so much so that the simple rule of halving the estimated distance and adding ten yards is more often than not the correct answer.

> A guess of 30 yards is really 25 yards.
> A guess of 40 yards is really 30 yards.
> A guess of 50 yards is really 35 yards.

Remember this and try it out in the field.

To underline the system of marking and gathering birds, here is a diagram showing guns advancing in line through a field. The two shot birds are marked by the letters R and L. The plan shows the marks that each of the guns should have fixed his eye on when the birds fell. From it, it is evident that the variety of different angles attained by the guns, especially the outside ones, can be invaluable in thick cover.

I repeat that this system, which should always be instinctively

MARKING AND GATHERING OF PARTRIDGES

Gun B walking up in field of roots gets a Right and Left at covey going away. He marks R on dotted line—gap at 2 and gap at 6; gun A marks on dotted line—blasted oak 4 and gate 8. Second partridge is marked by gun B on line corner of stack 1 and pylon 5; and by gun A on line hedgerow oak 3 and water tower 7.

applied by every man in a line of guns shooting partridges, needs modification if dogs are present, as they should be. If dogs are working, all the guns, including the shooter, should remain in

[227]

position, only assisting the dogs by helping them with their own marks to pick up the scent. It is fatal to foil the scent by stamping all round on the ground that a dog is working on. Human scent is very strong indeed and overlays almost any other sort of scent. The scent of a game bird is very finely perfumed, and even dogs are bothered to find it if the conditions are unfavorable. If you have got a runner, or several, and the dogs are unable to find them, very often the best practice is to walk the field again. If you are working in the roots, the chances are that you will put out your wounded bird at the end of it. If you have lost a bird and your best efforts cannot find it, remember to use the trick of dropping a handkerchief or a hat and go back, or get somebody else to go back, and look for it afterwards.

How to Shoot Pheasants

THE PHEASANT, with the probable exception of the ubiquitous pigeon, is responsible for a higher annual expenditure of cartridges than any other bird. However poor the season may be for other game birds, there are always pheasants; though, in a wet year, they too may be reduced in numbers.

It used to be thought that, without the protection of keepers and the regular introduction of fresh hand-reared stock, the pheasant couldn't hold his own as a wild bird in British coverts. But, during the Second World War, when sporting estates were necessarily allowed to run wild, when vermin increased, and when food shortages and the high price of game encouraged more ruthless hunting than ever before, it was notable how easily the wild pheasant held his own.

The hens even lived down their reputation of being bad mothers. In places where the hens were spared, the wild stock even increased. Now that hand-rearing, although on a limited scale to what it used to be, has been resumed, the pheasant is now probably the commonest game bird in the countryside. Every shooting man gets a chance to have a pot occasionally, and many enjoy pheasant shooting all through the season, from those pleasant autumn days walking up the outsides in October to the cream of the covert shooting when the leaf falls in November and December, and finally those "cocks-only" days at the end of the season which so often provide the tallest birds and the best shooting of all.

A pheasant is a larger bird than a grouse or a partridge, presents a more obvious target, gives you noisier notice of his approach, and should, in theory, be easier to hit. Yet one so often hears of good grouse or partridge shots who never seem to be at their best at pheasants, even at the beginning of the season or in the first days in the coverts when they are by no means difficult birds to shoot.

It is not always easy to find the exact reason why experienced shooting men, on occasion, miss pheasants; very often the grouse shot who has become accustomed to shooting low, fast, incoming birds, which have to be snapped very quickly, has also become accustomed to taking most of his weight on his left leg. Now, if he snaps in the same fast manner at a rising pheasant as he would at a grouse, he will almost invariably fire far behind. The reason is that his rigid left leg prevents him bending his body easily out of the vertical and slows his whole movement.

The bulk of shots at pheasants are overhead or high-angle shots, and the unconscious habits picked up while taking birds at low altitudes are likely to spoil precision completely when the shooter who has acquired them is dealing with birds which are flying moderately high.

Let's put the theory to the test: Take a gun in your hand and deliberately shift the bulk of your weight on to a rigid left leg. Make a snap at an imaginary overhead bird and follow the swing through for a second barrel. I think you will find that the movement requires a great deal of effort and that, at a certain point, there is often a perceptible check or rebound. Fresh effort has to be summoned up in order to pass what I can best describe as the "sticking point." It is obvious, I think, that in this pose you are not likely to hit fast high birds or even birds of ordinary height. Having carried out the experiment, which may well reveal a personal fault of your own, proceed to adopt the proper position.

Take your gun and hold it in the ready position but narrow a little your natural grouse stand. With your gun in the ready position, the whole weight of your body should be on the right leg, which is stressed but not rigid. This alteration of weight means that, for overhead birds and birds to the right, all the weight is on the right leg. Weight is only transferred to the left leg for shots over the left shoulder.

Now go into the garden and throw your gun at a rook or a pigeon passing over. Follow it with both hands until you have picked up its speed. At that point, your left hand should instinctively begin to mount the gun. As the gun reaches eye level, your right hand tightens grip a little and a swift final movement of both beds the gun to the shoulder and completes the action. You will find that you can carry out the whole of this movement without constraint, with little effort, and yet have freedom to reach overhead birds. In addition, you have all your time to devote to the bird and, as a consequence, you won't be flurried; you'll move smoothly and you won't jerk.

With correct gun-mounting, a miraculous improvement in shooting can be brought about simply by narrowing the position of the feet a little and settling yourself so that the body weight can be adjusted easily to either leg with the minimum of movement. If your stance is too wide and rigid, you will find you cannot transfer weight from one leg to the other without losing poise and dropping a shoulder. This in itself is sufficient to make you miss behind your bird.

It is a fact that, on the vast majority of shoots, really high birds are rare. There may be one or more stands where birds come fairly tall, but they are only relative to the average of the day. If a particular stand shows taller birds than the average during a shooting day, you will often notice that these higher birds are missed by men who have been shooting well and consistently at medium-height birds on the other stands. This is a very common phenomenon. But why?

The answer is that the high, fast pheasant is a very difficult bird to shoot indeed, and most of our ideas about appropriate allowances that we should make for him, when he is on the wing, are fundamentally wrong. But if you clear your mind of misapprehensions, you will soon get the hang of the game and find that shooting tall pheasants is a science that can be mastered.

The following diagram helps to explain some of the reasons why good average shots fail on these tall birds. In the first place, the average pheasant, even though he tops well-grown oak trees, is probably not more than twenty-five yards high, while the vast majority of driven birds are barely twenty yards high. A really high pheasant finds his "ceiling," or extreme shootable range, at a vertical height of forty yards. Good hillside drives

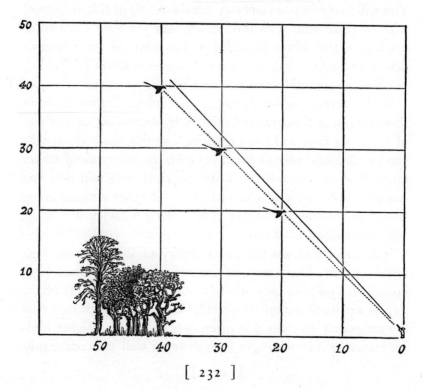

will occasionally produce birds that are really out of range for part, at least, of their journey across the line of guns.

In the diagrams on pages 232 and 234 the squares represent ten yards in each dimension and the line of the angle of vision is taken as 45 degrees. In the case of a bird flying on the twenty-yard height level, it cuts the line of vision about thirty yards from the gun, while the bird on the forty-yard height level comes into view nearly sixty yards away. The low bird has only twenty yards to travel before he is overhead, the high bird has forty yards to cover before he is over the guns. The greater height and distance are deceptive and the higher bird appears to be traveling at half the speed of the lower bird. Distance is easy to misjudge.

In the diagram overleaf, we have both birds (who move at equal speed) nearer the overhead position. The lower bird has only ten yards to go before he is vertically over the guns, but the higher bird has still twice that distance to cover. The type of shot who consciously estimates "forward allowances" now works out his personal equations. The table of allowances gives the approximate allowance for crossing birds at forty miles an hour as thirty-nine inches at twenty yards and ninety-six inches at forty yards. This would suggest that the shooter must make one and a half times as much allowance at forty yards as he does at twenty yards. This he would presumably do by swinging his gun-muzzle say one and a half times as much forward.

In practice, this means that a movement of two inches of the gun-muzzle will make a difference of forty inches at twenty yards and eighty inches at forty yards. In fact, the same relative movement is correct for birds at heights of twenty to thirty-five yards and only the tiniest fraction of extra movement of gun-muzzle will reach the bird at the ceiling limit of forty yards.

I hope I have said enough to demonstrate once again that the "conscious allowance" school can only involve you in endless confusion. Forget it. The reason that really high birds are missed is because guns tend to shoot at them when they are too far off, often not really in range, or because they shoot in front through trying to put into practice this misleading business of doubling the forward allowance.

High birds are never easy to kill owing to the wide spread of the shot and the decline in pellet energy in all but cartridges specially loaded for this type of shooting. In the ordinary way, the cheapest cartridge should kill at twenty yards, but, when it comes to tall birds, the velocity of the shot pellets is about two hundred and fifty feet per second lower than at twenty yards, and both penetration and pellet energy have declined in even greater proportion.

The indifferent cartridge, which may be quite satisfactory at low birds, lacks punch and driving power at tall birds, while, in addition, the bird itself is well protected by its bones and breast muscles. Weak pellets cannot penetrate to vital spots such as the lungs. The wing bones, too, are not easily broken or disabled and the main vital exposed area is the head and neck.

Held by the head and allowed to hang there, a pheasant appears to have a very long neck, almost as long as a duck. But contrast the difference in appearance between a pheasant and a duck in flight. The duck flies with the neck fully extended, offering a very vulnerable target, but the pheasant seems to contract its neck, or curve it, in flight and, as a consequence, the neck itself doesn't attract the eye as a target.

If you look at a real pheasant, not the drawings of pheasant, you will realize how the neck is contracted rather than projected and how very little of the vulnerable part is exposed. On occasion, if the guns are not lined out in an echoing or reverberating valley, you can actually hear the shot patter on a high pheasant and see him glide on undamaged, undisturbed, and giving no indication at all that he has been touched other than a transient flicker or dip that occurs when the sound waves of a discharge that missed him clean, so far as the pellets are concerned, checks his flight in the air.

Nobody knows quite how vulnerable a tall pheasant is to a shot charge. Very, very few birds, even from high stands, are really forty yards high, and of course a drop of five yards means a large increase in the target's vulnerability. The situation is complicated by the fact that, as I said in another chapter, few of us are good judges of height or distance. I have seen celebrated "high" stands where the average tall bird was thirty yards, yet almost everyone who shot there would have said that the birds were "out of range." A few, a very few, "high" stands exist, and they are almost all of them stands where the face of a hillside drops down in a precipitous slope. The birds, driven in over the top of it, run downhill a certain way before being flushed by wire or stops, then rise and fly over the guns below. They rise, as pheasants always rise, to clear the treetops, and this height may be (and, on a few downland shoots, actually is) nearly two hundred yards; six hundred feet above the guns waiting in the valley below. This isn't guesswork; you can check it on any ordnance map over the contour lines.

These particularly tall birds are wholly and incredibly out of shot. They fly down over the treetops and break somewhere below the last two contours over the valley below. They will come over the guns at heights which vary from forty yards to about forty-five yards, for very high birds, and twenty yards for low ones. The opposite side of the narrow downs at the bottom is normally steep woodland cover, and the valleys tend to widen towards the low line. Birds at the top end may be very high, but as the valley lengthens it widens, and the last birds beaten out will probably be considerably lower than those at the narrow end. These birds are all birds which are not rising but flying *down* a steep hillside and they are falling, not rising, shots. Very few are straight over the guns, and most of the birds plane down with fixed wings at a very high speed and with a most baffling twist or turn on it. The angle of descent is rapid and, if we plot it against our simple diagram of the level-flying pheasant and allow it to have movements in the third dimension as well, it is a very difficult shot for the uninitiated.

If the descending bird flies straight towards you, you are lucky. You should treat him exactly as you would treat a low-driven partridge. Mount the gun with the shortest possible movement of the barrels, snapping at the beak of the bird, when he looks big enough to eat, in front of you. The temptation, when you see a pheasant coming at you from a long way away, is to wait too long. If you fluff about with a bird like this, making up your mind *when* to shoot him, you will find that he is flicking his tail at you and is out of range before you can shoot at all. These descending birds coming down hillsides can move as fast as sixty miles an hour. You can swing your gun fast enough to catch them; but it is difficult. The proper moment to shoot your bird is when he is dead in front of you and, momentarily, at what appears to be a standstill. You have only got to move the butt of your gun a few inches from the ready position to your shoulder to kill him.

Once again, let me remind you not to be afraid to miss these fast-moving birds. If you are not afraid to miss, if you bring up your gun sharply and confidently and choose the right moment to fire, you will have the satisfaction of seeing a real screamer crashing down on his beak. The right moment is when the bird is directly in front of you.

But very few of these tall birds that you will meet planing down hillsides fly straight. The difficulty of most of the shots that they present is that they have a sharp curl on them as well. In that event, if you try to snap at them as they come towards you, you will miss on the right or left according to which way the bird is curling. The way to shoot these birds—and if you can shoot them consistently you can call yourself a first-class shot—is not to shoot them in the nose but on the side of the head as they curl past you. Your gun-mounting must be rapid and you must make sure that both hands are onto the bird, and the gun-barrels, too, as you mount. In the process of mounting, if you are mounting correctly with your eye on the bird and your whole body moving with him, you will find yourself bending down either to the right or to the left according to the side he curls away from you. If your gun-mounting is true, and your body moves down with the bird, and you shoot the moment the butt touches your shoulder, you will make a clean kill.

I have told you elsewhere that, when you are shooting at driven pheasants, or indeed in many cases when you are shooting at the ordinary going-away pheasant which has been flushed up from the hedgerow by a dog, you have got time to say slowly: "Come along, my beauty." But I want to emphasize that that sentence recited slowly is only effective in steadying your shooting if you are making a smooth gun-mounting with your body and hands as you say it and providing, too, that, as you speak the last syllable, your shoulder has come forward to meet the gun butt.

I know that's not always an easy thing to do. On our off-days the more we miss the more anxious and nervous we become and the more difficult it is to get a sweet gun-mounting and confident trigger pulling. Nearly every experienced pheasant shot knows that there are some days when he can promise with confidence that he will hit the next bird that comes over, however he comes; and other days when, if his life depended on it, he feels that he hasn't got a chance of touching a feather.

On your off-days, which is what I am principally concerned with in this book, it is quite a good policy to get yourself back into form and to re-educate yourself again not to fluff about with your gun, to sharpen your determination by pretending to yourself that you have lost your temper. Make up your mind that you will kill the next bird that comes over because you hate him more than any other bird in the world. Cough up a few choice words and then swing your gun onto him as if you intended to swipe him out of the sky. Suddenly, after all the careful poking which has made sure that you are always miles behind, you may well find that you are killing clean and killing with confidence.

But suppose that even that advice doesn't bring you the right results. Then it's almost certain that there is something wrong with your gun-mounting or your stance. Let's analyze how a really first-class shot at a first-class tall-pheasant stand sets about it.

The first thing you should notice is that the best pheasant shots take a rather narrow stance. This narrow stance stiffens the body, which is necessary for high birds because it is important to mount the gun in a very accurate line. There must be no sway or sideways wobble. The least unsteadiness carries the barrels to one side or the other of the bird. As I explained to you in the calculations of allowances, half an inch of muzzle movement means an error of fifteen to twenty inches at the business end. With a thirty-inch killing circle we cannot afford the slightest mistake in centering the charge.

Having noticed the stance of a first-class pheasant shot, watch the way he holds his head. First, he holds it high because naturally he wants to keep his head up to see the approaching target. But holding his head high he brings his eye well above the rib of the gun, thus automatically giving all the forward allowance required. Remember that the eye is always on the bird and only subconsciously aware of the gun-barrels. As the shot takes place, bird and barrel come into view together. If the eye is high above the rib, the bird is seen on the barrels before it is really there. But the gun is a fixed affair, firing at the same place. Now, as we know, at forty yards we want slightly more forward allowance as the shot takes longer to travel. The attached diagram shows what happens. The eye being held high over the rib, the allowance is naturally affected.

You may ask how it is that in the case of ordinary pheasants you're on the target at all if this theory is correct. The answer is that a shot at a middle-height oncoming pheasant is fired with confidence, or without conscious calculation, and probably some of the movement is unconsciously quick and exaggerated. The result is that natural overthrow "picks up" a bird we are "optically" behind. With tall birds there is usually lack of confidence and the subconscious chuck or overthrow, used in ordinary snap shooting, is temporarily inhibited.

Just thinking about making the shot slows down the process. There is a lack of rhythmic smoothness in the body swing (which must move in time with the bird) whilst the gun is coming up to make the sudden snap finish on a point of acceleration reached without check. One might describe it as a carefree *ac-*

celerating swing. As the bird comes nearer, the arc shortens and the apparent movement in time is swifter, even though the bird is really proceeding at a uniform velocity.

In a word, with high birds the stance has to be narrow and the shot must be taken at a point where the body can still move freely without check. The gun must come home to the shoulder and the shot fired before the spine and muscles begin to offer resistant stresses to the upward swing.

Try a little more dry practice on any suitable target in the open. Take a narrow stance and, with your gun at the ready position, squeeze the stock tightly between your elbow and your side, holding it firmly so that the inclination to begin gun-mounting with your arms before your body has begun to move is mechanically repressed. As your eyes are on the bird, you can, with your gun so held, point the gun at the bird whilst the stock is still under your arm. In fact, if your gun-mounting is correct, you should be on the bird from the moment the barrels start moving and your eye fixes on it.

In the shooting school we are often able to demonstrate this fact to pupils

THE

THEORY OF AUTOMATIC

ALLOWANCE

The shooter's eye sees the bird, but the angle of the barrels of the gun is in front of the target at the moment when bird and barrels come into view together. Thus, if the head is held correctly, the necessary forward allowance for a moving target is automatically provided for.

in actual practice. When a pupil is raising his gun to his shoulder and missing, because he is dwelling too long on his trigger pull (believing that he needs time to get the barrels of the gun onto the target), we instruct him to pull the trigger on the word of command. As soon as a clay pigeon comes over, and before the gun is on the pupil's shoulder, we order him to fire. In the end, he cottons onto the idea and does what he is told. With his gun in the half-mounted position, he finds, again and again, that he is shattering the clay. The lesson that that teaches is that if your eye is on the bird and you are mounting correctly, you haven't got to worry about anything at all. All you have to do is to remember, when you are shooting, that the gun that fits you is always "on." There is no necessity for effort or a duel between arms and body to make sure of it.

Once again:

Don't mount the gun first and swing second. Grip tightly with the left or forward hand, relax the right till the final snap to the shoulder.

Don't look at the gun. If you see the barrels, you have missed.

Don't look ahead of the bird or you will stop your gun swing. Shoot at it and don't shoot anywhere else.

I find that even experienced shooting men have the most misleading ideas of the spread and punch of the shot from a game-gun. In pheasant shooting especially it is important that everybody who hopes to kill his birds cleanly and well should appreciate the true state of affairs.

The spread of a normal game-gun is approximately an inch to a yard (e.g., forty inches at forty yards), the number of effective pellets likely to penetrate a pheasant are remarkably few. Sir Ralph Payne Gallway in his book *High Pheasants in Theory and Practice* didn't enjoy the modern convenience of a quarter of a century's improvement in pellets and cartridges. But he tells of an interesting experiment. Twenty dead cock pheasants were hoisted by kite to a forty yards overhead position and twenty rounds were fired at each bird. No less than four hundred rounds were fired and 115 thousand pellets expended, yet, on post mortem, the number of potentially fatal wounds on this score of birds was so low as to be calculable on the fingers of both hands. It is an instructive example. But, perhaps because Sir Ralph Payne Gallway hadn't my experience of the behavior of bullets in police work, a misleading one.

In fact, the resistance of dead flesh is several times greater than living flesh, and the computation of what is a mortal wound and what effect is due to temporarily disabling shot is a problem which gives rise to a good deal of theory, but not one on which any really scientific explanations are yet available.

But that's a side issue for the expert. If you are a good shot, familiar with your ground, you can shoot high pheasants as easily as the ordinary shot shoots the average bird, whatever the cause of their demise. There is no wizardry about it, it is a reasonably easy trick when you get it, and there is really no excuse for a man who goes into a high pheasant shoot continuing to fluff his birds.

With proper cartridges, and proper coaching, any shooting man should bring down anything in range. The eclectic, who desires high birds and high birds only, is not, as he would have us believe, the finest shot and the finest sportsman. He is an addict of the freak shot and, having learned his freak shooting, may put up a poor performance on lower birds. A snap shot, put up by a gun walking back with the beaters, may be a far better effort than the shooting of the tallest bird over the stand.

CHAPTER VII

How to Shoot Ground Game

W HEN a young sportsman is allowed to handle a gun in the field for the first time, it is almost certain that he will be given his chance in the type of shooting with the greatest danger factor of all. The ground shot at rabbits and hares is one in which even the most experienced shot of flying game is tempted to take chances. I don't know what it is about a bolting rabbit, or a hare at full stretch, that contrives to unbalance the judgment of otherwise safe shots; but the temptation to follow through to a dangerous angle and to let fly into a hedge without calculating where the shot charge will finish needs checking with the greatest firmness.

Without exception, the form of shooting with the greatest potential danger is when two or three men stand on opposite sides of a hedge waiting for ferrets to bolt rabbits. The most dangerous form of organized shooting is one of these battues at the end of the season when the farmers turn out to drive the hares.

Any shot made with the barrels of the gun pointing in the air is unlikely to kill anybody; although I think I have said enough to emphasize that an air-shot can be dangerous enough. But the moment a game-gun is leveled to the ground, the accident risk is doubled or even trebled. The charge can be placed squarely where it is intended. But a flint on the ground, or the trunk of a tree, can turn the shot in half a dozen directions. There are plenty of cases in which the shooter has killed the rabbit or hare he shot at; but the deflected remainder of the charge has caused serious accident.

In any shoot in which rabbits and hares are shot, with winged game as part of the drive, it is always dangerous to shoot in front unless the topography of the ground ensures that there is no possibility of a ricochet reaching the beaters. The best rule is never to shoot ground game during a drive except behind, when the hare or the rabbit has passed the line of guns. And remember not to mount your gun until you have made a complete round-about turn. To pick up the rabbit or the hare in front and follow through is not only abominably bad style (for you'll probably miss), but you needn't be surprised if the next gun in the line is wise enough to throw himself flat on his face as you do it.

Always beware of that tempting shot in roots, when the beaters are closing-in and the rabbits and hares are playing hide-and-seek in front of you. If you will only stand quiet, most of them will come through and you can take them behind. If you miss a chance you can still have the satisfaction of knowing that you didn't take a chance.

Beware of the rabbit that sneaks under the hedge in front of you. You can never be sure what is behind.

Beware of the rabbit, or the hare, that lollops towards you in a covert. Beaters, however often the keeper shouts at them, have a habit of breaking line. When they spot ground game, they are liable to be as irresponsible as you are and to charge forward through the undergrowth in the hope of knocking a rabbit on the head with a stick.

It is no case for you in civil law that the beater you wounded had no business to be where he was. Always assume, at a rabbit shoot or a hare drive, that the other man is liable to lose his head and act accordingly. Don't lose yours.

Far better to be one of those shots who complains that he can't hit ground game than make a reputation for hitting anything that moves.

Never go ferreting except with men whose judgment with a gun you can completely trust. Look out on back-end days when the farmers shoot up the hares. Even when you are alone, walking the hedgerows with a dog for rabbits, plodding through the plough in search of a hare for the pot, make up your mind that you are not alone and that the countryside isn't deserted. It is surprising the places that lovers select for their intimacies or that children get into when they are up to mischief.

On the whole, I think it is true that most shooting men enjoy good rabbit shooting and detest shooting hares. Rabbits, in ideal conditions and in safe company, can provide magnificent sport. It is only once in a while that a hare presents a shot which is really worth taking.

Theoretically, hares are usually so easy that a reasonable shot should never miss. In practice, hares are missed—and worse than that, wounded—again and again because (1) the shooter misjudges distance by underrating the size of the quarry, (2) the shot is made at an angle when it is difficult to make an immediately mortal wound.

A leveret, or a full-grown hare in poor condition, weighs nearly twice as much as a rabbit. A big hare can scale from eight to ten pounds, and hares are shot which are very much heavier.

In advising you on grouse shooting, I have told you to choose the moment to shoot when the bird looks big enough to eat. In advising you on shooting hares, I must warn you that hares, well beyond extreme ranges, still look big enough to eat. The moment to shoot, and not before, is when you can see the hare's big eyes.

When you are hare shooting, you must adopt a completely different attitude of mind to your attitude when you are shooting winged game in the coverts. As I told you, in the coverts you can generally assume that every partridge or pheasant that comes over your gun is likely to be in fair range and usually at much closer range than you would possibly believe. In hare shooting, the proper attitude is to convince yourself that the hare is normally out of range until you can pretty well see the whites of her eyes. I want to emphasize that because, as I said earlier, most hare shooting is easy shooting. Once in a while, when a hare is extended at full pace in front of you, you can pull off a shot at forty yards. Fully extended, the vulnerability of the hare is increased considerably. But, normally speaking, you won't get a shot at a hare at full gallop. The shot you will normally get is when a hare comes lolloping towards you, twenty yards at a time, stopping to sit up and look cautiously around her or to crouch down on the ground with ears laid back. Unless you choose to deal with the unpleasant business of wounding her and hearing her screaming on the ground, hold your fire until she is nearly on top of you.

The way to take the shot at a slowly-advancing hare—the advance will usually be slow—is to shoot the ground from underneath her. The technique is to aim the gun at what amounts to a sitting shot so that the charge blows up like a landmine underneath the target. In that way, you will make a clean kill. If you aim at the head, you will probably do no more than wound the hare in the rump.

Anyhow, if it is a drive, you will do far better to wait until the hare races past you and, on seeing you, increases pace. Under those conditions, you will get a reasonably sporting shot and you stand a very good chance of making a clean kill. The great secret of shooting running hares, as indeed it is the secret of shooting at all game, is not to look at the whole target but to select a part of it. If you try and take in the whole carcass of the hare, the chances are that you will wound her in the hind quarters. If you make up your mind that what you are shooting at is her ears, you'll make a clean kill in the head. The people who have the knack of shooting hares—the shooting of all sorts of game is a knack of one kind or another—are never deceived by the size of the animal. Consciously or unconsciously, they are pointing their gun-muzzles whilst gun-mounting and kill the hare in that clean fashion which makes her turn head-over-heels as she is hit.

But although a great many hares are shot during drives for pheasants and partridges, I suppose the greater number are still killed walking up and in those sometimes dangerous organized hare drives in which fifty, or perhaps a hundred, guns push the game from different directions towards a central point. From an agricultural point of view, the destruction of hares at the end of the season is very necessary, especially in downland country. If you take part in one of those shoots, in which most of the chances you get will be hares breaking from their forms under your feet, remember that by the time the other wing of the party is driving towards you the game will be as dangerous for you as for the hares. The secret of safe and accurate shooting is not to try to kill everything.

Walking up, you may carry your gun in the ready position. When a hare breaks from her form under your feet, come to a halt with feet together. Then, drawing the right foot backwards, mount your gun as if you were taking a normal snap shot at going-away partridges—the easiest shot of all. But, as you fix your eye on the hare moving away in front of you, you will find that your natural inclination is to look at her hind quarters, which is the part of her that you yourself see the largest. You must make a deliberate effort to train yourself to look not at the hind quarters, which are the least vulnerable part of a hare, but between her ears. From the moment that you can train yourself to plant a charge between the hare's ears, rather than at her rump, you will kill clean again and again.

It is important to emphasize that it is possible to make a mortal shot at a hare only to find that she shows no apparent sign of being hit at all. If you see flecks of down fly off her you can

[247]

reasonably assume that you've hit her. If she jinks, there's a strong possibility that she is seriously wounded.

In hare shooting, you have a special responsibility to keep your eye on the quarry you have shot at until she is quite out of sight. If you notice that, after a hare has been shot at, she runs about a hundred yards or so, then stops, then goes on again for a short distance and so on, you can be reasonably certain that she will be a dead hare before she reaches the next field. A hare that is untouched will travel at an even pace until she is completely out of view.

So these are the rules:

1. Don't shoot at a hare at all until you can see the animal's eyes.
2. Don't shoot even at forty yards, except to take a crossing shot when a hare's body is fully extended. In those conditions you will probably make a clean kill or miss altogether.
3. If you are in a stand, or you find yourself in circumstances where the hare is lolloping towards you, resist the inclination, if you can, to shoot her in front when she is crouching. If you must shoot under those conditions, aim the gun so that the charge is placed to lift her off the ground rather than at the animal herself. Alternatively, wait if you can until the hare sights you. You will then get a reasonable crossing shot or, if the beaters are moving up behind her, a going-away shot in which you can kill her under reasonably sporting conditions.
4. If a hare gets up under your feet and is going away from you, resist the natural inclination to fix the eye on the largest part of her, which is her rump. Train yourself to shoot her between the ears. She will give you plenty of time.
5. Above all, remember that a hare is the biggest animal in the shooting field. Just as you will generally over-estimate the range of pheasants or partridges, you will generally under-estimate the range of a hare. If you want to have the reputation for being a clean shot, don't raise your gun to a hare at all until you are sure that you can make a clean kill.

A rabbit is a far more vulnerable target than a hare. Normally speaking, if you center a gun on him at all, you will be unlucky if he manages to make his escape. Rabbit shooting also demands a higher standard of shooting altogether.

True, in certain circumstances (curiously enough, they are usually the conditions in which rabbit shooting is rather dangerous) killing them can be easy. But rabbit shooting at its best, in rough grass where the rabbits have been tainted out of their burrows, or in the coverts where, by clever beating, they can be driven forward across a narrow ride to a line of guns, is often comparable to the best sport that partridges or pheasants or grouse can provide.

The type of shooting that is most likely to defeat you is that best of shooting when you are standing on a corner covering a narrow ride in a covert with thick undergrowth on either side. This calls for snap shooting of the very highest quality. The rabbits are normally running in front of the beaters, so the gun knows from which side to expect them and the directions in which they will run.

It is hopeless, in these conditions, holding your gun pointing at one side of the ride or the other, as there is no body swing or carry through.

When you are expecting rabbits in a drive, your first move must be to keep as close into the hedge on their side as possible, so that, as far as possible, the advancing rabbits can't see you. So many rabbits run back, or accelerate, when they see a shooter rushing his gun to his shoulder. The expert rabbit shot stands still and keeps completely quiet, hides himself as much as he can, and remains in a constant state of alert. In that way he gets the greater proportion of easy shots, the rabbits are not alarmed and cross the ride at a normal pace; often at less than normal pace.

What the bad shot does is to stand in the middle of the ride jerking his gun at every noise, with his head moving all the time as he searches the covert. Suddenly a rabbit dashes across twenty yards ahead. The unwise shot half-raises his gun, lowers it, looks regretfully at the spot where the rabbit crossed, and then curses because another rabbit dashes across the ten-yard mark. He makes a hasty snatch and, of course, his charge is placed yards behind.

The secret of shooting rabbits, when they are likely to pop out at any point around you, is to take a firm stand, keep still, and remain in position. The good shot does not shift his head about. He stands there relaxed, with his gun at the ready. His gaze is straight along the ride, or in the gap, where he expects to get the chance of a shot. His eyes are not focused on anything in particular. He is ready to snap at ten, twenty, or thirty yards.

In normal shooting, I estimate the average distance at which rabbits are killed is about twelve yards. Pace out the next ten rabbits you shoot and discover if I am wrong. I suggest that 95 per cent of all rabbits shot are killed at twenty yards range and under. A long shot at a wide-crossing rabbit that pleases you very much may look like forty yards but, if you pace it out, you will find that it is usually rather less than thirty.

If you miss a rabbit, you can usually assume that you have missed high and behind. High because your hands were in the wrong place and the weight of your legs was out of correct balance, behind because you faulted in concentration and gun-mounting.

In ground-game shooting, the gun is held in the ready position with the barrels pointing directly in front of you. But you should adopt the ready position with this difference: YOU SHOULD SHORTEN YOUR REACH BY DRAWING BACK YOUR LEFT HAND AT LEAST ONE INCH FROM THE NORMAL POSITION WHICH YOU ADOPT FOR WINGED GAME.

At the moment of gun-mounting, you should move the weight of your body forward on the left foot. Indeed, your whole frame should move perceptibly forwards and downwards as you drop the barrel of the gun onto the target.

Try it in dry practice. Shorten your left-hand grip so that you can most comfortably and quickly drop the barrels of the gun for a ground shot. Then lean forward with the weight on the left foot so that your whole body moves sweetly onto the target below you. If you can acquire this movement, so that you adopt it instinctively for ground game, you will pull off snap shots at rabbits, with time to spare, which will surprise you as much as the lookers-on.

If you still miss, you can assume that you are making the familiar error of thinking about where the gun is pointing and not where the rabbit is going. Concentrate not on the whole rabbit but on a part of it; preferably, for a crossing shot, his front legs. *Don't* hold on to the trigger and *don't* make forward allowances which, while you are thinking about them, will ensure you shoot behind. Let the natural overthrow of the gun do its work.

Curiously enough, you will often discover that guns who are completely experienced in shooting winged game will have their eyes wiped by keepers or farmers who probably couldn't hit a crow unless they caught it napping on a tree. The reason is simple. If you adopt the same stance and grip that you are accustomed to for winged game, your shot charge will go over and in the stern of a rabbit or a hare. The farmer, or the keeper, who is accustomed to shooting ground game and has got into the habit of holding his gun a little short and leaning forward on the left foot to make the ground shot, makes a kill every time. Because they tend to hold their guns short and to crouch rather than to make a natural upward swing of the whole body to a bird passing over, many good vermin destroyers make a poor show when they are given the opportunity of showing their mettle against driven game. Everything in game shooting is a matter of knowing how to deal with different targets in different conditions.

CHAPTER VIII

How to Shoot Wildfowl

How NOT to shoot wildfowl might be a more suitable title for this chapter. There is a tendency in the many excellent text-books on wild-fowling practice to put almost too much emphasis, if that were possible, on the necessity for personal camouflage; on ways of building blinds and digging-in, and the choice of clothes to face the rigors of the hardiest sport with a gun that a man can choose.

But the dawn excursions and evening attacks, the waiting hours in freezing weather, the muddy discomfort will be all to no purpose—however tough the gunner and however effectively he sinks himself into the background of the mud flats and the marshes—if, when he hears at last the whistle of pinions and gets a fair chance at a duck, he fails to make a successful shot.

Gunners miss: (1) Because they tend to over-gun themselves with weapons which are too heavy or too long in the barrel for the job; (2) Because they often conceal themselves so efficiently that, when the unforgiving moment comes, they haven't allowed room for themselves to swing a gun with comfort; (3) Because they completely misjudge distance.

Let's take the last first. I have emphasized that, in driven-game shooting, the tallest and widest birds are seldom out of range of the guns in the line. In upland shooting, the only variety of game which is consistently and regrettably shot-at at outside ranges is the hare. The reason that inexperienced sportsmen shoot at hares at sixty yards and more is because they unconsciously assume that because a hare looks as big as a rabbit at extreme ranges, it's shootable.

Wild-fowlers consistently shoot duck, geese, and other fowl at wild ranges because:

1. They get trigger happy after a long wait.
2. The absence of landmarks in typical wild-fowling areas makes every object that appears seem nearer than it actually is.
3. The variation in the size of different species of fowl is such that a Brent goose crossing at one hundred yards looks as big as a mallard at twenty yards; and a mallard at sixty yards looks as big as a teal at twenty yards.
4. On the morning and evening flights the ducks move most freely in the deceptive half-light between daylight and darkness.

The cure for the wild-fowler who continually commits the crime of pricking birds at extreme ranges—and, incidentally, pushing them well up and out of range of any other gunner who happens to be on the marshes—is to give up shooting until he can identify pretty well any species of fowl by silhouette and characteristic flight. It is unforgivable to go flighting without that ornithological wisdom. The best wild-fowlers are always first-class naturalists.

To be a first-class shot at wildfowl calls for many qualities besides sheer gunmanship; for that reason alone, wild-fowling has an appeal which, when it gets a man, usually grips him like a fever. The successful wild-fowler must be ornithologist, astronomer, meteorologist, commando, and longshoreman, too.

But what I am concerned about is what is called in another place "the end product." Assuming that you do everything else right—that you choose the right creek on the right morning; that you establish a good blind; and that you have that mixture of good luck and good judgment which puts you on the flight line the ducks are using—you must still shoot straight.

[253]

To what extent is the drill given in this book going to help you in successful shooting at wildfowl? What modifications are necessary?

Let it be said at once that whether you are lying on your face or on your back, whether you are crouched in a hole in the ground or down at the bottom of a creek, you will miss if your gun-mounting is at fault. But it is evident that, in the conditions in which wild-fowling is usually carried out, you won't be in a position to give attention to pieces of finesse like footwork and body movement. WHAT YOU MUST DO, IN EFFECT, IS TO LEARN TO SWING YOUR GUN WITH YOUR HANDS AND SHOULDERS ALONE.

You won't do that unless you are the complete master of gun-handling and gun-mounting in the natural standing position, when all the conditions are in your favor. In other words, even though you may find yourself crouched against a sea wall, you must still mentally think of yourself as if you were handling your gun in the most comfortable and natural position. Your body, from the waist upwards, must still move with the bird and you must be more careful than ever, in a cramped position, to check that you are not bringing your cheek to your gun but bringing the gun to your cheek. Head movement is the besetting sin of wild-fowlers who have had to wait a very long time for the chance of a shot.

To check on your personal style I recommend you to assume the sort of position with gun in your hand in front of a mirror that you will probably have to assume in a blind when you are after wildfowl. Pick a point on the ceiling well over your head and try swinging your body as smoothly as you can from the waist at the same time mounting the gun until you come onto your target.

As you practice, watch your head. If your head is coming down to the gun or going back too far, as it often does in wild-fowling, you have discovered the reason why you are missing. If you feel that you are not following your bird with your chest, in the same way that you should feel you are following your bird with your whole body when you can assume a natural stance, you can be sure that, on the marshes, you will be missing behind. Notice, as you squat in a cramped position in front of the mirror, how important it is that when your legs are immovable, you should have complete freedom of your arms.

Remember that point when you make a blind. No matter how cleverly you fool the fowl, you are wasting your time unless you settle yourself in a position where you have got this freedom of arm and chest movement which is so important. It is possible in a completely restricted position to make a going-away snap shot, but very few shots at wildfowl are going-away snap shots. Most of them are crossing shots and straight-on shots and in most cases the birds are moving fast. Always try to shoot at the beak and trust your eye to make the necessary overthrow.

The greatest problem of the wild-fowler, whose game is often scarce and, on so many morning or evening flights, not even existent at all, is that, when he gets a chance, he commits all the crimes of over-anxiety. If you try and make too sure of your bird, you will inevitably hang on the trigger and start poking the gun about making wild and incalculable "forward allowances." Your gun must sweep the sky onto your bird in the same way, and at the same pace, that the birds sweep over you. I am only too well aware that it isn't easy; but that's what you've got to do.

Apart from the necessity of making sure that your blind is not only a good blind, but that you yourself are established in a position in which you can swing your arms with comfort, the consideration of the clothes you wear is of major importance. Too many wild-fowlers dress exclusively for the weather. You must take care to put on only enough sweaters, coats, and scarves to keep warm. If you put on too much, you will inevitably sacrifice the freedom in your arms and pad out your shoulder to such an extent that, even a gun which fits you in normal conditions, may be as much as half an inch too long in the stock. Wear loose-

[255]

fitting clothes for preference, rather than clothes that hug onto your body like thick wool sweaters and heavy tweeds. The secret of keeping warm and still remaining active which the bomber pilots used in the war should be noted by everyone: wear thin silk next to the skin and a layer of wool on top of that. It is surprising how the combination of the two will keep your body warm and your muscles active while, at the same time, giving you plenty of freedom to swing your gun. Alternatively, if you must pad yourself out against the weather, it would be better, when you are wild-fowling, to use a shorter stocked gun than you normally use on the inland shooting field.

Traditionally, wild-fowlers have a tendency to use the heaviest caliber guns they can carry. In the old days, anything less than an 8- or a 10-bore would have been called a toothpick and, even in these days, I am surprised by the number of wild-fowlers who still prefer to go out shooting with old heavy 12s and antique weapons of various kinds which must reduce the performance of even the best shot considerably.

No gun that you take out can possibly be ideal for all purposes. A modern 10-bore probably has a range of at least ten yards better than the 12, and they can be built as light today as the heavy 12-bores of yesterday. But very few men can afford to have a battery of guns for all sorts of purposes. In most cases the wild-fowler wants a gun which will serve him reasonably well, and in all sorts of conditions, from the beginning of the season to the end and from the stubbles to the widgeon grass. From every point of view I believe that the best 12-bore you can afford, even with normal loads, is in the long run likely to be just as efficient as the most arm-breaking 8- or 10-bore cannon such as our forebears favored in the past.

The reason is simple. Ease of handling, in the difficult conditions in which wild-fowlers have to shoot, is far more important than the capacity of the gun to push a charge a few yards farther or throw up a pattern with a few more shots. More that that, I believe you will get twice as many shots with a 12-bore as you will with an 8-bore because, with the latter gun, so many chances are missed through slow gun-mounting. Further, I would recommend you to use a gun with short barrels. The increase of the speed that it will give you in your gun-mounting will make yards of difference to the range at which you are usually able to take your bird. Nevertheless, the powerful charge, and the longest possible range and the greatest penetration, does seem to have an effect on the morale of the average wild-fowler.

The man who cannot afford a battery of guns and to whom the cost of cartridges is a serious consideration should try to own a long-chambered 12. It is handier than the heavier guns and, although there is a slight loss of range, you have still got a powerful charge; in addition, you can get onto your bird more quickly and in a long day you won't find it so tiring carrying it.

Remember that, with ordinary game-guns and ordinary game-cartridges, birds can be killed up to sixty yards. Wildfowl in winter plumage need a greater penetration of shot than inland game birds, but you can overcome this very largely by increasing the size of shot. If you get yourself a long-cased 12-bore firing two-and-three-quarter inch or three-inch cartridges I don't think you will ever regret it. Besides being an excellent all-purpose wildfowl gun, it is also a valuable gun for shooting high pheasants and big hares. Bored right half choke and left full choke, short cases *can* be used provided care is taken to clean the chambers as well as the barrels at the end of the day.

Whatever gun you take out on the marshes, remember that the action of the sea air is such that you must take far more care of it than is necessary if you are only using a gun for inland shooting. Personally, when I am flighting, I wipe the whole of the actions over with oil before going out. Other wild-fowlers even go so far as to have their barrels painted, partly as an extra protection from the action of the salt, but also to reduce the glint of the barrels which might turn the duck; although, in practice, by the time the duck sees the barrels of your gun coming up, he ought to be dead. Every wild-fowler should be even more particular than most shooting men to see that his gun is completely overhauled by a competent gunsmith at the end of each season.

To sum up:

(1) CAMOUFLAGE. In your anxiety to camouflage yourself so that the duck can't see you, don't restrict your movements to such an extent that you have very little chance of bringing your gun to bear in time on a fast-flying duck at all.

(2) CLOTHES. Don't muffle yourself up to such an extent that you restrict the freedom of your arms or pad out your shoulder so that you artificially make the stock of a well-fitting gun too long for you. Either have the stock shortened or, better, wear silk against the skin and only thin wool or cloth on top of that.

(3) GUN-MOUNTING. In dry practice learn to swing your gun from the waist, keep your head still, and sweep your birds out of the sky.

(4) DISTANCES. Generally speaking, wildfowl tend to look bigger and seem nearer than they really are. Don't make yourself a reputation as a man who pricks his birds. You must learn the hard way to gauge the relative ranges of game which, in a morning's shooting, may range from a jack snipe to a wild goose.

(5) THE GUN. Although you may be tempted to carry as heavy and powerful a gun as you can, remember that you need to be a very strong man indeed to carry a caliber as large as 8-bore. In most cases you will do much better with a 12-bore with short barrels, preferably chambered for magnum cartridges. What you lose in range you will gain from the fact that you will bring up your gun quicker; you will get onto your bird when he is ten yards nearer; you won't tire so easily; and, if you have got a long drag home when half a pound can make a difference, a light gun will be on your side.

(6) CARE OF GUNS. A wild-fowler should bestow far more care on his weapon than a man who only engages in inland shooting. The action of the salt can do terrible damage in an incredibly short length of time. Wipe your gun with Rangoon oil when you go out and, when you come home, clean it in every corner patiently and thoroughly. In addition, always remember that one of the many hazards of wild-fowling is the hazard to the gun itself. Setting out before dawn, fumbling with cartridges in the half light, you may well get careless. Whatever you do, never load your gun without holding up the barrels to what light there is and making sure that you haven't scooped up a lump of mud or got some other obstruction into the tubes. Indeed, whenever you are shooting, it's a good habit to adopt the mannerism of many experienced shots who, before they load their gun, will peep quickly up the barrels and give a sharp blow. The blowing through the tubes is, of course, quite unnecessary; but, somehow, the habit comes easily and it is an extra guarantee that you are keeping your eye on what you are up to.

In certain conditions, you may have the opportunity to shoot duck from a punt or on marshes where the sport so closely resembles normal driven game shooting that it is unnecessary to give different advice to that I have given for shooting pheasants, partridges, and grouse. All it is necessary to say is that, if you have the good fortune to attend one of those magnificent shoots where the duck come as thick as pheasants out of the coverts at Holkham, it is of the greatest importance that you don't start shooting except at a prearranged signal by the host or the keeper. Nothing will make you more unpopular on an organized duck shoot than if you start blinding off at tall birds when the first few wisps of them come over. Duck can very easily rise out of range. The moment to begin shooting is when the guns are in position and the duck are coming over at heights when they present reasonable shooting for the whole party.

When duck are plentiful, the golden rule is to resist with iron will the temptation to open fire at the very high overhead birds you sight first; even if you calculate that they are within killable range. If you do that, the duck that follow will swing skywards and fly still higher; probably out of range altogether. The shooter's reward for resisting a fancy shot at the start of the morning flight is that the duck that follow will all come down to normal range and, if they really want to come in, will give you good shooting over a long period.

Shooting from a boat has problems of its own. Some men prefer to shoot sitting down. But, if you can stand steadily in a rocking boat without falling over, you are more likely to shoot better that way than otherwise. It's all a matter of personal taste. The best position for you is the one in which you feel you can shoot most comfortably against the rock of the boat. In specialized shooting of this kind, it is always well to remember that it is certain that there will be local rules as to the time to shoot, the technique of picking up, and the exchange of signals, usually by whistles, between guns. Make sure, if you have the good fortune to be invited as a guest to a shoot of this kind, to learn precisely what the local rules are.

Shooting as I do in various parts of the world, I am never ashamed not only to speak to my host privately, but to get him to explain to all the guns present exactly how the shooting will be conducted. Sometimes guns are too shy to admit that they don't know the form. Sometimes hosts are too polite to say in advance what the form is. You will be popular with everybody if you see to it that the position is crystal clear.

CHAPTER IX

Various

"VARIOUS" can include an odd partridge in the bag at a covert shoot or, as I once remember, an odd pheasant when we were reducing the population of moor hens in an East Anglian duck decoy. But, generally speaking, "various" means the odd and interesting additions to the main bag, such as woodcock and snipe, wood pigeons, jays, gray squirrels, and other vermin.

Some shoots make a practice of having a small forfeit from each gun for every head of vermin that is shot; the spoils to be proportionately divided among the guns who killed them. It's good fun if you are in company where the guns can be trusted not to take chances in their anxiety not to miss the chance at a jay, a magpie, or a gray squirrel leaping across the tree branches. It can be very dangerous if guns get over-excited, crouching down, as I have so often seen them, to snap at a jay switchbacking with its rising and falling flight just over the heads of the beaters. Better to lose two bits and let the next man take the risky chance.

Never forget the story told of the head keeper who, on celebrating his hundredth birthday, was interviewed by the press. Asked to what he attributed his great age, he replied that it was because he had never failed to throw himself flat on his face at the cry of "woodcock." I hope that that anecdote sticks in your mind as a reminder that, at the call of "cock" from the beaters, the vital thing is to keep your head. It's a great pity that wood-cock have a false reputation that they are difficult to shoot and, further, that they carry those pin feathers which shooting men are so anxious to put up in the ribbon of their hats.

Woodcock have a slow and easy flight and when they give a chance of a shot, it is usually at close range. But they tend to fly low and to weave their way through woodland where every branch can deflect a shot charge. In their anxiety to bag one, shooting men constantly forget every basic rule they have learned. They shoot on sight and they snap without considera-tion. I don't think it would be an exaggeration to say that some-body takes a chance nearly every time a woodcock flits down the line.

Let the other man have the cock if he must. If he misses, you yourself can have the satisfaction of wiping his eye after giving yourself time to make sure that you take the bird in a safe arc of fire. The crossing shot is the one to watch; that's the dangerous one. The bird that flies straight over can, and should be, snapped like a partridge in front.

Don't hustle. There is no need. I repeat that woodcock are slow fliers, and in woodland, when they zigzag between the gaps in the trees, the gaps are usually even helpful in concentrating your eyes on the bird. Notice how often you will make a clean kill at a pheasant hustled up by a spaniel in thick woodland when there is only one narrow area of sky in which you get a good sight of him. In fact, the cloaking of trees has the effect of forcing you to concentrate on looking at the bird. And if you look at the bird, and only the bird, you'll always be on him with your gun-barrels.

Snipe are far more difficult to shoot than woodcock; but there's a knack to snipe shooting, too. When a wisp of snipe blows off a marsh in the wind, you *must* be quick. Your gun should be at the ready position whenever you expect snipe, and you should shoot at the moment when the bird turns in the air after its initial spring from the ground to show you the white of its rump. It's the same moment that the snipe drops a spot of lime as it throws over to settle into its characteristic zigzag flight. If you wait until the bird settles on its course, you will be just plumb lucky if you make a kill. To be certain, you must catch it when it hangs momentarily in the air between the lift from the ground and the going-away flight.

Experienced snipe shots count it so important to kill their bird at the psychological moment that many of them will shoot before their gun is properly settled to the shoulder. I don't recommend the practice (nor do I think it necessary), but it emphasizes the necessity of shooting at snipe at the right time rather than at the moment when you yourself have had time to get ready for it. When you are snipe shooting you must be on your toes. Within a fraction of a second of the bird breaking out of the marsh, with its characteristic scauping call, your gunstock should be on its way to your shoulder.

Finally, you will always make incalculable misses at snipe if you shoot with shot larger than number seven. Number eight is preferable if you are out on a day when you are concentrating on shooting snipe and snipe only. But number seven is the minimum if you want consistent results. The pattern thrown by number five or number six, if it is the slightest degree off center, has gaps in it which are well within the bulk of the target.

Throughout this book I have deliberately refrained from discussing naturalist's lore and the artifices of getting up to game which are the essential corollaries of good shooting. Unless you are something of a naturalist, unless you know how to find game and get within range of it, half of the sport will be lost and, apart from driven game, you will only get in range of half the potential targets. But that can be learned and it has already been widely discussed in many admirable textbooks. I am concerned with helping you to shoot straight.

For that reason I am assuming that, if you go out after pigeons, you will know how to pick a flight line, how to build a blind, how to set up decoys, and how to pick the crops that the "woodies" are likely to be feeding on at different seasons. The shooter who doesn't study the habits of pigeons had just as well not go out after them at all. And shooters who haven't learned how to get among them usually reveal it by declaring that pigeon shooting doesn't provide first-class sport.

If you know how to set about it, pigeon shooting, which anybody with a box of cartridges and the confidence of a friendly farmer can enjoy, offers one of the finest sports with a gun a man can have. More than that, if you are a good pigeon shot, and that also implies that you know how to get among them and to judge the proper moment to shoot them when they are coming in to feed or roost, you can shoot anything that flies.

Not long ago, when one of the British Government Research Stations wanted wood pigeons to make post-mortems with a view to finding out whether they were in any way responsible for carrying disease, I remember they offered three cartridges for every bird brought in. In my view any man who can kill on an average of one wood pigeon to three cartridges must be a first-class shot.

Wood pigeons have the reputation of requiring a heavy charge of shot to kill them. That's not strictly true. What is true is that pigeons have such a loose plumage that they bulk twice as big as they are. When you shoot at them, and they leave a puff of feathers behind them, you may think to yourself as they carry on, what a lot of punishment they can take. The probability is that you haven't touched them.

Pigeon feathers are so loosely attached that a soft-mouthed gun dog will collect an inconvenient bunch of them all round his jaws and tongue just from carrying a dead pigeon twenty yards or so. For that reason many dogs are reluctant to retrieve pigeons at all. For that reason, when a few feathers fly on charge, shooters get the notion that the birds they are shooting at are hard hit and are surprised when they carry on.

If you hit the breast of a pigeon, or break a wing, he will come down quick enough. But remember that he is half the size you think he is and you must shoot twice as accurately.

If you can put up a good performance with pigeons, you can take it from me that you can put up a good performance at every game bird that flies. From a blind among the wheatsheafs, from the stand on the edge of a covert when the birds are coming into roost, you will get every sort of shot you are ever likely to meet in the shooting field. Indeed, with pigeons you will be lucky if you get a straight advancing bird. They nearly all have a curl on them. They can gain height quicker than any of the game birds and, on the wing, their aerobatics are quick enough to defeat a hawk. If you make the slightest mistake in gun-mounting, if the alignment of your gun is to the slightest degree out of the true, if you drop your head, if you don't swing your gun sweetly in pace with the movement of the bird, you will miss them. If you kill a fast oncoming pigeon cleanly, you can congratulate yourself that you have brought off a shot in which the slightest fault in gun-handling would have beaten you.

It's true that, in certain conditions, pigeon shooting can be relatively easy; personally, it's not the easy shooting that I would have for choice. But, if you are shooting over a field of cabbages in hard weather, if you have got a blind under a skeleton tree which is the sort of observation post pigeons always favor in the harvest field, the chances are that in addition to flying shots you will get a lot of chances at birds when they are roosting or on the ground. Theoretically speaking, nobody should miss a sitting bird. In practice, it is surprising how often people do. But there is a simple trick to remember. If you are firing at a roosting pigeon don't shoot at his head, shoot at his pink legs. If you put the charge into his legs you will kill him through the head. If he is sitting on the ground, in the stubble for example, treat him as I

[265]

told you to treat a crouching hare. If you shoot at his head your charge will go over him. The secret is to place your charge so that it lifts the ground from under his crop.

If you want to become a good pigeon shot, and assuming that you take the trouble to place yourself where you stand a good chance of getting at them, it's not much good going out with the notion of being over economical with cartridges. The secret of mastering pigeons is to keep on shooting at them. The shots that are really worth taking are the shots which the miserly cartridge user wouldn't dream of wasting sixpence on. True, you can kill pigeons with comparative certainty by knocking them out of the trees where they are at roost, or off the shocks when they are feeding on the corn. The sport is to try and shoot them when they are flying past and wild.

Indeed, the all-round shooting man is one who can kill all varieties of game in all sorts of conditions. And, if you master the drill in this book, you ought to be able to do so in all conditions pretty well anywhere.

In fact, I am well aware that men who can shoot quite brilliantly when they are walking by themselves along the hedgerows fold up completely when they are invited to an organized drive through the coverts. That is largely a matter of nerve; but it is also an indication that the drill of gun-mounting and gun-handling has not become the habit it ought to have.

When you miss a bird or a rabbit or a hare don't be content to say "damn." You shouldn't be satisfied with yourself until you can say to yourself: "I was behind that bird about one foot. The reason I was behind was because I dropped my head as I mounted the gun and I think that I held my trigger just a fraction too long. I think I missed, in fact, because I was a little over-anxious. Next time I'll bring up my gun smoothly; I'm not going to worry whether I hit or miss but I am going to make up my mind that, whatever else I do, I'm going to keep my eye on the target." You will find that this personal reasoning with yourself, whether you are at an organized shoot or walking alone over the stubbles, will help you to shoot better.

When the British Metropolitan Police are training the drivers of police cars, they teach them, as part of the drill, to say out loud all the thoughts that come into their minds as they drive along the road. For example, the driver will say: "There's a child on the pavement in front of me who might easily cross the road without warning. There's a lorry there coming out of that side road which may or may not halt as it should. I'll act on the assumption that the driver won't halt. Look out, here's a pedestrian crossing."

You couldn't do better than to apply the same technique to yourself when you are shooting. Think all the time what you are doing and tell yourself what you are doing right and what you are doing wrong. Above all, remember that there is a great deal more to first-class shooting than straight shooting. The men who bring in most of the bag are not necessarily the best shots. They are the men who anticipate before the drive begins where and how, in the light of the conformation of the ground and the state of the wind, birds are likely to fly. They are the men who seem to know instinctively when something is going to show.

I remember a great partridge shot saying to me that, when he was walking up, he could sense when he was drawing close to a covey of partridges and when it was likely to get up. That was simply another way of saying that he had become so experienced that, as he walked over the ground, he could calculate where partridges were likely to be in different conditions and at different times of the day. That knowledge enabled him in most cases to kill two birds before the next man down the line had realized that a covey had been flushed at all. You can learn this field know-how far better when you are walking out with a gun by yourself. Learn to consider the possibilities of every tree, of every patch of bramble. Learn to read by the behavior of your dog what he smells moving over the ground. Learn which way the fur and feather is likely to run, or fly, in different conditions. If you know that, you will make up for many faults in shooting. If you don't know that, however excellent a shot you are, you will be shooting at a disadvantage. And you won't have a fraction of the fun you will if you learn the subtleties of the great sport of game shooting.

Conclusion

I HAVE read somewhere that one third of the cars at present in use in England would not survive a strict test of road-worthiness. Whether or not this statement is true in the matter of cars, I would wager my last cartridge that, if all the shotguns in regular use in the countryside were submitted to expert examination, at least 10 per cent of them would be condemned as thoroughly dangerous.

It is only necessary to attend an average rough shoot to meet people carrying suicidal antiquities which, by all the rules of ballistics, ought to explode in their hands the moment they pull the trigger. Every farm in the country includes in its deadstock some calamitous fowling piece of a former generation. And there must be thousands of people using soft metal hammer guns, made for a few pounds on the Continent, which are potentially lethal to the holder after the discharge of a few hundred rounds.

Hardly any of these guns, with the problematical exception of the cheaper foreign firearms of recent manufacture, have been proofed for use with modern smokeless powder. If you pick one up, you will find that, in most cases, the barrels fit so loosely to the stock that you can see daylight between the action face and the chambers. Locks are untrustworthy, the barrels pocked with rough holes, and the woodwork swollen from the metal like an old man's joints.

On many occasions I have seen men out shooting with old hammer guns lashed together with bits of wire and even string. I know a gamekeeper at the moment who is using a gun in which the barrels are punctured like a colander. Every time he fires, puffs of smoke spurt out through the pits in the paper-thin tubes. Yet, if you give the owners of these guns the friendly warning that every time they shoot they are liable to be blinded by back blast or lose their fingers through a burst barrel, they seem to take a perverse pride in the accident risk. And, invariably, they will tell you that their own gaspipe is the "hardest hitting gun" they have ever handled.

I often wonder what they mean. Since the punch behind the charge comes entirely from the combustion of the propellant inside the cartridge, all that any gun can do is to guide the shot in an even pattern in the direction in which the barrels are pointing. Admittedly, the constriction, or otherwise, of the shot pattern is controlled by the degree of choke in the barrel. Admittedly, too, some guns throw better shot patterns than others. But you only need to glance at the muzzles of those ancient weapons to recognize that the barrels are completely "shot out." The charge must spout out of them as erratically as if the shot were thrown by hand.

Nevertheless, I am the first to admit that many of these old guns do, in fact, stand up to considerable use (or misuse) without serious accident, and their owners, on occasion, shoot passably well. The explanation, if you can call it so, is that the men who use these old guns are usually enthusiastic sportsmen with an uncanny skill of their own and the guns themselves are quite often the rusty remnant of the uncanny skill of some great old craftsman. Against all reasonable possibility, the guns hold together and contain a charge long after the margin of safety has vanished altogether. But it is not good enough.

It was A. P. Herbert, I believe, who, as a subaltern in the

First World War, warned his men when they went into action "to treat all Germans with the gravest suspicion." The same might be said of old hammer guns with Damascus barrels. Some of them, not many, are proofed for standard pressures developed by modern cartridges. But the guns should be checked; and, fortunately, it is the easiest matter in the world to do so.

Any gun made in Great Britain carries proof marks on the flats of the barrels and the actions. If a gun in good condition is stamped "nitro proofed" or "N.P.," it is safe to use with smokeless powder. If not, it should be sent to a reputable gun-maker for reproofing. If the barrels burst, as they probably will, under the maximum pressures imposed in proofing, the owner should count himself lucky. It might have happened when he had the gun in his hand. If the barrels stand the test, the owner will have the satisfaction of knowing that he can shoot the gun in perfect safety and that its market value has been appreciably increased by the nitro-proofing stamp.

Indeed, whether the gun is old or new, I repeat that it should be sent without fail to a gun-maker at the end of every season for examination and overhaul. It is marvellous how many years a good gun will shoot without the benefit of expert attention. But it is alarming, too, to discover how many little things need seeing to in a gun after, perhaps, one season's shooting.

But, if my parting words are to warn you about using unsafe guns, I must also add that guns are not only unsafe in themselves. Everybody who keeps a gun in the house has a responsibility. Those who have to keep guns in the same house as children have a very special one.

My own view is that it is useless to hope that a child growing up in a country house, and in an atmosphere of country sports, can be permanently kept out of reach of game-guns. The gun cabinet may be locked, but sooner or later any child in the country will get the opportunity to pick up a firearm; if not in his own house, in somebody else's. Neither, I think, is it fair to suppress a small boy's healthy curiosity for an object that glitters and bangs in such a fascinating fashion as a shotgun.

My own idea is that the most intelligent approach to the problem is to recognize the fact that, to a small boy, a gun is irresistible and to take the earliest opportunity to gratify his hands. Once he learns what a gun is for, it is time to canalize his interests in a similar toy.

I don't want to advise fathers but, when little boys put greasy fingers on the barrels of my own guns, I always make a point of giving them a demonstration of how they work. I make no attempt to move them out of reach. I let them look up the barrels to see that they are properly polished. And, with a pair of snap caps, I let them pull the triggers and watch the ejectors work. That's one way of making sure that guns have no particular mystery for children.

How soon a boy should be allowed the use of a real gun is entirely a matter of individual development. I remember seeing a boy using a .410 with safety at the age of seven, which is supposed to be the time when children come to the use of reason. But I think that, while seven is about the right age to put a boy on a pony for the first time, fourteen is soon enough to give him a gun. I should be reluctant, even then, to let him shoot without someone to keep an eye on him.

The old rule, for training a boy in the use of a gun was to start him off on shooting days carrying an empty one; with the promise that if he handled it safely all day he would be permitted one cartridge.

For their first gun, most boys are given a .410. On humane grounds, I am not an enthusiast for guns of that bore. Four-tens are limited in their effectiveness. In the hands of any but a skilled shot an undue proportion of game is pricked. Apart from the undesirability of wounding without killing, the .410 tends to encourage young shots to pop off at song birds.

CONCLUSION

Personally, I would always give a boy the largest bore gun he is able to handle with comfort. These days, what I usually recommend is a light 12-bore chambered for 2-inch cases. Twenty-bores are going out of fashion, largely because 20-bore cartridges have a way of accidentally slipping into the top of the chamber of a 12-bore gun.

In my opinion, people who give boys the use of hammer guns, especially old ones, are bad parents.

I would also like to repeat what I have already said in the chapter on how to shoot rabbits; that rabbit or rat shooting to ferrets, which is usually the kind of shooting that most boys are first introduced to, is almost certainly the most dangerous form of shooting there is. Boys should not be allowed to ferret without the most careful supervision.

Finally, the day that any parent first gives his son a gun, may I remind him that he should take out a sportsman's insurance policy for him forthwith. The premium is very low and, indeed, I can't for the life of me understand why everybody who goes shooting does not protect himself and his gun in this obvious way.

Having warned you about safe guns and made my comments about the age when boys should be allowed to touch guns and handle them for the first time, I feel that my last responsibility in this book is to say something on behalf of the game which provides us with so much sport and so much good food.

Let me quote to you an extract from the report of a British Government Committee on Cruelty to Wild Animals:

"The shooting of wild animals of all kinds is very widely practised both as a method of control and for sport. If the animal fired at were always killed outright, shooting would be one of the most humane methods of control, but this is by no means always the case and there can be no doubt that it may involve great suffering if the animal is wounded and escapes, particularly if it is not followed up and killed. This happens less frequently with experienced shots, but we think that a great deal of shooting is done by people who lack the necessary skill and experience. Despite the high cost of cartridges, many people who lack the necessary skill are accustomed to try their hand with a gun from time to time, and there is a tendency for these people, and also for some who shoot more frequently, to fire at too great a range or to use the wrong type of cartridge. At present anyone who takes out a gun licence can use a gun no matter how unskilled he may be, and some witnesses have suggested that nobody should be allowed to shoot until he has passed the shooting test. This suggestion is in our view impractical.

"Most of the opponents of field sports advocate shooting as an alternative method of control and consider it to be more satisfactory and more humane than hunting or any other method. We agree that, in many circumstances, shooting is a very important valuable method of controlling a number of animals such as the fox, but at the same time we are convinced that for the reasons we have given inexpert shooting causes a great deal of unnecessary suffering. Also we do not accept the view which was expressed to us by some witnesses that a normal animal does not normally suffer from its wounds to any appreciable extent. . . . We realize, however, that shooting is a convenient method of control on which farmers, gamekeepers and others concerned with the control of pests depend to a great extent. It is a common practice for farmers to walk round their land with a gun and to shoot any rabbits or other pests as the opportunity arises, and this helps considerably to keep the land free from pests and consequently to safeguard food. Because of this it is clearly contrary to the national interest for us to recommend that shooting should be prohibited, nor has any witness proposed this. As it would be quite impos-

sible to attempt to regulate shooting by laying down minimum ranges and other details of that sort, there is no recom-
mendation for legislation that we can usefully make, but we
think that more should be done to instruct people in the use
of guns. We suggest, therefore, that the animal welfare
organizations might give some consideration to the cruelty
involved in shooting and . . . might compile a pamphlet on
the proper use of guns and the avoidance of cruelty arising
from their use. It might be possible for such a pamphlet to
be issued with gun licences."

I hope that the advice I have given in this book will do something to implement the wishes of the Government Committee;
but it is interesting that the report falls into the common error
which will be immediately recognized by readers of this book.
The idea that somebody who is completely inexperienced in the
use of guns is likely to cause unnecessary suffering to the game
he shoots at is a fallacy. The man who is completely inexperienced can, generally speaking, be relied upon to miss altogether.
All he is likely to hurt is his own shoulder, or mouth, through
bad gun-mounting.

The special problem that shooting presents as a sport is that
the man who is most likely to wound an animal is the experienced shot who is off his day. If you don't know how to shoot,
you'll never be within ten yards, for example, of a driven
pheasant. If you're a shot on the top of your form, you will
consistently kill him in the air. But if you are an experienced shot
who is not on the top of form, then you will again and again
wound pheasants without killing them by hitting them behind.
There is no solution that I know of to this problem, except to
shoot better.

On occasions, I have known an experienced shot who realized
that he was off form put down his gun. On others, I have known
men ask their host to put a reliable shot behind to clean up any

birds which they had the misfortune to tail. On most well-organized shoots, the dogs are there to pick up runners as quickly as possible.

Apart from these precautions, there is a responsibility on every man who goes shooting to see to it that for the sake of the game, as well as his host, that he doesn't accept an invitation to shoot at all unless he is in good physical condition. In the old days of the big covert shoots, the crack shots would only drink very sparingly on the evening before they shot. They didn't sit up all night playing cards, they went to bed early, they took care of themselves; and, in many cases, they put in dry practice, or a few rounds at clay pigeons, before they started out in the morning.

Shooting is indeed a great field sport and it would be a sad day if it were ever interfered with. The most humane form of shooting, and the way in which the larger part of the game harvest is gathered for the food market, is driven game shooting, because most of the birds are shot in front and, if they are hit at all, they are usually picked up. The form of shooting which provides the greatest number of wounded birds is going-away shooting when a man is by himself or when he is walking up with a line of guns. From the point of view of the man with the gun, walking up is the easiest form of shooting. From the point of view of the game, it is the form of shooting in which the greatest care should be taken not to shoot without a fair chance and to see to it that the dogs are put on at once to any bird which is a runner.

To sum up for the last time:

1. *Keep fit*. You can't hope to shoot at your best and you have no business to accept a shooting invitation if you are tired and nervy and if you are not at the top of your form.

2. When you are shooting hare or wildfowl, remember that the natural fault is to think that the quarry is much nearer to you than it is. Better not to shoot at all than to take a chance at extreme ranges.

3. The man who wounds birds isn't the inexperienced shot, who

[276]

is chiefly dangerous not to the game at all, but to the guns who have the misfortune to be out with him. The man who "tails" birds is usually the experienced shot who is off his day. The more you study drill and practice the drill that I have given in this book, the more seldom will you have an off-day.

4. Use the best gun that you can afford and don't begrudge the extra expense of using a gun that fits you. Don't fool about with a battery of guns of one kind or another. The best gun is the one you are most used to and the gun that you yourself shoot best with.

5. Take as much trouble to wear clothes which give you maximum freedom of body movement as you do over your gun.

6. Practice . . . practice . . . practice. There is nobody in reasonable physical condition, with eyes good enough to distinguish the difference between a pheasant and a partridge at thirty yards, who can't with training become a reasonably good average shot. Further, age is not a limiting factor.

I am conscious that, in this book, I have been guilty of repetition. I have done it deliberately. This is a drill book, and the secret of drill is repetition until the movements are rooted in the mind of the person who has to carry them out.

Index

INDEX

[v]